Contents

The authors

Victor Ceserani was formerly Head of School of Hotel Keeping and Catering, Ealing College of Higher Education. He has been an examiner for City and Guilds Advanced Cookery (706/3) and is a well-known judge at national food and cookery competitions and a Fellow of the Hotel, Catering and Institutional Management Association. He is also an Honorary Member of the Association Culinaire Française, the Academie Culinaire de France, the City and Guilds of London Institute, and an Honorary Fellow of Ealing College of Higher Education.

In 1968/9 he held the appointment of Visiting Professor at Michigan State University where he also gained the Degree of Master of Business Administration. He has been apprentice chef at the Ritz Hotel, commis chef at the Orleans Club and chef at Boodle's, all rightly renowned for the excellence of their cuisine.

Ronald Kinton trained at Westminster Technical College and was employed as a chef at the head offices of ICI Ltd and at the Waldorf Hotel and Claridges. He was formerly Senior Lecturer at the School of Hotel Keeping and Catering, Ealing College of Higher Education where he taught for fifteen years. He subsequently taught at Garnett College, the College of Education (Technical) concerned with the teaching of catering teachers. He obtained a BEd Honours degree in which his special studies related to catering education.

Acknowledgements

The Publishers would like to thank: Michael Barber for arranging the photographs and Ted Poole, The College, Swindon, for permission to reproduce them, on pages 50, 74, 107, 108, 113, 114, 115, 117, 118, 122, 125 and 129; Steve Richards for permission to reproduce the photograph on this page.

The Publishers regret they have been unable to trace the copyright of the photographs of the Terrace kitchens, The Dorchester, London, on pages 105 and 116.

Cookery: an introduction

Victor Ceserani MBE, MBA, FHCIMA
Former Head of School of Hotel Keeping and Catering
Ealing College of Higher Education

Ronald Kinton BEd (Hons), FHCIMA
Formerly of Garnett College,
College for Teachers in Further and Higher Education

Edward Arnold

First published in Great Britain 1987 by
Edward Arnold (Publishers) Ltd,
41 Bedford Square, London WC1B 3DQ

Edward Arnold (Australia) Pty Ltd,
80 Waverley Road, Caulfield East,
Victoria 3145, Australia

Reprinted 1988

British Library Cataloguing in Publication Data
Ceserani, Victor
Cookery: an introduction.
1. Cookery
I. Title II. Kinton, Ronald
641.5'7 TX663

ISBN 0-7131-7491-9

Text set in 10/11 Mallard
by Colset Pte. Ltd., Singapore
Printed and bound at The Bath Press, Avon

Introduction

This book is written as an introduction to professional cookery and its purpose is to assist young people in their initial training and older people in their retraining to become competent cooks. It is our intention that this book will help students on courses taking maybe only a few months to become employable in that short time. The ability to do well in the practical situation is more likely to be present if there is understanding of the principles or rules of cookery and knowledge of why these principles or rules need to be followed.

The first things a person learning to cook needs to know is why food is cooked and *what* the effects are when heat is applied to food – that is, how to cook. Certain rules must be known and followed if success is to be achieved. These principles or rules apply in developing hygienic and safe practices at the same time as carrying out cooking procedures such as boiling, frying, roasting, etc.

To be a good cook requires not only competency in the technical skills and understanding of the theoretical knowledge of cooking; it also requires the right attitude to the customer or consumer, to the people with whom you work and to employers. Social skill is shown by a person's ability to get on with other people in society. Politeness, reliability, tact, loyalty, co-operativeness, willingness, and trustworthiness are but a few of the qualities which help to make technically good cooks employable cooks.

We have attempted to produce a simple, basic but clear book as an introduction to the theory and practice of cookery. For the next stage of learning we suggest the use of *The Theory of Catering* and *Practical Cookery*. Both these books are published by Edward Arnold and each has a companion book, *Questions on The Theory of Catering* and *Questions on Practical Cookery*, to assist learning.

We consider cooking should be enjoyable, and learning to cook should also be enjoyable. We hope that by using this book you will find that this is so and that you become a successful cook. A successful cook, we suggest, is one who is both professional and able, and, having obtained a job, is competent in keeping it and improving in knowledge and experience. Such a cook will obtain job satisfaction from doing a job well because of having the right attitude to it. We wish you success and hope this book will be helpful.

There is an index of recipes and a general index at the end of the book. Recipes are for 4 portions unless otherwise stated. All eggs should be size 3.

1

Self-assessment, competency and employability check-list

Students need to know what they should achieve by the end of their course. Continuous assessment by the teacher enables progress to be monitored and discussed. This should take place at regular intervals in order that the student may be kept fully aware of his or her level of competence.

In addition, students may wish to record their own progress and competency. Therefore, we have provided boxes to be completed in the index at the end of the book. It is suggested that each box should be marked when the student believes that an acceptable standard of knowledge and/or skill has been achieved. Each box can contain one of 3 indications:

1. ◪ one stroke for initial knowledge and/or skill;
2. ☒ a cross to show that more skill and understanding has been reached;
3. ▩ a completed box when the student feels confident of his or her ability.

2

Principles and processes of cookery

General objective To have a knowledge and understanding of the principles and processes of cookery.
Specific objectives To be able to explain how each method affects foods; to state which foods are cooked by each method; to explain why cooks need to use the various principles and processes of cookery.

A good cook has to use skills to produce food which looks good, tastes good, and does good; in other words, healthy food.

The recipes in this book are based on the traditional classical methods. If, however, any of these recipes are required to be prepared incorporating contemporary healthy eating principles they can be adjusted by replacing certain commodities, e.g. polyunsaturated oil or margarine in place of butter or dripping, wholemeal flour in place of or partly in place of white flour, natural yoghurt in place of cream, skimmed milk in place of full cream milk, unrefined sugar in place of refined sugar, low fat cheese in place of full fat cheese. Always use the minimum of salt or low sodium salt.

Reasons for cooking food

1. To make food more digestible.
2. To make food more attractive to the eye.
3. To make food enjoyable to eat.
4. To give food an appetising smell, thus stimulating the digestive juices.
5. To give variety to the texture of foods.
6. To develop flavour.
7. To preserve food.

To cook food, heat is supplied by using hot water, hot fat or dry heat. The principles and processes of cookery are:

1. Boiling
2. Poaching
3. Steaming
4. Stewing
5. Braising
6. Roasting
7. Grilling
8. Frying (shallow)
9. Frying (deep)
10. Baking
11. Microwave
12. Pot roasting
13. Cook-freeze/cook-chill

When applying the principles and processes of cookery, the following points need to be observed:

1. Attention to detail – weighing, timing, recipes.
2. An understanding of the equipment used.
3. Ability to evaluate the product being cooked – quality, size, shape, etc.
4. Knowing and applying the principles of safety and hygiene.
5. Understanding and practising the qualities which make a good roast cook, pastry cook, etc.

Variation in the exact definitions and classifications of the principles and processes of cookery may be met with. This is because:

a) some words used in French or English may not exactly correspond, e.g. boiled chicken in English may be called poached chicken, or *poulet poché* in French;
b) some usage in domestic situations is not

always the same as in catering establishments, e.g. stewed fruit, poached fruit and *compôte* of fruit may well refer to the same dish.

If there is difficulty in finding a recipe, refer to the general recipe index.

Oven Temperature Chart

	Regulo 1 – 9	°C	°F
Slow or cool	¼	110	225
	½	130	250
	1	140	275
	2	150	300
Moderate	3	160	325
	4	180	350
	5	190	375
	6	200	400
Hot	7	220	425
	8	230	450
	9	250	500

Recipes – their principles and practice

Recipes are instructions. They

a) list the ingredients needed and the amounts required,
b) explain the procedures to follow in preparation and cooking,
c) explain how the dish should be presented,
d) specify how many portions the recipe will produce.

Pastry recipes are precise and should be carefully followed. Recipes for use in the kitchen are good guides, but ingredients vary in quality and size, and factors such as evaporation, variations in heat, etc., affect the results. Therefore, personal judgement in the use of these recipes is necessary. It is helpful to think of ratios where possible, e.g. equal fat to flour for puff pastry, 1 part fat to 2 parts flour for short pastry; to consider relationships, e.g. vegetable soups such as cauliflower, potato, carrot will have similar quantities of basic ingredients. Some recipes have the same base, e.g. white sauce. To this can be added parsley, onions, hard boiled egg, cream, cheese, etc., to produce other sauces.

Recipes need to be adjusted according to experience. A recipe book should be an accurate guide to the process to be followed. However, it should be remembered that, for example, no two ovens are exactly identical, the quality of meat for grilling will vary, the size of portions will differ in various establishments and according to the number of courses being eaten.

Questions – recipes

1. What do you understand by *ratio*?

2. Complete these words to make the whole. Which two words do the omitted letters make?

   CONSIS ENCY
   GARNIS ING
   TEXTUR
   FLAVOU
   PRES NTATION
   AC OMPANIMENT
   Y ELD
   AP EARANCE
   S ASONING

3. Recipes must always be weighed exactly. Which recipes need particular attention?

4. What may cause the liquid in a recipe to vary in the cooking process?

   a) evaporation
   b) incorrect measuring
   c) spillage.

5. When following a recipe a cook must learn h——— control so as to achieve satisfactory results.

Answers can be found on page 152.

3

Kitchen terms

Since the beginning of the twentieth century many French chefs have worked in Britain and inevitably used their own language in the kitchens. As a result of this many French words have remained in kitchen use and the following list includes a small number of these words and terms. Also included are a number of English words which have particular reference to food in some form or another.

General objective To know and understand the basic terms used in cookery.

Specific objectives To be able to explain the commonly used terms listed, and to be able to use them correctly.

Accompaniments — Items offered separately with a dish of food.

A la carte — Dishes prepared to order and priced individually.

Au gratin — Sprinkled with cheese or breadcrumbs and browned.

Bacteria — Single-celled micro-organisms, some of which are harmful, e.g. they cause food poisoning. Others are useful, e.g. in cheese-making.
Bacteria – plural.
Bacterium – singular.

Bain-marie
- a) A container of water to keep foods hot without fear of burning.
- b) A shallow container of water for cooking foods in order to prevent them burning or over-cooking.
- c) A deep, narrow container for storing hot sauces, soups and gravies.

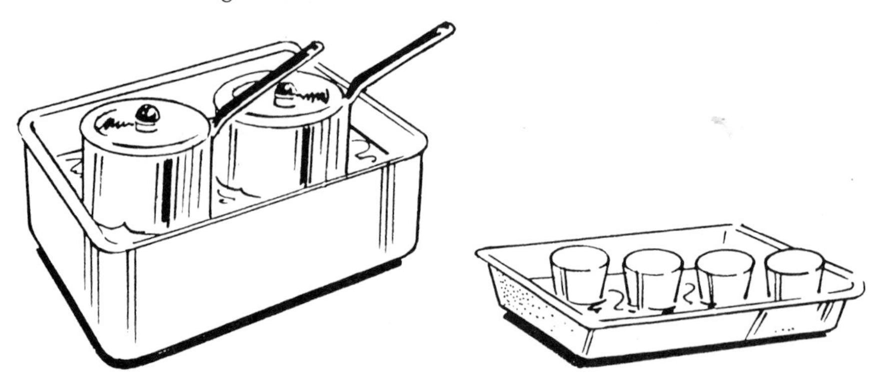

Basting — Spooning the hot fat or juices over food during cooking.

Bed of roots — Carrots and onion sliced thickly.

Beurre noisette	Nut-brown butter as used with fish meunière.
Blanch	To blanch, to whiten or to make soft.
Blanquette	A white stew cooked in stock, from which the sauce is made, e.g. blanquette de veau.
Bouchées	Small puff pastry cases.
Bouquet garni	A faggot of herbs – parsley, thyme and bay leaf, usually tied inside pieces of leek and celery.
Brine	A preserving solution of water, salt, saltpetre and aromates used for meats, e.g. silverside, brisket, tongue.
Brunoise	Small dice.
Carbohydrate	This is a nutrient which has three groups: sugar, starch and cellulose. The first two provide the body with energy, and cellulose provides roughage.
Casserole	An earthenware, fireproof dish with a lid.
Choux paste	Mixture for making éclairs, etc.
Cocotte	Porcelain or earthenware fireproof dish.
Compôte	Stewed, e.g. compôte des fruits (stewed fruits).
Concassée	Coarsely-chopped, e.g. parsley, tomatoes.
Consommé	Basic clear soup.
Contrefilet	Boned sirloin of beef.
To cook out	The process of cooking flour in a roux, soup or sauce.
Correcting	Adjusting the seasoning, consistency and colour.
Court-bouillon	A well-flavoured cooking liquor for fish.
Crêpes	Pancakes.
Croquettes	Cooked foods moulded into a cylindrical shape, coated in egg and crumbs, and deep fried.
Croûtons	Cubes of fried or toasted bread served with soup; also triangular pieces with spinach, and heart-shaped pieces with certain vegetables and entrées.
Dariole	A small mould, e.g. as used for cream caramel.
Darne	A slice of round fish on the bone.
Déglacer (deglaze)	To swill out a pan (in which food has been fried) with wine, stock or water in order to use the sediment for the accompanying sauce or gravy.
Demi-glace	Equal quantities of espagnole and brown stock, reduced by half.
Drain	To place food in a colander.
Escalope	Thin slice, e.g. escalope de veau (veal escalope).
Flan	Open fruit tart.
Friture	A pan that contains deep fat.

Garnish	Trimmings – on the dish.
Gâteau	A cake of more than one portion.
To glaze	a) To colour a dish under the salamander, e.g. fillets of sole bonne femme. b) To finish a flan or tartlet, e.g. with apricot jam. c) To shine certain vegetables with butter, e.g. glazed carrots, turnips, button onions.
Hors-d'oeuvre	Appetising first-course dishes.
Jardinière	Vegetables cut into batons.
Julienne	Cut into fine strips.
Jus-lié	Thickened gravy.
Macédoine	a) A mixture – fruit or vegetables. b) Cut in $\frac{1}{2}$ cm ($\frac{1}{4}$ in.) dice.
Masking	To cover with a sauce.
Menu	Bill of fare.
Meunière	Term for certain shallow fried foods.
Mirepoix	Roughly-cut onion, carrots, celery, and a sprig of thyme and a bay leaf.
Mise-en-place	Basic preparations prior to serving.
Mousse	A dish of light consistency, hot or cold.
Navarin	Brown stew of lamb or mutton.
Paner	To pass through seasoned flour, beaten egg and white breadcrumbs.
Pass	To cause to go through a sieve or strainer.
Paysanne	To cut into even, thin pieces – triangular, round or square.
Plat du jour	Special dish of the day.
Protein	The nutrient which is needed for growth and repair.
Prove	To allow a yeast dough to rest in a warm place so that it can rise and expand.
Pulses	Vegetables grown in pods (dried).
Purée	A pulp.
Ragoût	Stew, e.g. ragoût de boeuf (beef stew).
Reduce	To concentrate a liquid by boiling.
Refresh	To make cold under running cold water.
Roux	A thickening of cooked flour and fat.
Salamander	This is a type of grill heated from above.
Sauté	a) To toss in fat, e.g. pommes sautées. b) To cook quickly in a sauté or frying pan. c) A brown stew of a specific type, e.g. kidney sauté.

Shredded	Cut in fine strips, e.g. lettuce, sorrel, onion.
Simmer	To cook just below boiling point.
Strain	To separate the liquid from the solids by passing through a strainer.
To sweat	To cook in fat or oil under a lid without colouring.
Table d'hôte	A meal at a fixed price.
Tronçon	A slice of flat fish on the bone.
Velouté	a) A basic sauce. b) A soup of velvet or cream consistency.

4

Boiling

General objective To have a knowledge and understanding of boiling.
Specific objectives To give the definition and the principles of boiling; to explain the reasons for boiling; to demonstrate the ability to apply boiling as a method of cookery; to list the foods cooked by boiling; to state the effects of boiling on foods; to describe the advantages of boiling; to explain soaking, skimming, blanching, refreshing, draining, simmering, straining, passing; to select equipment, and state its care and use; to explain and apply efficiency and safety procedures; to use recipes associated with boiling.

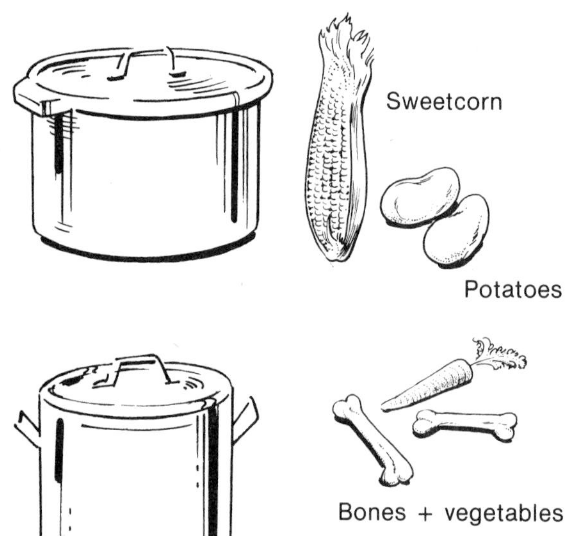

Definition

Boiling is the cooking of foods in just sufficient liquid, which may be stock, water or milk, to cover the food.

The principles of boiling

Once the liquid has come to the boil, the heat should be lowered so that the liquid boils very gently – this is called *simmering*. Items such as sauces, stocks or soups, once brought to the boil, should then simmer.

Foods to be boiled may be placed either in cold liquid or in boiling liquid, brought to the boil and then allowed to simmer.

1. The method of placing food in cold liquid is used for

a) extracting maximum flavour from the food, e.g. *stocks*;
b) softening hard root vegetables, e.g. carrots, swedes, parsnips;
c) preventing food breaking up, e.g. whole fish.

2. The method of placing food in liquid which is already boiling is used for

a) sealing in the flavour of the food, e.g. leg of mutton, cuts of fish on the bone;
b) green vegetables, in order to cook them quickly so that they retain flavour and goodness (referred to as nutritive value).

Equipment used for boiling

Stockpots
Saucepans
Bratt pans
Fast boiling pans
Jacket boilers
Induction cookers
Combined forced air convection/microwave cookers

Efficiency and safety

All equipment (including small equipment) must be kept clean by thoroughly washing with hot water containing detergent, rinsing with clean hot water, and then drying. Equipment must be used carefully according to manufacturer's instructions. Unsafe equipment must never be used. Any faults must be reported.

1. To conserve fuel always select a suitably sized pot.
2. Cover pan with a lid as appropriate.
3. Control temperature to simmering point wherever possible to reduce shrinkage and evaporation.
4. Top up boiling liquid as required.
5. Check that pressure gauges and safety valves (if fitted) are in working order.

Care must be taken when placing foods into boiling liquid and when removing lids from pans of boiling water, or severe scalds from the hot water or steam can result. When moving pans containing boiling liquid move them carefully and do not jerk them.

Suitable foods cooked by boiling

Stocks

Bones, vegetables and water are brought to the boil and simmered to extract the flavour; the liquid then forms the basis for many uses such as in soups, sauces and stews, etc.

Soups

Soups vary from the unthickened variety, such as clear soup (*consommé*), to those containing pieces of vegetables (broths) and those thickened by the vegetables (e.g. potatoes in a potato soup) or thickened with a roux (e.g. tomato soup). In all cases they are brought to the boil and then simmered.

Sauces

Many sauces are produced by boiling when the liquid – stock, milk or water – is thickened.

Eggs

Eggs can be soft or hard boiled. The cooking times are approximately 3 minutes for soft boiled and 10 minutes for hard boiled when started in boiling water.

Pasta and Rice

Spaghetti, macaroni, noodles and other forms of pasta are boiled in plenty of slightly salted boiling water before being drained and finished in various ways. Pasta should not be overcooked.

Rice can also be boiled in boiling, slightly salted water. It must not be overcooked, as it is important that the grains remain separate.

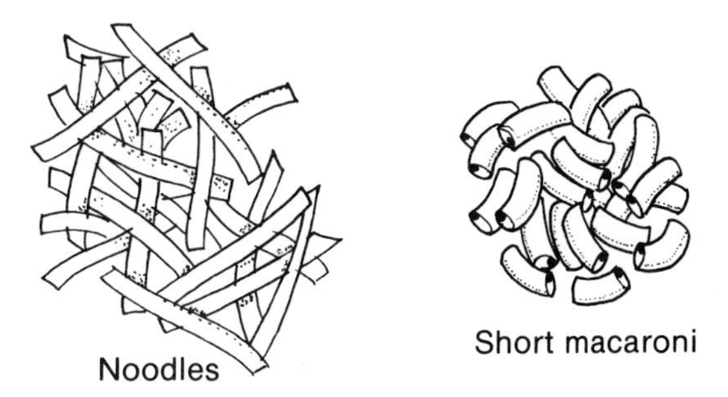

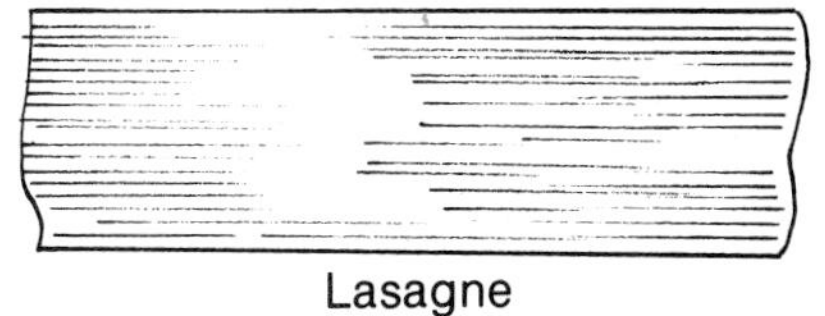

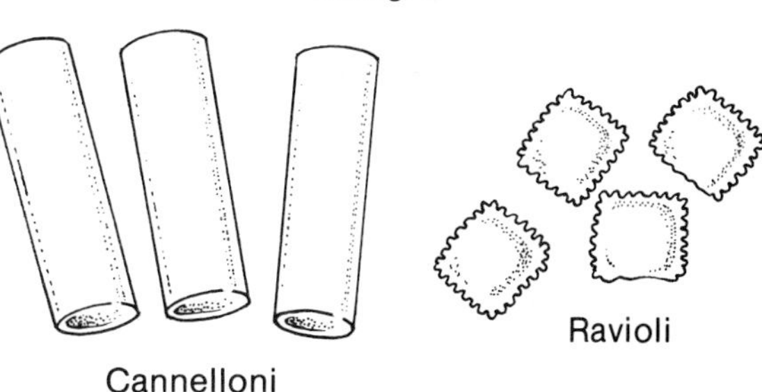

Pasta

Fish

Fish may be

a) boiled whole, e.g. salmon, trout, smoked haddock, shellfish;
b) cut in slices on the bone, e.g. turbot, brill, cod, salmon.

When boiling fish it is essential that the cooking liquid is simmering, otherwise the fish will break up. Gentle cooking is important. Sufficient liquid just to cover the fish is necessary. Whole fish are covered with cold liquid and slowly brought to simmer, cut fish are placed in simmering liquid and allowed to cook gently.

Meat

As boiling is a slow, moist method of cookery, it is suitable for older, tougher joints of meat and poultry, which would be tough and difficult to eat if cooked by roasting, grilling or frying. Meat to be boiled may be unsalted or salted. Silverside, brisket of beef, ox tongue, ham and bacon (gammon, hock, collar) are preserved by *pickling* in *brine* (a salt solution). Because of this it is advisable to soak the joints in cold water for several hours to reduce the salt content, otherwise the meat when cooked can taste too salty. The meat being soaked should be kept in a refrigerator or cool larder. The water used for soaking the meat is thrown away and fresh water is used for cooking the meat.

Unsalted meat, such as thin flank of beef, leg of mutton or leg of pork, is boiled with vegetables and herbs. The liquid in which the meat is boiled retains a good flavour and is served with the meat. This liquid, known as stock, is also used for sauces.

Poultry

Two types of chicken are generally used for boiling: large birds weighing over 2 kg (4.5 lb) or tough, old fowls. Older, tougher chickens are cheaper and when boiled can be made tender. They can be three-quarters cooked by boiling, and then roasted. In either case the chickens yield a good, well flavoured stock which has many uses.

Uses of boiled chicken

1. Served in portions with braised rice and sauce made from the chicken stock.
2. Cut into pieces, in a sauce made from the stock and served in small (*bouchées*) or large (vol-au-vent) puff pastry cases.
3. Minced or chopped for poached eggs, pancakes, croquettes.
4. Sandwiches, salads.
5. Soups and sauces.

Vegetables

To retain colour, flavour and goodness, vegetables should be boiled steadily in lightly salted water for the minimum amount of time, so that they remain slightly crisp or firm and look fresh and appetising.

Vegetables grown *above* the ground (green vegetables) should be started in rapidly boiling water with the lid on the pan, quickly brought back to the boil and the lid removed. They should then be allowed to boil gently and they must *never* be overcooked.

Vegetables grown *below* the ground (root vegetables) are started in cold, lightly salted water. Root vegetables should not be overcooked – they become soft and mushy, look unappetising, and lose their flavour, colour and nutritive value.

Stocks

General objectives To know the importance of stocks and understand their use in the kitchen.
Specific objectives To explain the preparation, care and use of stocks; to produce clear and well flavoured stocks.

Recipes for stock

Stock is a liquid containing some of the soluble nutrients and flavours of food which are extracted by prolonged and gentle simmering. The one exception is fish stock, which requires only 20 minutes' simmering. Stocks are the foundation of many important kitchen preparations, e.g. soups, sauces, gravies, therefore the greatest possible care should be taken in their production.

1. Unsound meat or bones and decaying vegetables will give stock an unpleasant flavour and cause it to deteriorate

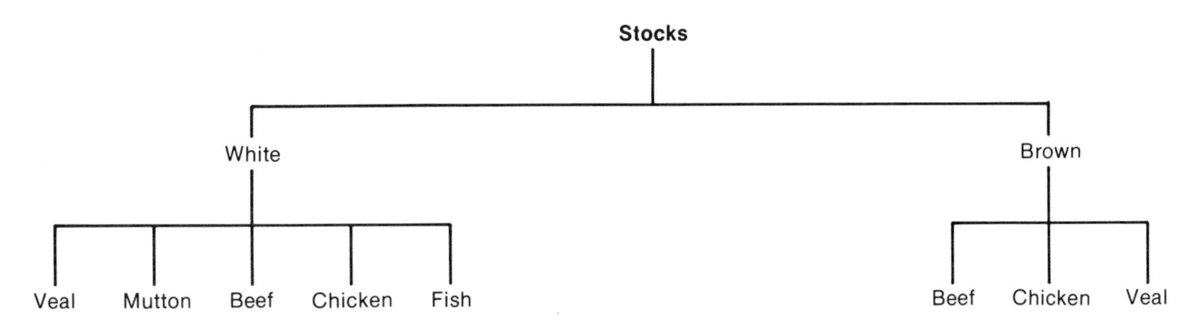

quickly.
2. Scum should be removed, otherwise it will boil into the stock and spoil the colour and flavour.
3. Fat should be skimmed off, otherwise the stock will taste greasy.
4. Stock should always simmer gently; if allowed to boil quickly, it will evaporate and go cloudy.
5. Stock should not be allowed to go off the boil, otherwise, in hot weather, there is a danger of it going sour.
6. Salt should not be added to stock.
7. When making chicken stock, if raw bones are not available, then a boiling fowl can be used.
8. If stock is to be kept, strain, reboil, cool quickly and place in the refrigerator.

White stocks, e.g. beef, veal, chicken, are used for white soups, sauces and stews.
Brown stocks, e.g. beef, veal, chicken, are used for brown soups, sauces, gravies and stews.
Fish stock is used for fish soups and sauces.

General proportions of ingredients for all stocks except fish stock are as follows:

2 kg	4 lb	raw bones
4 litres	1 gal	water
$\frac{1}{2}$ kg	1 lb	vegetables (onion, carrot, celery, leek)
		bouquet garni (thyme, bay leaf, parsley stalks)
		12 peppercorns

General method for all white stocks (except fish stock)

1. Chop up the bones, remove any fat or marrow.
2. Place in a stock pot, add the cold water and bring to the boil.
3. If the scum is dirty, then blanch and refresh by placing under running cold water until clean. Clean the pan, re-cover with cold water and bring to the boil.
4. Skim, wipe round sides of the pot and simmer gently.
5. Add the washed, peeled, whole vegetables, bouquet garni and peppercorns.
6. Simmer for 6 to 8 hours.
7. Skim and strain.

During the cooking, a certain amount of evaporation must take place, therefore add $\frac{1}{2}$ litre (1 pt) cold water just before boiling point is reached. This will also help to throw the scum to the surface and make it easier to skim.

General method for all brown stocks

1. Chop the bones and brown well on all sides by either:
   a) placing in a roasting tin in the oven, or
   b) carefully browning in a little fat or oil in a frying-pan.
2. Drain off any fat and place the bones in stock pot.
3. Brown any sediment that may be in the bottom of the tray, deglaze with $\frac{1}{2}$ litre (1 pt) of boiling water, simmer for a few

minutes and add to the bones.
4. Add the cold water, bring to the boil and skim.
5. Wash, peel and roughly cut the vegetables, fry in a little fat or oil till brown, strain and add to the bones.
6. Add the bouquet garni and peppercorns.
7. Simmer for 6 to 8 hours.
8. Skim and strain.

For brown stocks a few sound, squashed tomatoes and washed mushroom trimmings may also be added to improve the flavour.

Method for fish stock

Proportions of ingredients for fish stock are as follows:

50 g	2 oz	margarine, butter or oil
200 g	8 oz	onion
2 kg	4 lb	white fish bones (preferably sole, whiting or turbot)
4 litres	1 gal	water
		1 bay leaf
		juice of $\frac{1}{2}$ lemon
		parsley stalks
		6 peppercorns

1. Melt the fat or oil in a thick-bottomed pan.
2. Add the sliced onions, the well washed fish bones and the remainder of the ingredients.
3. Cover with greaseproof paper and a lid and sweat (cook without colour to extract flavour) for 5 minutes. Remove greaseproof paper.
4. Add the water, bring to the boil, skim and simmer for 20 minutes, then strain.
5. If fish stock is allowed to cook for longer than 20 minutes, the flavour is not improved and may be spoiled.

Recipes for sauces

General objectives To understand the purpose of sauces and to know the various types, hot and cold, and how they are made.
Specific objectives To state when and how sauces are made and to explain with what foods they are served; to demonstrate the production of each sauce to a satisfactory standard, with particular regard to consistency; to list the derivatives of the basic sauces.

A sauce is a liquid which has been thickened by (a) roux (b) cornflour or arrowroot (c) beurre manié (kneaded butter and flour) or (d) egg yolks, etc. All sauces should be smooth, glossy in appearance, definite in taste and light in texture, that is to say the thickening medium should be used in moderation.

The roux

A roux is a combination of fat, or oil, and flour which are cooked together. There are 3 degrees to which a roux may be cooked, namely (a) white roux (b) blond roux or (c) brown roux.

A boiling liquid should never be added to a hot roux, as the result may be lumpy and the person making the sauce may be scalded by the steam produced.

White roux

Uses: béchamel sauce (white sauce), soups.
Equal quantities of margarine, butter or oil and flour cooked together (without colouring) for a few minutes to a sandy texture.

Blond roux

Uses: veloutés, tomato sauce, soups.
Equal quantities of margarine, butter or oil and flour cooked for a little longer than a white roux (but also without colouring) to a sandy texture.

Brown roux

Uses: Espagnole (brown sauce), soups.
200 g (8 oz) dripping to 250 g (10 oz) flour (white or wholemeal) per 4 litres (gallon) of brown stock, cooked together slowly to a light-brown colour. Overcooking brown roux causes a loss of its thickening property. It will also cause too much roux to be used to achieve the required thickness and will give an unpleasant flavour.

Other thickening agents for sauces

1. Cornflour, arrowroot.
   Uses: jus-lié and jam sauces.
   These are diluted with water, stock or milk as appropriate, then stirred into the boiling liquid and allowed to reboil for a

few minutes.

2. Beurre manié.
   Uses: chiefly fish sauces.
   Equal quantities of butter or margarine and flour kneaded to a smooth paste and mixed into a boiling liquid.
3. Egg yolks.
   Uses: mayonnaise, fresh egg custard sauces.
   Refer to the appropriate recipe, as the yolks are used in a different way for each sauce.

White sauce 1 litre (1 quart)

Known as béchamel

This is the basic white sauce made from milk and a white roux.

100 g	4 oz	margarine, butter or oil
100 g	4 oz	flour
1 litre	1 qt	milk or skimmed milk
		1 studded onion*

1. Melt the fat or oil in a thick-bottomed pan.
2. Mix in the flour.
3. Cook for a few minutes over a gentle heat without colouring.
4. Allow to cook slightly.
5. Gradually add the warmed milk and stir till smooth.
6. Add the onion.
7. Allow to simmer for 30 minutes.
8. Remove the onion, and pass the sauce through a conical strainer.
9. Cover with a film of butter or margarine to prevent a skin forming.

*Studded with a piece of bayleaf pierced with a clove

Velouté 1 litre (1 quart)

Chicken, veal, fish

This is a basic white sauce made from white stock and a blond roux, as follows:

100 g	4 oz	margarine, butter or oil
100 g	4 oz	flour
1 litre	1 qt	stock (chicken, veal, fish as required)

1. Melt the fat or oil in a thick-bottomed pan.
2. Mix in the flour.
3. Cook out to a sandy texture over gentle heat without colour.
4. Allow the roux to cool.
5. Gradually add the boiling stock.
6. Stir until smooth and boiling.
7. Allow to simmer for approximately 1 hour.
8. Pass through a fine conical strainer.

A velouté sauce for chicken, veal or fish dishes is usually finished with cream and, in some cases, also egg yolks.

Sauces made from veloutés

Suprême sauce $\frac{1}{2}$ litre (1 pint) *8 – 12 portions*

Uses: served hot with boiled chicken, vol-au-vent, etc. This is a velouté made from chicken stock flavoured with well washed mushroom trimmings.

$\frac{1}{2}$ litre	1 pt	chicken velouté
25 g	1 oz	mushroom trimmings (white)
60 ml	$\frac{1}{8}$ pt	cream
		1 yolk
		2 – 3 drops lemon juice

1. Allow the velouté to cook out with the mushroom trimmings.
2. Pass through a fine strainer.
3. Reboil (contd. on p. 14).

Milk + white roux = white sauce

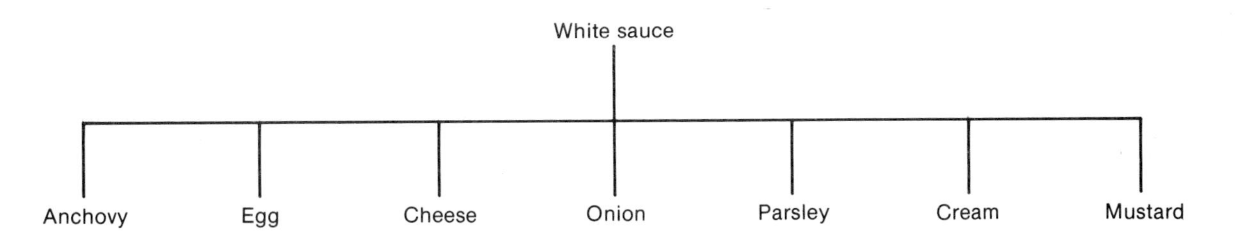

Sauces made from béchamel (quantities for $\frac{1}{2}$ litre (1 pint), *8 – 12 portions*)

Sauce	*Served with*	*Additions per $\frac{1}{2}$ litre (pt)*
Anchovy	Poached or fried fish	1 tbsp anchovy essence.
Egg	Poached fish	2 hard-boiled eggs in small dice.
Cheese	Fish or vegetables	50 g (2 oz) grated cheese, 1 yolk. Mix well in boiling sauce, remove from heat. Strain if necessary but do not allow to reboil.
Onion	Roast or boiled mutton	100 – 200 g (4 – 8 oz) chopped or diced onions cooked without colour either by boiling or sweating in fat or oil.
Parsley	Poached fish and vegetables	1 tbsp chopped parsley.
Cream	Poached fish and boiled vegetables	Add cream or milk to give the consistency of double cream.
Mustard	Grilled herrings	Add diluted English mustard to make a fairly hot sauce.

4. Mix the cream and yolk in a basin (liaison).
5. Add a little of the boiling sauce to the liaison.
6. Return all to the sauce, do *not* reboil.
7. Mix, finish with lemon juice and correct the seasoning.

White wine sauce (for fish)

$\frac{1}{4}$ litre ($\frac{1}{2}$ pint)

250 ml	$\frac{1}{2}$ pt	fish velouté
		2 tbsp dry white wine
50 g	2 oz	butter
		2 tbsp cream
		salt, cayenne
		few drops lemon juice

1. Boil the fish velouté.
2. Whisk in the wine.
3. Remove from the heat.
4. Gradually add the butter.
5. Stir in the cream.
6. Correct the seasoning and consistency; add the lemon juice.
7. Pass through a fine strainer.

Fish stock + blond roux = fish velouté → White wine sauce / Mushroom sauce / Shrimp sauce

Brown sauce

1 litre (1 quart)

Known as Sauce espagnole

This is the basic brown sauce made from brown stock and brown roux, as follows:

50 g	2 oz	good dripping or oil
60 g	$2\frac{1}{2}$ oz	flour (white or wholemeal)
25 g	1 oz	tomato purée
1 litre	1 qt	brown stock
100 g	4 oz	carrot
100 g	4 oz	onion

1. Melt the dripping or oil in a thick-bottomed pan.
2. Add the flour, cook out slowly to a light brown colour, stirring frequently.
3. Cool and mix in the tomato purée.
4. Gradually mix in the boiling stock.
5. Bring to the boil.
6. Wash, peel and roughly cut the carrots and onions.
7. Lightly brown in a little fat or oil in a frying-pan.
8. Drain and add to the sauce.
9. Simmer gently for 4 to 6 hours.
10. Skim when necessary. Strain.

Care should be taken when making the brown roux not to allow it to cook too quickly, otherwise the starch in the flour (which is the thickening agent) will burn, and its thickening properties will be weakened. Over-browning should be avoided, as this tends to make the sauce taste bitter.

Demi-glace sauce 1 litre (1 quart)

This is a refined basic brown sauce and is made by simmering 1 litre (1 qt) espagnole and 1 litre (1 qt) brown stock, and reducing by a half. Skim off all impurities as they rise to the surface during cooking. Pass through a fine conical strainer, reboil, correct the seasoning.

Chasseur sauce $\frac{1}{4}$ litre ($\frac{1}{2}$ pint) 4 – 6 *portions*

25 g	1 oz	butter or oil
10 g	$\frac{1}{2}$ oz	chopped shallots
50 g	2 oz	sliced button mushrooms
60 ml	$\frac{1}{8}$ pt	white wine (dry)
100 g	$\frac{1}{4}$ lb	tomatoes (concassée)
250 ml	$\frac{1}{2}$ pt	demi-glace
		chopped parsley and tarragon

1. Melt the butter or oil in a small sauteuse.
2. Add the shallots and cook gently for 2 to 3 minutes without colour.
3. Add the mushrooms, cover with a lid, and gently cook for 2 to 3 minutes.
4. Strain off the fat.
5. Add the wine and reduce by half.
6. Add the tomatoes.
7. Add the demi-glace, simmer for 5 to 10 minutes.
8. Correct the seasoning and add the tarragon and parsley.

Usually served with fried steaks, chops, chicken, etc.

Brown onion sauce $\frac{1}{4}$ litre ($\frac{1}{2}$ pint) 4 – 6 *portions*

25 g	1 oz	fat or oil
100 g	4 oz	sliced onions
	$\frac{1}{2}$ pt	2 tbsp vinegar
250 ml	$\frac{1}{2}$ pt	demi-glace

1. Melt the fat or oil in a sauteuse.
2. Add the onion, cover with a lid.
3. Cook gently till tender.
4. Remove the lid and colour lightly.
5. Add the vinegar and completely reduce.
6. Add the demi-glace, simmer for 5 to 10 minutes.
7. Skim and correct the seasoning.

May be served with minced beef, steaks or fried liver.

Miscellaneous sauces (including gravies)

Curry sauce $\frac{1}{4}$ litre ($\frac{1}{2}$ pint) 4 – 6 *portions*

50 g	2 oz	chopped onion
		$\frac{1}{4}$ clove of garlic
10 g	$\frac{1}{2}$ oz	oil, dripping, butter or margarine
10 g	$\frac{1}{2}$ oz	flour (white or wholemeal)
5 g	$\frac{1}{4}$ oz (approx)	curry powder
5 g	$\frac{1}{4}$ oz	tomato purée
375 ml	$\frac{3}{4}$ pt	stock
25 g	1 oz	chopped apple
		1 tbsp chopped chutney
5 g	$\frac{1}{4}$ oz	desiccated coconut
10 g	$\frac{1}{2}$ oz	sultanas
		salt

1. Gently cook the onion and garlic in the fat or oil in a small sauteuse, without colouring.
2. Mix in the flour and curry powder.
3. Cook gently to a sandy texture.
4. Mix in the tomato purée; cool.
5. Gradually add the boiling stock and mix to a smooth sauce.
6. Add the remainder of the ingredients; season lightly with salt.
7. Simmer for 30 minutes.
8. Skim and correct the seasoning.

This sauce has a wide range of uses, e.g. with prawns, shrimps, vegetables, eggs, etc. For poached or soft-boiled eggs it may be strained, and for all purposes it may be finished with 2 to 3 tbsp cream or yoghurt.

Roast gravy $\frac{1}{4}$ litre ($\frac{1}{2}$ pint) 4 – 6 *portions*

200 g	8 oz	raw bones	
250 ml	1 pt	stock or water	
50 g	2 oz	onion	roughly cut
25 g	1 oz	celery	roughly cut
50 g	2 oz	carrot	roughly cut

For preference use beef bones for roast beef gravy and the appropriate bones for lamb, veal, mutton and pork.

1. Chop bones and brown in the oven or brown in a little fat or oil on top of the stove or frying-pan.
2. Drain off all fat.
3. Place in saucepan with the stock or water.

4. Bring to boil, skim and allow to simmer.
5. Add the lightly browned vegetables, which may be fried in a little fat or oil in a frying-pan, or added to the bones when partly browned.
6. Simmer for 1½ to 2 hours.
7. Remove the joint from the roasting tin when cooked.
8. Return the tray to a low heat to allow the sediment to settle.
9. Carefully strain off the fat, leaving the sediment in the tray.
10. Return the tray to the stove and brown carefully.
11. Add the brown stock and allow to simmer for a few minutes.
12. Correct the colour and seasoning.
13. Strain and skim.

Thickened gravy ¼ litre (½ pint) *4 – 6 portions*
Known as *jus-lié*

200 g	8 oz	raw veal or chicken bones	
25 g	1 oz	celery	roughly chopped
50 g	2 oz	onion	
50 g	2 oz	carrot	
		½ bay leaf	
		sprig of thyme	
5 g	¼ oz	tomato purée	
500 ml	1 pt	stock or water	
10 g	½ oz	arrowroot or cornflour	

1. Chop the bones and brown in the oven or in a little fat or oil in a sauteuse on top of the stove.
2. Add vegetables and herbs and brown well.
3. Mix in the tomato purée and stock.
4. Simmer for 2 hours.
5. Dilute the arrowroot in a little cold water.
6. Pour into the boiling stock stirring continuously until it reboils.
7. Simmer for 10 to 15 minutes.
8. Correct the seasoning.
9. Pass through a fine strainer.

Tomato sauce ¼ litre (½ pint) *4 – 6 portions*

10 g	½ oz	fat or oil	
50 g	2 oz	onion	roughly cut
50 g	2 oz	carrot	
25 g	1 oz	celery	
		½ bay leaf	
		sprig of thyme	
10 g	½ oz	bacon scraps (optional)	
10 g	½ oz	flour (white or wholemeal)	
25 – 50 g	1 – 2 oz	tomato purée	
375 ml	¾ pt	stock	
		½ clove garlic	
		salt and pepper	

1. Melt the fat or oil in a small sauteuse.
2. Add the vegetables, herbs and bacon, and brown slightly.
3. Mix in the flour and cook to a sandy texture. Allow to colour slightly. Cool.
4. Mix in the tomato purée.
5. Cool.
6. Gradually add the boiling stock; stir to the boil.
7. Add the garlic; season.
8. Simmer for 1 hour.
9. Correct the seasoning.
10. Pass through a fine strainer.

This sauce has many uses, e.g. served with spaghetti, eggs, fish, meats, etc.

Jam sauce ¼ litre (½ pint)

200 g	8 oz	jam
100 ml	4 oz	water
10 g	½ oz	cornflour

1. Boil jam and water together.
2. Adjust the consistency with a little cornflour or arrowroot diluted with water.
3. Reboil until clear and pass through a conical strainer.

Custard sauce ¼ litre (½ pint)

10 g	½ oz	custard powder
250 ml	½ pt	milk
25 g	1 oz	castor sugar

1. Dilute the custard powder with a little of the milk.
2. Boil the remainder of the milk in a saucepan.
3. Pour a little of the boiled milk on to the diluted custard powder.
4. Return to the saucepan of milk.
5. Stir to the boil and mix in the sugar.

Fresh egg custard sauce ¼ litre (½ pint)

		2 egg yolks
25 g	1 oz	castor sugar
		2 – 3 drops vanilla essence
250 ml	½ pt	milk

1. Mix yolks, sugar and essence in a basin.
2. Whisk on the boiled milk.
3. Return to a thick-bottomed pan.
4. Place on a low heat and stir with a wooden spoon till it coats the back of the spoon. Do *not* allow to boil.
5. Pass through a fine strainer.

Chocolate sauce

10 g	$\frac{1}{2}$ oz	cornflour
250 ml	$\frac{1}{2}$ pt	milk
25 g	1 oz	chocolate (block) or
10 g	$\frac{1}{2}$ oz	cocoa powder
35 g	$1\frac{1}{2}$ oz	sugar
5 g	$\frac{1}{4}$ oz	butter

1. Dilute the cornflour with a little of the milk; mix in the cocoa or grated chocolate.
2. Boil the remainder of the milk.
3. Pour a little of the milk on to the cornflour.
4. Return to the saucepan.
5. Stir to the boil.
6. Mix in the sugar and butter.

Recipes for soup

Soups are served for luncheon, dinner, supper and snack meals. A portion is usually between 200 – 250 ml ($\frac{1}{3}$ – $\frac{1}{2}$ pt), depending on the type of soup and the number of courses to follow.

Consommé – a clear soup prepared from a beef or chicken stock.
Broth – a good stock (beef, mutton or chicken) garnished with diced vegetables, diced meat or chicken and rice or barley.

Thick soups – these cover a wide variety of soups.
Purée – a passed soup, thickened by the dried or fresh vegetable of which it is chiefly composed.
Cream -- a soup of creamy consistency which can be either:

a) half béchamel and half vegetable purée, or
b) purée soup, finished with cream, milk or yoghurt.

Clear soup (basic recipe) *4 portions*

Also known as *consommé*

200 g	8 oz	chopped or minced beef
		salt
		1 egg white
1 litre	1 qt	cold white or brown beef stock
100 g	4 oz	mixed vegetables (onion, carrot, celery, leek)
		bouquet garni
		3 – 4 peppercorns

1. Thoroughly mix the beef, salt, egg white and $\frac{1}{4}$ litre ($\frac{1}{2}$ pt) cold stock in a thick-bottomed pan.
2. Peel, wash and finely chop the vegetables.
3. Add to the beef with the remainder of the stock, the bouquet garni and the peppercorns.
4. Place over a gentle heat and bring slowly to the boil, stirring occasionally.

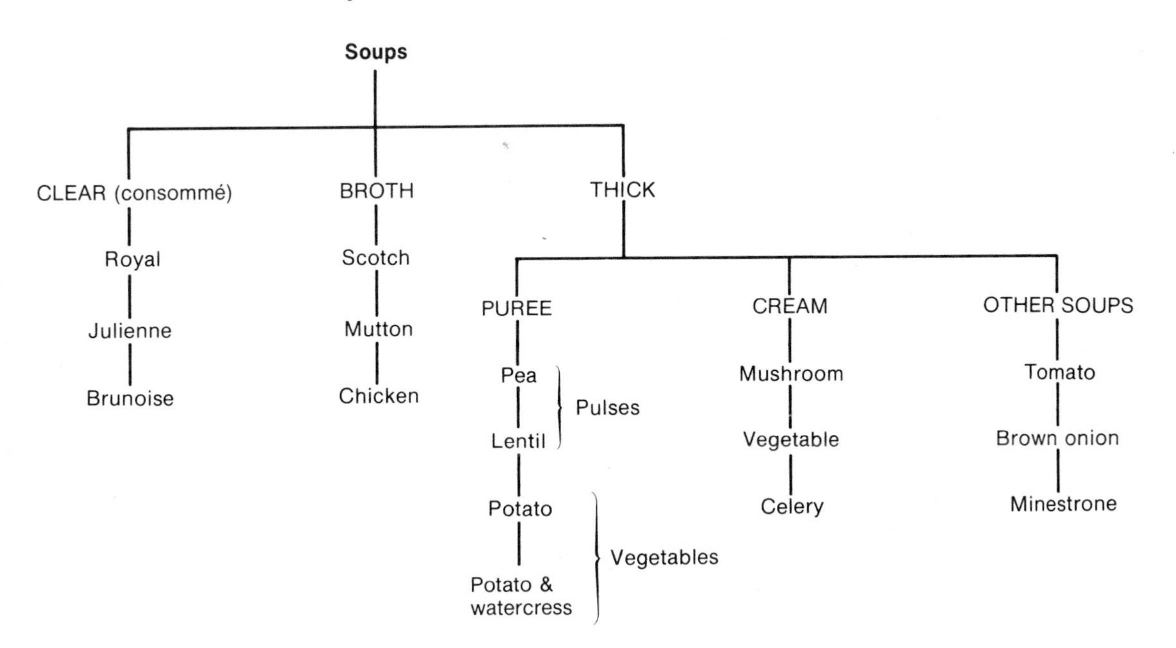

5. Allow to boil rapidly for 5 – 10 seconds.
6. Give a final stir.
7. Lower the heat, so that the consommé is simmering very gently.
8. Cook for $1\frac{1}{2}$ – 2 hours *without* stirring.
9. Strain carefully through a double muslin.
10. Remove all fat, using both sides of 8 cm (3 in.) square pieces of kitchen paper.
11. Correct the seasoning and colour, which should be delicate amber.
12. Degrease again, if necessary.
13. Bring to the boil and serve.

A consommé should be crystal clear. The clarification process is caused by the albumen of the egg white and meat coagulating, rising to the top of the liquid and carrying other solid ingredients. The remaining liquid beneath the coagulated surface should be gently simmering.

Cloudiness is due to some or all of the following:

a) poor quality stock;
b) greasy stock;
c) unstrained stock;
d) imperfect coagulation of the clearing agent;
e) whisking after boiling point is reached, whereby the impurities mix with the liquid;
f) not allowing the soup to settle before straining;
g) lack of cleanliness of pan or cloth;
h) any trace of grease or starch.

Consommés are varied in many ways by altering the stock, e.g. chicken, chicken and beef, etc, and also by the addition of numerous garnishes.

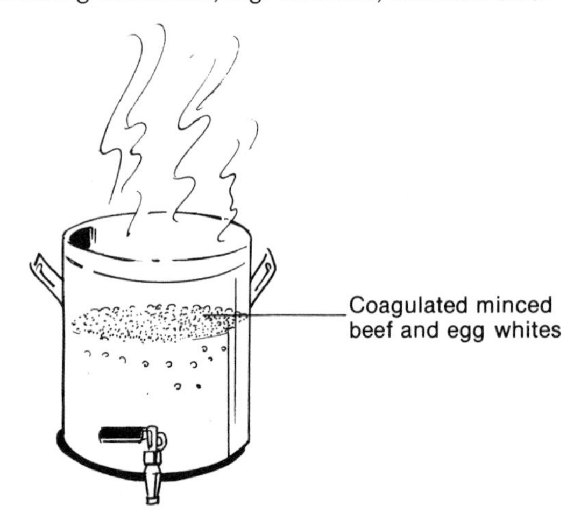

Royal

A royal is a savoury egg custard used for garnishing consommé. It should be firm but tender, the texture smooth, not porous. When cut, no moisture should be apparent. When this happens it is a sign of overcooking.

1. Whisk up 1 egg; season with salt and pepper and add the same amount of stock or milk.
2. Pass through a fine strainer.
3. Pour into a buttered dariole mould.
4. Stand the mould in a pan half full of water.
5. Allow to cook gently in a moderate oven until set, approximately 15 minutes.
6. Remove when cooked; when quite cold turn out carefully.
7. Trim the edges and cut into neat slices 1 cm ($\frac{1}{2}$ in.) thick, then into squares or diamonds.

Clear soup julienne

Basic consommé with a garnish of 50 g (2 oz) carrot, turnip and leek cut into 4 cm ($1\frac{1}{2}$ in.) long fine strips, which have been previously cooked in a little salted water, then refreshed to preserve the colour. The garnish must be added to the consommé at the last moment.

Clear soup brunoise

Basic consommé, with a garnish of 50 g (2 oz) carrot, turnip and leek cut into 2 mm ($\frac{1}{12}$ in.) dice, cooked as for julienne. Add to the consommé at the last minute.

Broths

Scotch broth *4 portions*

25 g	1 oz	barley
1 litre	2 pt	white beef stock
200 g	8 oz	vegetables (carrot, turnip, leek, celery, onion)
		bouquet garni
		salt, pepper
		chopped parsley

1. Wash the barley.
2. Simmer in the stock for approximately 1 hour.
3. Peel and wash the vegetables and cut into neat 3 mm ($\frac{1}{8}$ in.) dice.

4. Add to the stock with the bouquet garni and season.
5. Bring to the boil, skim and allow to simmer until tender, approximately 30 minutes.
6. Correct the seasoning, skim, remove the bouquet garni, add the chopped parsley and serve.

Mutton broth
As for Scotch broth, using mutton stock in place of beef.

Chicken broth
As for Scotch broth, using chicken stock, and garnishing with rice and diced chicken in place of barley.

Purée soups (pulses)

Green pea soup (with dried peas) *4 portions*

200 g	8 oz	green split peas
$1\frac{1}{2}$ litres	3 pt	stock or water
50 g	2 oz	carrot (whole)
		bouquet garni
25 g	1 oz	green of leek
50 g	2 oz	onion
50 g	2 oz	knuckle ham or bacon
		salt, pepper
		croûtons
		1 slice stale bread
50 g	2 oz	butter or margarine

1. Wash the peas and soak if necessary.
2. Place in a thick-bottomed pan; cover with cold water or stock.
3. Bring to the boil and skim.
4. Add the remainder of the ingredients and season.
5. Simmer until tender; skim when necessary.
6. Remove the bouquet garni, carrot and ham.
7. Pass through a sieve or liquidise.
8. Pass through a medium conical strainer.
9. Return to a clean saucepan, reboil, correct the seasoning and consistency; skim if necessary.
10. Serve accompanied by $\frac{1}{2}$ cm ($\frac{1}{4}$ in.) diced bread croûtons, toasted or shallow fried in butter.

Yellow pea soup (dried peas)
Proceed as for green pea soup, using yellow split peas and omitting the leek. The carrot need not be removed and can be sieved or liquidised with the peas.

Lentil soup 4 portions

200 g	8 oz	lentils
1 litre	2 pt	stock or water
50 g	2 oz	onion
		bouquet garni
		salt, pepper
50 g	2 oz	carrot
50 g	2 oz	knuckle of ham or bacon (optional)
		1 tsp tomato purée
		croûtons
		1 slice stale bread
50 g	2 oz	butter or margarine

Method of cooking and serving as for green pea soup.

Purée soups (vegetable)

Potato soup *4 portions*

25 g	1 oz	butter, margarine or oil
50 g	2 oz	onion
50 g	2 oz	white of leek
1 litre	2 pt	white stock or water
400 g	1 lb	peeled potatoes
		bouquet garni
		salt, pepper
		chopped parsley
		croûtons
		1 slice stale bread
50 g	2 oz	butter or margarine

1. Melt the fat or oil in a thick-bottomed pan.
2. Add the peeled, washed and sliced onion and leek, cook for a few minutes without colour with a lid on.
3. Add the stock and the peeled, washed, sliced potatoes and the bouquet garni, and season.
4. Simmer for approximately 30 minutes.
5. Remove the bouquet garni, skim.
6. Pass the soup firmly through a sieve, then pass through a medium conical strainer or liquidise.
7. Return to a clean pan, reboil and correct the seasoning and consistency.
8. To serve, sprinkle on a little chopped parsley. Serve toasted or fried croûtons separately.

Potato and watercress soup
1. Ingredients as for potato soup, plus a small bunch of watercress.
2. Pick off 12 neat leaves of watercress and plunge into a small pan of boiling water for 1 to 2 seconds. Refresh under cold water immediately. These leaves are to garnish the finished soup.

3. Add the remainder of the picked and washed watercress, including the stalks, to the soup at the same time as the potatoes and finish as for potato soup.

Cream soups

Vegetable *4 portions*
The following recipe is suitable for cauliflower, celery, leek, onion or turnip soup.
To produce cream of vegetable soup either (a) in place of ½ litre (1 pt) stock, use ½ litre (1 pt) thin béchamel, or (b) finish with milk, cream or yoghurt, simmer for 5 minutes, and serve.

200 g	8 oz	named soup vegetable, sliced
100 g	4 oz	sliced onions, leek and celery
50 g	2 oz	butter, margarine or oil
50 g	2 oz	flour (white or wholemeal)
1 litre	2 pt	white stock or water
		bouquet garni
		salt, pepper

1. Gently cook all the sliced vegetables, in the fat or oil under a lid, without colour.
2. Mix in the flour and cook slowly for a few minutes, without colour. Cool slightly.
3. Gradually mix in the hot stock.
4. Stir to the boil.
5. Add the bouquet garni and season.
6. Simmer for 45 minutes approx. Skim when necessary.
7. Remove the bouquet garni, pass firmly through the sieve and through a medium strainer or liquidise.
8. Return to a clean pan, reboil and correct the seasoning and consistency, and serve.

Mushroom soup *4 portions*

100 g	4 oz	onion, leek and celery
50 g	2 oz	margarine, butter or oil
50 g	2 oz	flour (white or wholemeal)
1 litre	2 pt	white stock (preferably chicken)
100 g	4 oz	white mushrooms
		bouquet garni
		salt, pepper

1. Gently cook the sliced onions, leek and celery in the fat or oil in a thick-bottomed pan, without colouring.
2. Mix in the flour; cook over a gentle heat to a sandy texture, without colouring.
3. Remove from the heat, and cool slightly.
4. Gradually mix in the hot stock.
5. Stir to the boil.
6. Add the well washed, chopped mushrooms and bouquet garni, and season.
7. Simmer 30 – 45 minutes. Skim when necessary.
8. Remove the bouquet garni.
9. Pass through a sieve or liquidise.
10. Pass through a medium strainer.
11. Return to a clean saucepan.
12. Reboil, correct the seasoning and consistency, add milk or cream, and serve.

Other soups

Leek and potato soup *4 portions*

400 g	1 lb	leeks (trimmed and washed)
25 g	1 oz	butter
750 ml	1½ pt	white stock
200 g	8 oz	potato
		salt, pepper

1. Cut the white and light green of leek into ½ cm (¼ in.) squares.
2. Slowly cook in the butter in a pan with a lid on until soft, but without colouring.
3. Add the stock and the potatoes, cut into paysanne. Season with salt and pepper. Simmer until cooked and serve.

Tomato soup *4 portions*

50 g	2 oz	butter, margarine or oil
25 g	1 oz	bacon trimmings (optional)
100 g	4 oz	onion
100 g	4 oz	carrot
50 g	2 oz	flour (white or wholemeal)
50 g	2 oz	tomato purée
1¼ litres	2½ pt	stock
		bouquet garni
		salt, pepper
		croûtons
		1 slice stale bread
50 g	2 oz	butter or margarine

1. Melt the margarine or butter in a thick-bottomed pan.
2. Add the bacon, rough diced onion and carrot; brown lightly.
3. Mix in the flour and cook to a sandy texture.
4. Remove from heat; add the tomato purée.
5. Return to heat.
6. Gradually add the hot stock.
7. Stir to the boil.
8. Add the bouquet garni; season lightly.
9. Simmer for approximately 1 hour. Skim when required.
10. Remove the bouquet garni.
11. Pass firmly through a sieve then through a fine conical strainer, or liquidise.
12. Return to a clean pan, correct the seasoning

and consistency. Bring to the boil.
13. Serve $\frac{1}{2}$ cm ($\frac{1}{8}$ in.) dice fried or toasted croûtons separately.

Brown onion soup *4 portions*

600 g	$1\frac{1}{2}$ lb	onions
25 g	1 oz	fat or oil
10 g	$\frac{1}{2}$ oz	flour (white or wholemeal)
1 litre	2 pt	brown stock
		salt, mill pepper
		$\frac{1}{4}$ of a French (bread) stick
50 g	2 oz	grated cheese

1. Peel the onions, halve and slice finely.
2. Melt the fat or oil in a thick-bottomed pan, add the onion and cook steadily over a good heat until cooked and well browned.
3. Mix in the flour and cook over a gentle heat, browning slightly.
4. Gradually mix in the stock, bring to the boil, skim and season.
5. Simmer for approximately 10 minutes until the onion is soft. Correct the seasoning.
6. Pour into an earthenware tureen or casserole, or into individual dishes.
7. Cut the French stick, 2 cm (1 in.) diameter into slices, and toast on both sides.
8. Sprinkle the toasted slices of bread liberally over the soup.
9. Sprinkle with more grated cheese and brown under the salamander. Serve.

Minestroni *4 portions*

300 g	12 oz	mixed vegetables (onion, leek, celery, carrot, turnip, cabbage)
50 g	2 oz	fat or oil
$\frac{3}{4}$ litre	$1\frac{1}{2}$ pt	white stock
		bouquet garni
		salt, pepper
25 g	1 oz	peas
25 g	1 oz	French beans
25 g	1 oz	spaghetti
50 g	2 oz	potatoes
		1 tsp tomato purée
100 g	4 oz	tomatoes (skinned, diced)
50 g	2 oz	fat bacon
		chopped parsley
		1 clove garlic

1. Cut the peeled and washed vegetables into paysanne.
2. Cook slowly without colour in the fat or oil in a pan with a lid.
3. Add the stock, bouquet garni and seasoning. Simmer for approximately 20 minutes.
4. Add the peas, and the beans cut in diamonds, and simmer for 10 minutes.
5. Add the spaghetti in 2 cm (1 in.) lengths, the potatoes cut in paysanne, the tomato purée and the diced tomatoes, and simmer gently until all the vegetables are cooked.
6. Meanwhile finely chop the fat bacon, parsley and garlic, and form into a paste.
7. Mould the paste into pellets the size of a pea and drop into the boiling soup.
8. Remove the bouquet garni. Correct the seasoning.
9. Serve grated cheese (Parmesan) and thin, toasted slices of French stick separately.

Egg recipes

Hard-boiled eggs

1. Plunge the eggs into a pan of boiling water.
2. Reboil and simmer for 8 to 10 minutes.
3. Refresh until cold under running water.

If high temperatures or a long cooking time are used to cook eggs, an unsightly blackish ring around the yolk will form. Stale eggs will also show a black ring around the yolk.

Curried eggs

50 g	2 oz	rice (long grain)
		4 hard-boiled eggs
250 ml	$\frac{1}{2}$ pt	curry sauce (page 15)

1. Wash the rice.
2. Add to plenty of boiling salt water.
3. Stir to the boil and allow to simmer gently till tender, approximately 12 – 15 minutes.
4. Wash well under running water, drain and place on a sieve and cover with a cloth.
5. Place on a tray in a moderate oven or on a hot plate until hot.
6. Place the rice in an earthenware dish.
7. Reheat the eggs in hot salt water, cut into halves and dress neatly on the rice.
8. Coat the eggs with sauce and serve.

Boiled eggs

Allow 1 or 2 eggs per portion.

Method 1 – place the eggs in cold water, bring to the boil, simmer 2 – $2\frac{1}{2}$ minutes, remove from the water and serve at once in an egg cup.

Method 2 – plunge the eggs in boiling water, reboil, simmer 3 – 5 minutes.

Boiled eggs are always served in the shell.

Soft-boiled eggs

Plunge the eggs into boiling water, reboil, simmer for 5½ minutes. Refresh immediately. Remove the shells carefully. Reheat when required for ½ minute in hot salt water.

The recipes given for poached eggs (page 31 – 32) can be applied to soft-boiled eggs.

Pasta recipes

Pasta may be served for lunch, dinner or supper, or as a snack meal, and can also be used as a garnish for other dishes.

General points for cooking and serving pasta

1. Always cook in plenty of boiling salted water.
2. Stir to the boil. Do not overcook; pasta should be firm to the bite (*al dente*).
3. If not to be used immediately, refresh and reheat carefully in hot salted water when required.
4. Drain well in a colander.
5. With most pasta, grated cheese (preferably Parmesan) should be served separately.
6. Allow 10 g (½ oz) pasta per portion as a garnish.
7. Allow 25 – 50 g (1 – 2 oz) pasta per portion for a main course.

Spaghetti with tomato sauce

100 g	4 oz	spaghetti
250 ml	½ pt	tomato sauce (page 16)
25 g	1 oz	grated cheese

1. Plunge spaghetti into a saucepan containing plenty of boiling salted water.
2. Allow to boil gently.
3. Stir occasionally with a wooden spoon.
4. Cook for 12 to 15 minutes approx.
5. Drain well in a colander.
6. Return to a clean, dry pan.
7. Mix in the tomato sauce.
8. Correct the seasoning and serve grated cheese separately.

Spaghetti bolognese

25 g	1 oz	fat or oil
50 g	2 oz	chopped onion
100 g	4 oz	lean minced beef
125 ml	¼ pt	jus-lié or demi-glace
50 g	2 oz	tomato purée
		salt, mill pepper
		a little marjoram or oregano
100 g	4 oz	spaghetti

1. Place half the fat or oil in a sauteuse.
2. Add the chopped onion and cook for 4 to 5 minutes without colour.
3. Add the beef and cook, colouring lightly.
4. Add the jus-lié or demi-glace and tomato purée.
5. Simmer till tender.
6. Correct the seasoning.
7. Meanwhile cook the spaghetti in plenty of boiling salted water.
8. Allow to boil gently.
9. Stir occasionally with a wooden spoon.
10. Cook for approximately 12 to 15 minutes.
11. Drain well in a colander.
12. Return to a clean pan containing the remaining fat or oil.
13. Correct the seasoning and serve, coated with the sauce.

Macaroni cheese

100 g	4 oz	macaroni
100 g	4 oz	grated cheese
500 ml	1 pt	thin béchamel
		½ tsp diluted English mustard
		salt, mill pepper

1. Plunge the macaroni into a saucepan containing plenty of boiling salted water.
2. Allow to boil gently.
3. Stir occasionally with a wooden spoon.
4. Cook for approximately 15 minutes.
5. Drain well in a colander.
6. Return to a clean pan.
7. Mix with half the cheese. Add the béchamel and mustard and season.
8. Place in an earthenware dish.
9. Sprinkle with the remainder of the cheese.
10. Brown lightly under the salamander and serve.

Macaroni may also be prepared and served as for spaghetti bolognese.

Plain boiled rice *4 portions*

100 g	4 oz	rice (long grain)
$1\frac{1}{2}$ litres	3 pt (at least)	water

1. Wash the long-grain rice.
2. Add to plenty of boiling salt water.
3. Stir to the boil and allow to simmer gently till tender, approximately 12 – 15 minutes.
4. Wash well under running water, drain and place on a sieve and cover with a cloth.
5. Place on a tray in a moderate oven or in the hot plate until hot.

Risotto *4 portions*

50 g	2 oz	fat or oil
25 g	1 oz	chopped onions
100 g	4 oz	rice (short grain)
185 ml	$\frac{3}{8}$ pint approx	white stock (preferably chicken)
25 g	1 oz	grated Parmesan cheese
		salt, mill pepper

1. Melt the fat or oil in a small sauteuse.
2. Add the chopped onion.
3. Cook gently without colour for 2 to 3 minutes.
4. Add the washed and well drained rice.
5. Cook without colour for 2 to 3 minutes.
6. Add the stock, season lightly.
7. Cover with a lid.
8. Allow to simmer on the side of the stove.
9. Stir frequently and if necessary add more stock until the rice is cooked.
10. When cooked, all the stock should have been absorbed into the rice and evaporated.
11. A risotto should be more moist than a pilaff.
12. Finally, mix in the cheese with a fork, correct the seasoning and serve.

Fish recipes

Boiled cod

1. If using whole cod, cut into 1 – 2 cm ($\frac{1}{2}$ – 1 in.) slices on the bone (cod cutlets). Where required, tie with string.
2. Place the prepared fish into a shallow pan of simmering salted water containing lemon juice.
3. Simmer gently until cooked, approximately 7 – 10 minutes.
4. Remove the centre bone and string before serving.
5. Serve with a suitable sauce, e.g. parsley, egg, anchovy.

Boiled salmon $\frac{1}{2}$ kg (1 lb) uncleaned salmon yields *2 – 3 portions*

Salmon may be obtained in varying weights from $3\frac{1}{2}$ – 15 kg (7 – 30 lb). Size is an important consideration, depending on whether the salmon is to be cooked whole or cut into slices (darnes). A salmon of any size may be cooked whole. When required for darnes, a medium-sized salmon will be more suitable.

Fish cooking liquid Known as *court bouillon*

1 litre	1 qt	water
10 g	$\frac{1}{2}$ oz	salt
50 g	2 oz	carrots (sliced)
		1 bay leaf
		2 – 3 parsley stalks
60 ml	$\frac{1}{8}$ pt	vinegar
		6 peppercorns
50 g	2 oz	onions (sliced)
		sprig of thyme

Simmer all the ingredients for 30 to 40 minutes. Pass through a strainer, use as required.

Boiled cut salmon

When cooking salmon in cut portions:

1. Place in a simmering court bouillon and simmer gently for approximately 5 minutes. Drain well; remove the centre bone.
2. Serve garnished with picked parsley, and a plain boiled potato.
3. Accompany with sliced cucumber and a suitable sauce, e.g. Hollandaise sauce.

Meat recipes

Boiled salt beef, carrots and dumplings *4 portions*

400 g	1 lb	silverside, brisket, or thin flank
200 g	8 oz	carrots
200 g	8 oz	onions
100 g	4 oz	suet paste (page 37)

1. Soak the meat in cold water to remove excess brine for 1 to 2 hours.
2. Place in a saucepan and cover with cold water; bring to the boil and skim. Simmer for 45 minutes.
3. Add whole, peeled onions and carrots, and simmer gently until cooked.
4. Divide the suet paste into 8 even pieces; lightly mould into balls.
5. Add the dumplings and simmer for a further 15 to 30 minutes.
6. Serve by carving the meat across the grain, garnish with carrots, onions and dumplings, and moisten with a little of the cooking liquor.

Brine

$2\frac{1}{2}$ litres	4 qt	cold water
15 g	$\frac{3}{4}$ oz	saltpetre
$\frac{1}{2}$ – 1 kg	1 – 2 lb	salt

Boil the ingredients together for 10 minutes, skimming frequently. Strain into a china, wooden or earthenware container. When the brine is cold, add the meat. Immerse the meat for up to 10 days. Keep in a refrigerator.

Boiled fresh beef *4 portions*

600 g	1 lb 8 oz	thin flank or brisket
		salt, pepper
		1 head celery
200 g	8 oz	leek
		small cabbage
200 g	8 oz	onion
200 g	8 oz	carrot
100 g	4 oz	turnip

1. Blanch and refresh the meat.
2. Place in a clean pan and cover with cold water.
3. Bring to the boil and skim, season and allow to simmer.
4. Prepare all the vegetables by tying the celery and leek into bundles, tying the cabbage to keep it in one piece, and leaving the rest of the vegetables whole.
5. After the meat has simmered for 30 minutes add the celery, onions and carrots and continue cooking for 30 minutes.
6. Add the leek, cabbage and turnips and continue cooking till all is tender, approximately 2 – $2\frac{1}{2}$ hours in all.
7. Serve by carving the meat in slices against the grain, garnish with the vegetables and pour a little liquor over the meat.

Tripe and onions *4 portions*

400 g	1 lb	tripe
500 ml	1 pt	milk and water
200 g	$\frac{1}{2}$ lb	onion
		salt, pepper
25 g	1 oz	flour or cornflour

1. Wash the tripe well.
2. Cut into neat 5 cm (2 in.) squares.
3. Blanch and refresh.
4. Cook the tripe in the milk and water with the sliced onions.
5. Season and simmer $1\frac{1}{2}$ – 2 hours.
6. Gradually add the diluted flour or cornflour, stir with a wooden spoon to the boil.
7. Simmer for 5 to 10 minutes, correct the seasoning and serve.

An alternative thickening is $\frac{1}{8}$ litre ($\frac{1}{4}$ pt) of béchamel in place of the cornflour and milk.

Boiled bacon hock, collar or gammon

1. Remove any bones that may interfere with carving the meat after it is cooked.
2. Soak the bacon in cold water for 24 hours before cooking.
3. Change the water.
4. Bring to the boil, skim and simmer gently, approximately 25 minutes per $\frac{1}{2}$ kg (1 lb), and 25 minutes over.
5. Allow to cool in the liquid.
6. Remove the rind and brown skin.
7. Carve into thin slices and serve with a little of the cooking liquid.

Bacon may be served with pease pudding (see page 26) and a suitable sauce, such as parsley sauce.

Poultry recipes

Boiled chicken and rice, suprême sauce *4 portions*

2 – $2\frac{1}{2}$ kg	4 – 5 lb	1 boiling fowl
50 g	2 oz	onion
50 g	2 oz	carrot
		bouquet garni
		6 peppercorns
75 g	3 oz	butter or margarine
1 litre	2 pt	chicken stock
		few drops of lemon juice
75 g	3 oz	flour
		4 tbsp cream or yoghurt

50 g	2 oz	butter or oil
50 g	2 oz	chopped onion
200 g	8 oz	rice (long grain)
500 ml	1 pt	chicken stock

1. Place the cleaned and trussed chicken in cold water.
2. Bring to the boil and skim.
3. Add peeled, whole, washed vegetables, the bouquet garni, peppercorns and salt.
4. Simmer till cooked. To test, remove the chicken from the stock and hold over a plate to catch the juices from the inside of the bird. There should be no sign of blood. Also test the drumstick with a trussing needle, which should penetrate easily to the bone.
5. Prepare $\frac{1}{2}$ litre (1 pt) of velouté from the cooking liquor; simmer for 1 hour. Correct the seasoning and pass through a fine strainer.
6. Finish with cream or yoghurt.
7. Prepare a pilaff of rice (see page 45).

To serve, cut into portions. Dress the rice neatly on the plate or serving dish, arrange the portions of chicken on top and coat with sauce.

Vegetable recipes

Beetroot

Select medium size or small beetroots, and carefully twist off the green leaves. Wash well in cold water, cover with water and simmer gently until the skin is easily removed by rubbing between the fingers. Do not cut or prick with knife, as the beetroots will 'bleed' and turn pale. Beetroots may also be cooked in a steamer.

Broccoli

Cook and serve as for any of the cauliflower recipes. Green and purple broccoli, because of their size, need less cooking time than cauliflower.

Buttered carrots, turnips or swedes

4 portions

400 g	1 lb	carrots, turnips or swedes
		salt, sugar
25 g	1 oz	butter
		chopped parsley

1. Peel and wash the vegetables.
2. Cut into neat even pieces.
3. Place in a pan with a little salt, a pinch of sugar and butter. Barely cover with water.
4. Cover with a buttered paper and allow to boil steadily in order to evaporate all the water.
5. When the water has completely evaporated check that the vegetables are cooked. If not, add a little more water and continue cooking. Do *not* overcook.
6. Toss the vegetables over a fierce heat for 1 to 2 minutes in order to give them a glaze.
7. Serve sprinkled with chopped parsley.
8. Overcooking will lessen the vitamin content. This point is true when cooking any green vegetables.

Brussels sprouts

$\frac{1}{2}$ kg (1 lb) will yield 3 – 4 portions

1. Using a small knife, trim the stems and cut a cross 2 mm ($\frac{1}{12}$ in.) deep. Remove any discoloured leaves.
2. Wash well.
3. Cook in boiling salted water, approximately 5 – 15 minutes according to size. Do *not* overcook.
4. Drain well in a colander and serve.

Cauliflower

Allow 1 medium sized cauliflower for 4 portions

1. Trim the stem and remove outer leaves.
2. Hollow out the stem with a peeler.
3. Wash well.
4. Cook in boiling salted water, approximately 15 – 20 minutes. Do *not* overcook.
5. Drain well; cut into neat even portions and serve.

Cauliflower may be served plain or with a cream or Hollandaise sauce.

Cauliflower with cheese sauce

Known as Cauliflower Mornay

1. Cut the cooked cauliflower into 4 portions.
2. Reheat in a pan of hot salted water and drain well. Place on tray or serving dish.
3. Coat with $\frac{1}{4}$ litre ($\frac{1}{2}$ pt) Mornay (cheese) sauce (see page 14).
4. Sprinkle with grated cheese.
5. Brown under the grill.

Marrow $\frac{1}{2}$ kg (1 lb) will yield 2 – 3 portions

1. Peel the marrow using a peeler.
2. Cut in half lengthwise.
3. Remove the seeds with a spoon.
4. Cut into even pieces approximately 5 cm (2 in.) square.
5. Cook in boiling salted water for approximately 5 – 15 minutes.
6. Drain well and serve as for any of the cauliflower recipes.

Leaf spinach $\frac{1}{2}$ kg (1 lb) will yield 2 portions

1. Remove the stems and discard them.
2. Wash the leaves very carefully in plenty of deep water several times as necessary.
3. Cook in boiling salted water until tender, approximately 5 minutes. Drain well and serve.
4. If not for immediate service, refresh under cold water and squeeze dry into a ball.
5. When required for service, place into a pan containing 25 – 50 g (1 – 2 oz) butter, loosen with a fork and reheat quickly without colouring. Season with salt and mill pepper and serve.

Spinach purée

1. Cook, refresh and drain spinach as above.
2. Pass through a sieve, mincer or mouli, or liquidise.
3. Reheat in 25 – 50 g (1 – 2 oz) butter, mix with a wooden spoon. Season and serve

Broad beans $\frac{1}{2}$ kg (1 lb) will yield approximately 2 portions

Shell the beans and cook in boiling salted water until tender, approximately 10 – 20 minutes. Do *not* overcook. Drain well and serve. If the inner skins are tough they should also be removed.

Haricot beans $\frac{1}{2}$ kg (1 lb) will yield 6 – 8 portions

1. Soak the beans if necessary in cold water overnight in a cool place.
2. Change the water.
3. Cover the beans with cold water and bring to the boil.
4. Skim when necessary.
5. Add 50 g (2 oz) carrot, 50 g (2 oz) onion, 50 g (2 oz) bacon trimmings (optional) and a bouquet garni to every $\frac{1}{2}$ kg (1 lb) beans.
6. Continue simmering gently until tender; add salt.
7. Drain well and serve.

French beans $\frac{1}{2}$ kg (1 lb) will yield 3 – 4 portions

1. Top and tail the beans, carefully and economically.
2. Using a large sharp knife, cut the beans into thin strips approximately 5 cm × 3 cm (2 × $\frac{1}{8}$ in.).
3. Wash.
4. Cook in boiling salted water until tender, approximately 5 – 15 minutes. Do *not* overcook.

Peas (fresh) $\frac{1}{2}$ kg (1 lb) will yield approximately 2 portions

1. Shell and wash the peas.
2. Cook in boiling salted water with a sprig of mint until tender, approximately 5 – 15 minutes. Do *not* overcook.
3. Drain well and serve.

Basic tomato preparation

Known as tomato concassée

This is a cooked preparation which is usually included in the normal *mise-en-place* of a kitchen, as it is used in a great number of dishes.

400 g	1 lb	tomatoes
25 g	1 oz	chopped shallot or onion
25 g	1 oz	fat or oil
		salt, pepper

1. Remove the eyes from the tomatoes.
2. Plunge into boiling water for 5 to 6 seconds. Refresh immediately.
3. Remove the skins, cut in halves across the tomato and remove all the seeds.
4. Roughly chop the flesh of the tomatoes.
5. Meanwhile cook the chopped onion or shallot without colouring in the fat or oil.
6. Add the tomatoes and season.
7. Simmer gently on the side of the stove until the moisture has evaporated.

Pease pudding

200 g	8 oz	yellow split peas (soaked)
$\frac{1}{2}$ litre	approx. 1 pt.	water
50 g	2 oz	onion

50 g	2 oz	carrot
50 g	2 oz	bacon trimmings (optional)
50 g	2 oz	butter or margarine (optional)
		salt, pepper

1. Place all the ingredients, except the butter or margarine, in a saucepan with a tight-fitting lid.
2. Bring to the boil, cook in a moderate oven (150 – 200°C) for approximately 2 hours.
3. Remove onion, carrot and bacon and pass the peas through a sieve, or emulsify.
4. Return to a clean pan, mix in the butter or margarine, and correct the seasoning and consistency (this should be firm).

Mixed vegetables *4 portions*

100 g	4 oz	carrot
50 g	2 oz	turnips
50 g	2 oz	French beans
50 g	2 oz	peas

1. Peel and wash the carrots and turnips.
2. Cut into $\frac{1}{2}$ cm ($\frac{1}{4}$ in.) dice or batons.
3. Cook separately in salted water and refresh.
4. Top and tail the beans.
5. Cut into $\frac{1}{2}$ cm ($\frac{1}{4}$ in.) dice, cook and refresh.
6. Cook the peas and refresh.
7. Mix the vegetables together and when required reheat in hot salted water.
8. Drain well and serve.

Potato recipes

$\frac{1}{2}$ kg (1 lb) old potatoes will yield approximately 3 portions
$\frac{1}{2}$ kg (1 lb) new potatoes will yield approximtely 4 portions

Plain boiled potatoes

1. Wash, peel and again wash the potatoes.
2. Cut, shape or turn into even-sized pieces, allowing 2 – 3 pieces per portion.
3. Cook carefully in salted water for approximately 20 minutes.
4. Drain well and serve.

Parsley potatoes

1. Prepare and cook potatoes as for plain boiled.
2. Brush liberally with melted butter, sprinkle with chopped parsley and serve.

Mashed potatoes

1. Wash, peel and rewash the potatoes. Cut to an even size.
2. Cook in salted water.
3. Drain off the water, place a lid on the saucepan and return to a low heat to dry out the potatoes.
4. Pass through a medium sieve or a special potato masher.
5. Return the potatoes to a clean pan.
6. Add 25 g (1 oz) butter per $\frac{1}{2}$ kg (1 lb) and mix in with a wooden spoon.
7. Gradually add 30 ml ($\frac{1}{8}$ pt) warm milk, stirring continuously until a soft, creamy consistency is obtained.
8. Correct the seasoning and serve.

Duchess potatoes (basic recipe)

1. Wash, peel and rewash the potatoes. Cut to an even size.
2. Cook in salted water.
3. Drain off the water, place a lid on the saucepan and return to a low heat to dry out the potatoes.
4. Pass through a medium sieve or a special potato masher or mouli.
5. Place the potatoes in a clean pan.
6. Add 1 yolk per $\frac{1}{2}$ kg (1 lb) and stir in vigorously with a wooden spoon.
7. Mix in 25 g (1 oz) butter or margarine per $\frac{1}{2}$ kg (1 lb).

Piping duchess potato

8. Correct the seasoning.
9. Place in a piping bag with a large star tube.
10. Pipe out into neat spirals approximately 2 cm (1 in.) in diameter and 5 cm (2 in.) high on to a lightly greased baking sheet.
11. Place in a hot oven (230 – 250°C) for 2 to 3 minutes in order to slightly firm the edges.
12. Remove from the oven and brush with eggwash.
13. Brown lightly in a hot oven or under the grill and serve.

Marquis potatoes

1. Pipe out duchess mixture in the shape of an oval nest 5 × 2 cm (2 × 1 in.).
2. Glaze as for duchess potatoes.
3. Place a spoonful of cooked tomato (page 26) in the centre, sprinkle with a little chopped parsley and serve.

Sweet recipes

Fruit fool *4 portions*

Method 1: apple, gooseberry, rhubarb, etc.

400 g	1 lb	fruit
60 ml	$\frac{1}{8}$ pt	water
100 g	4 oz	sugar

Cook to a purée and pass through a sieve.

25	1 oz	cornflour
$\frac{1}{4}$ litre	$\frac{1}{2}$ pt	milk
25 g	1 oz	sugar

1. Dilute the cornflour in a little of the milk. Add the sugar.
2. Boil remainder of the milk.
3. Pour onto the diluted cornflour; stir well.
4. Return to the pan on low heat and stir to the boil.
5. Mix with the fruit purée. The quantity of mixture should not be less than $\frac{1}{2}$ litre (1 pt).
6. Pour into four glass coupes and allow to set.
7. Decorate with a rose of whipped, sweetened cream.

Method 2:

400 g	1 lb	fruit in purée
100 g	4 oz	castor sugar
$\frac{1}{4}$ litre	$\frac{1}{2}$ pt	fresh whipped cream

Mix together and serve in coupes.

Rhubarb fool in coupe, and rosette of cream

Rice pudding – ingredients as for baked rice pudding (see page 81)

1. Boil the milk in a thick-bottomed pan.
2. Add the washed rice; stir to the boil.
3. Simmer gently, stirring frequently until the rice is cooked.
4. Mix in the sugar, flavouring and butter, and serve.
5. If required, pour into a pie dish, place on a baking sheet, brown lightly under the salamander and serve.

Semolina pudding *4 portions*

$\frac{1}{2}$ litre	1 pt	milk or skimmed milk
35 g	$1\frac{1}{2}$ oz	semolina
50 g	2 oz	sugar (white or unrefined)
10 g	$\frac{1}{2}$ oz	butter or margarine
		2 – 3 drops lemon juice or lemon essence

1. Boil the milk in a thick-bottomed pan.
2. Sprinkle in the semolina and stir to the boil.
3. Simmer for 15 to 20 minutes.
4. Add the sugar, butter and flavouring (an egg yolk if desired).
5. Pour into a pie dish.
6. Brown under the salamander and serve.

Sago pudding, tapioca pudding, ground rice pudding

These are made in the same way as for semolina pudding, using sago, tapioca or ground rice in place of semolina, and vanilla essence instead of lemon essence.

Questions – Boiling

1. When boiling foods they should be
   a) half covered with liquid,
   b) three-quarters covered with liquid, or
   c) fully covered with liquid?

2. Why is it necessary to soak pre-salted foods for a few hours before cooking?

3. Boiling chickens are more expensive than roasting chickens. True or false?

4. When boiling cut fish are they started in cold or hot liquid?

5. Which temperature of liquid is higher, simmering or boiling?

6. Which of the following is started in hot liquid, and which in cold liquid? Green vegetables, fresh beef.

7. When boiling green vegetables, which is correct?
   a) cover with lid and simmer till cooked;
   b) use no lid and simmer till cooked;
   c) bring to boil with lid on, remove lid and cook quickly;
   d) cover with lid and boil rapidly.

8. Name 4 different foods cooked by boiling.

9. Which of these are suitable for boiling? Bacon joints, silverside of beef, leg of mutton, ox tongue, ham.

10. Green vegetables when correctly cooked should be
   a) mushy,
   b) well done,
   c) slightly firm,
   d) firm?

Answers can be found on page 152.

5

Poaching

General objectives To have a knowledge and understanding of poaching.
Specific objectives To give the definition and the principles of poaching; to explain the purpose of poaching; to demonstrate poaching as a method of cookery; to state the foods which are poached; to explain the effect of poaching on food; to describe the advantages of poaching; to explain the techniques used in poaching; to specify the selection, use and care of equipment; to explain and apply efficiency and safety procedures; to use recipes associated with poaching.

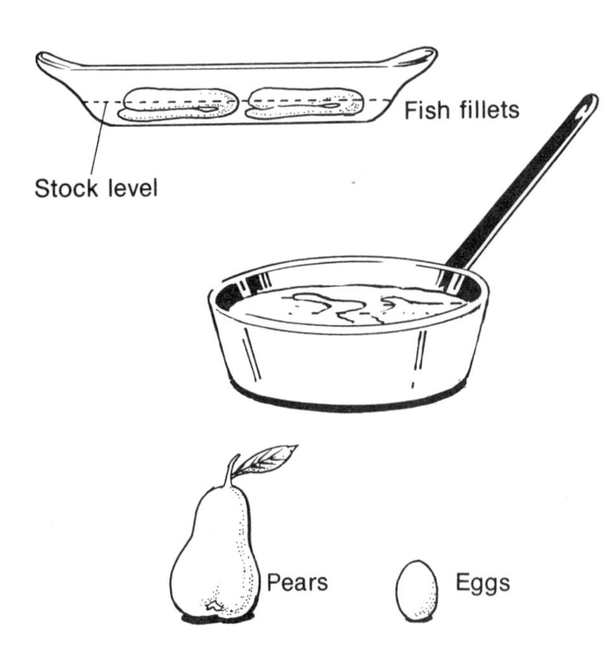

Definition

Poaching is the cooking of foods in a suitably sized container in the minimum amount of liquid (water, stock, milk or wine).

The principles of poaching are as follows:

1. The food must cook slowly.
2. The liquid should never boil but be kept as near to boiling point as possible.
3. Food should be covered with greaseproof paper or foil during cooking. (Poached eggs are an exception to this principle.)

When poaching is carried out with these rules observed, the maximum flavour and nutritive value of the food is retained.

Equipment used for poaching

Shallow pans, trays, ovenproof dishes and small equipment must be clean and hygienically stored when not in use. These items of equipment are cleaned in hot detergent water, rinsed, drained and dried before storing.

Safety

Take care to prevent burns and scalds when poaching, e.g. trays tilting when being removed from the oven.

Examples of foods cooked by poaching

Fish, fruit and eggs.

Fish
Most fish can be poached. They are usually filleted, but some fish can be poached whole. The fish is placed in a lightly buttered dish, barely covered with fish stock, wine or milk, and covered with lightly buttered greaseproof paper. It is then cooked in the oven. The fish may be garnished and lemon juice or wine added before cooking; usually the cooking liquid is used to form part of the coating sauce. Careful handling of the fish is necessary to avoid breaking it.

Poached eggs

Fruits
A wide variety of fresh fruits can be poached: e.g. plums, pears, apricots, apples and peaches can be cooked whole, and apples, pears and rhubarb can be cut into pieces and poached.

Whether whole or in pieces, sufficient stock syrup is added just to cover the fruit and, when required, lemon juice to retain colour and cloves for added flavour. The fruit is covered with kitchen paper, foil or a lid and cooked slowly in the oven to prevent it from breaking up. In some establishments fruit cooked in this manner is referred to as stewed fruit, or *compôte* of fruit.

Dried fruits, such as prunes or apricots, after being soaked in cold water may be poached and they do not break up as easily as fresh fruit. They can be brought to the boil on top of the stove and the cooking finished in the oven or on top of the stove.

Eggs
Poached eggs are the exception to the above rules. They are gently cooked in approximately 8 cm (3 in.) of steadily simmering water containing a little vinegar.

Eggs cooked in individual shallow metal pans fitted over a small amount of boiling water are in reality cooked by steaming.

Poached egg recipes

Only fresh eggs should be used for poaching because they have a large amount of thick white and consequently have little tendency to spread in the simmering water.

A well prepared poached egg has a firm, tender white surrounding the slightly thickened, unbroken yolk. The use of a little vinegar (an acid) helps to set the egg white, so preventing it from spreading; it also makes the white more tender and whiter. Too much vinegar will discolour and give the eggs a strong vinegar flavour.

1. Carefully break the eggs, one by one, into a shallow pan containing at least 8 cm (3 in.) gently boiling water to which a little vinegar has been added (1 litre (1 qt) water to 1 tbsp vinegar).
2. Simmer until lightly set, approximately $2\frac{1}{2}$ – 3 minutes. Drain well and serve.
3. If not required for immediate use, remove carefully with a perforated spoon into a bowl of cold water.
4. Trim the white of egg if necessary.
5. Reheat, when required, by placing into hot salted water for approximately $\frac{1}{2}$ to 1 minute.
6. Remove carefully and drain on a clean cloth.
7. Use as required.

Poached eggs with cheese sauce

Known as poached eggs Mornay

4 eggs
4 short paste tartlets, or

		4 half-slices of buttered toast
250 ml	$\frac{1}{2}$ pt	cheese sauce (see page 14)

1. Poach the eggs; drain well.
2. Place tartlets or buttered toast in a serving dish (the slices of toast may be halved, cut round with a cutter, and the crust removed).
3. Add the hot, well-drained eggs.
4. Completely cover with sauce, sprinkle with grated Parmesan cheese. Brown under the salamander and serve.

Poached eggs with cheese sauce and spinach

Known as poached eggs florentine

$\frac{3}{4}$ kg	1 lb 8 oz	spinach
		4 eggs
250 ml	$\frac{1}{2}$ pt	cheese sauce

1. Remove the stems from the spinach.
2. Wash very carefully in plenty of water several times if necessary.
3. Cook in boiling salted water until tender for approximately 5 minutes.
4. Refresh under cold water; squeeze dry into a ball.
5. When required for service, place into a pan containing 25 – 50 g (1 – 2 oz) butter or oil, loosen with a fork and reheat quickly without colouring; season with salt and mill pepper.
6. Place in the serving dish.
7. Place the eggs on top, and finish as for eggs Mornay.

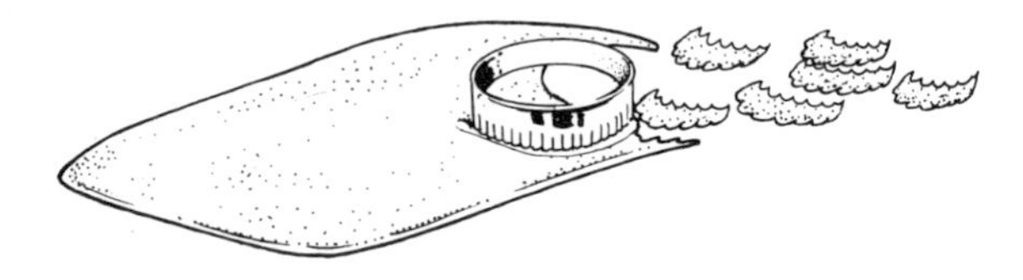

Puff-paste fleurons

Poached fish recipes

The following recipes may be used for portioned fillets of any white fish. The method of making the sauce can also be varied (see page 13).

For service always place a little sauce under the fish before masking; this keeps the fish moist, preventing it from overcooking and sticking to the dish, thus facilitating service. The type of fish should always be named on the menu, e.g. fillets of lemon sole Duglèré.

Fillets of fish with white wine sauce

4 portions

50 g	2 oz	butter
10 g	$\frac{1}{2}$ oz	finely chopped shallot
500 – 600 g	1 – 1$\frac{1}{4}$ lb	fish fillets
60 ml	$\frac{1}{8}$ pt	fish stock
60 ml	$\frac{1}{8}$ pt	dry white wine
		juice of $\frac{1}{4}$ lemon
250 ml	$\frac{1}{2}$ pt	fish velouté
		2 tbsp cream

1. Butter and season an earthenware dish.
2. Sprinkle with the chopped shallot.
3. Add the fillets of fish.
4. Season, add the fish stock, wine and lemon juice.
5. Cover with buttered, greaseproof paper.
6. Poach gently in a moderate oven (150 – 200°C), 5 – 10 minutes.
7. Drain the fish well; place on a little sauce on the serving dish and keep warm.
8. Bring the cooking liquor to the boil with the velouté.
9. Correct the seasoning and consistency, and pass through a fine strainer.
10. Mix in the butter, and add the cream.
11. Coat the fillets with the sauce. Garnish with puff-paste crescents – known as fleurons.

Fillets of fish Duglèré

4 portions

50 g	2 oz	butter
10 g	$\frac{1}{2}$ oz	*finely* chopped shallots
500 – 600 g	1 – 1$\frac{1}{4}$ lb	fish fillets
200 g	8 oz	tomatoes concassée
		pinch chopped parsley
		salt, pepper
60 ml	$\frac{1}{8}$ pt	fish stock
60 ml	$\frac{1}{8}$ pt	dry white wine
		juice of $\frac{1}{4}$ lemon
250 ml	$\frac{1}{2}$ pt	fish velouté

1. Butter and season an earthenware dish.
2. Sprinkle in the chopped shallots.
3. Add the fillets, tomatoes and chopped parsley.

4. Season with salt and pepper.
5. Add the fish stock, wine and the lemon juice.
6. Cover with buttered greaseproof paper.
7. Poach gently in a moderate oven (150 – 200°C), 5 – 10 minutes.
8. Remove the fillets and the garnish; drain well. Place on a little sauce on the serving dish and keep warm.
9. Pass and reduce the cooking liquor in a small sauteuse, add the fish velouté, then incorporate the butter.
10. Correct the seasoning and consistency.
11. Coat the fillets with the sauce and serve.

Fillets of fish Mornay *4 portions*

500 – 600 g	1 – 1½ lb	fish fillet
125 ml	¼ pt	fish stock
250 ml	½ pt	béchamel sauce
		yolk or sabayon
50 g	2 oz	grated cheese
		salt, cayenne
25 g	1 oz	butter
		2 tbsp cream

1. Prepare fillets, place in a buttered, seasoned earthenware dish or shallow pan, such as a sauté pan.
2. Add the fish stock, and cover with buttered greaseproof paper.
3. Cook in a moderate oven (150 – 200°C), approximately 5 – 10 minutes.
4. Drain the fish well, place on the serving dish and keep warm.
5. Bring the béchamel to the boil, whisk in the yolk and remove from the heat. Add cheese and sufficient cooking liquor to correct the consistency. Do *not* reboil, otherwise the egg will curdle.
6. Correct the seasoning and pass through a fine strainer.
7. Mix in the butter and cream.
8. Mask the fish, sprinkle with grated cheese and brown under the grill.

Poached smoked haddock *4 portions*

400 – 600 g	1 – 1½ lb	smoked haddock
250 ml	½ pt	milk
250 ml	½ pt	water

1. Trim off all fins from the fish.
2. Cut into 4 even pieces.
3. Simmer gently in the milk and water.
4. When cooked, the backbone should be easy to remove.
5. Remove the backbone and serve.

Poached fruit recipes

Poached fruits *4 portions*

Also known as compôte of fruits

100 g	4 oz	sugar	stock syrup
¼ litre	½ pt	water	stock syrup
		½ lemon	stock syrup
400 g	1 lb	fruit	

Apples, pears

1. Boil the water and sugar.
2. Quarter the fruit; remove the core and peel.
3. Place in a shallow pan in stock syrup.
4. Add a few drops of lemon juice; cover with greaseproof paper.
5. Allow to simmer slowly, preferably in the oven. Cool and serve.

Soft fruits – raspberries, strawberries

1. Pick and wash the fruit, and place in a glass bowl.
2. Pour on the hot syrup.
3. Allow to cool and serve.

Stone fruits – plums, damsons, greengages, cherries

Wash the fruit, barely cover with stock syrup and cover with greaseproof paper or a lid. Cook gently in a moderate oven until tender.

Rhubarb

Trim off the stalk and leaf, and wash. Cut into 5 cm (2 in.) lengths and cook as for apples, adding extra sugar if necessary.

Gooseberries

Top and tail gooseberries; wash and cook as for stone fruit, adding extra sugar if necessary. Check by tasting.

Blackcurrants, redcurrants

The currants should be carefully removed from the stalks, washed and cooked as for stone fruits.

Dried fruits – prunes, apricots, apples

Dried fruits should be washed and soaked in cold water overnight. Gently cook in the liquor with sufficient sugar to taste. A piece of cinnamon stick and a few slices of lemon may be added to the prunes.

Questions – Poaching

1. Give a brief description of poaching as a method of cookery.
   Slow cook in minimum amount of water
2. What food is the exception in poaching?
   EGGS
3. The cooking liquid from poached fish should always be used to form part of the sAUCE to be served with the fish.
4. Poached fruits are sometimes referred to by two other names. One is stewed, the other is c.OMPO.TE
5. Poached eggs are cooked in which depth of water?

   a) 2.5 cm (1 in.) b) 5 cm (2 in.)
   c) 8 cm (3 in.) ✓ d) 10 cm (4 in.)
6. How much liquid is required, and what degree of movement of the liquid occurs when poaching? WATER TO JUST COVER
7. Why are poached foods such as fish covered with a buttered paper?
   STOP DRYING OUT

Answers can be found on page 152.

6

Steaming

General objectives To have a knowledge and understanding of steaming.
Specific objectives To state the definition and principles of steaming; to explain the reasons for steaming; to demonstrate steaming as a method of cookery; to list the foods cooked by steaming; to state the effects of steaming on food; to state the advantages of steaming; to describe the techniques of steaming; to choose suitable equipment and state its care and use; to explain and apply efficiency and safety procedures; to use recipes associated with steaming.

Definition

Steaming is cooking in moist heat (steam).

Principles of steaming

There are 3 ways in which food can be steamed.

1. The food, e.g. fillets of fish or chicken, is placed in a covered, perforated container, or on a plate covered by another plate, over a saucepan of boiling water. The steam rising from the boiling water cooks the food.
2. Portions of food are placed in a dish or pan on a garnish of vegetables and herbs moistened with a little stock/wine and covered with a tight-fitting lid. The dish or pan is then placed over a sufficient degree of heat to generate steam. Modern styles of cookery in which light, non-rich single dishes are required frequently use this method of cooking, particularly for fish dishes and chicken dishes.
3. Large equipment is used in commercial catering which cooks by steam. Steamed puddings must be covered with foil or greaseproof paper to protect them from the condensed steam which turns to water and which would make the pudding soggy.

   Metal-hinged cylindrical moulds known as pudding sleeves are sometimes used; these eliminate the need for paper or foil.

   Foods cooked in a steamer include potatoes, beetroot, meat and sweet puddings.

   Pressure steamers operate under higher steam pressure than the large steamers. The higher the steam pressure the more quickly the food cooks, thus saving fuel. Because of the speed of cooking, vegetables retain colour, flavour and goodness.

Examples of foods cooked by steaming

a) fish, chicken;
b) meat and sweet puddings;
c) potatoes, beetroots and other vegetables.

When steamed, foods such as fish and chicken are more digestible and are therefore suitable for invalids and people with weak digestion. Items such as puddings, e.g. meat or Christmas pudding, require a long cooking time and steaming is suitable.

Potatoes can be steamed in their skins and can be cooked in large quantities on steamer trays.

Safety

If the steamer has a water well it is essential to check that it contains sufficient water before lighting the steamer and that the water supply is maintained, otherwise the steamer will burn dry and be seriously damaged. Always take care when opening steamer doors as steam may jet out sharply and cause a severe scald.

Steaming

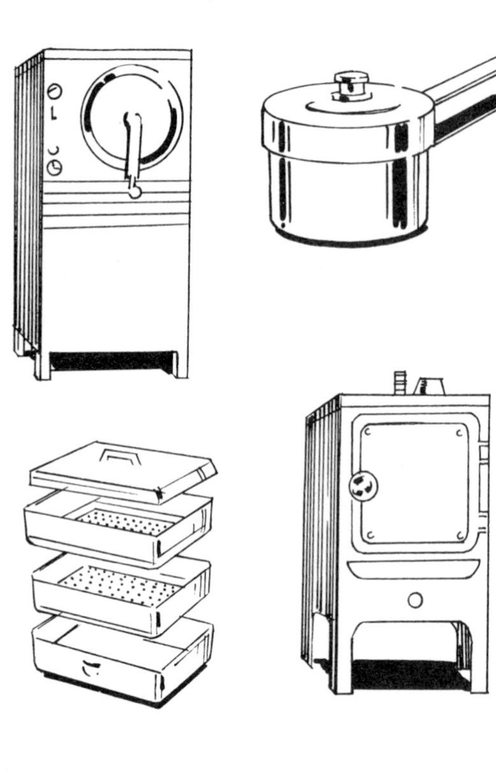

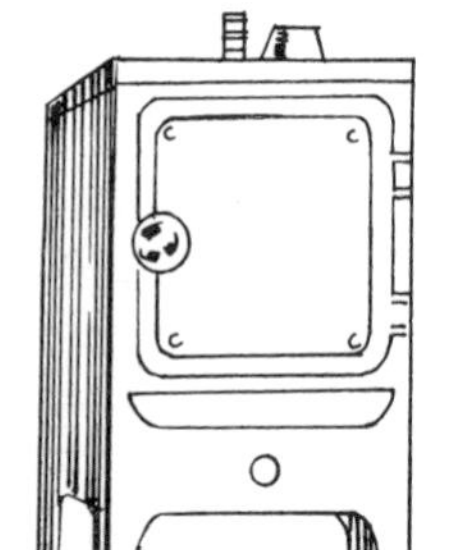

Runner beans

Beetroot

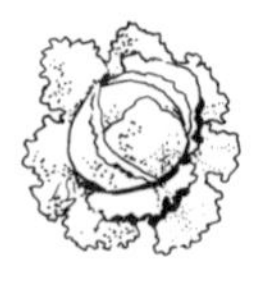

Cabbage

Potatoes

Fish fillet

Chicken 'supreme'

Cleaning

Steamer trays, runners and the insides of the steamer must be washed after use in hot detergent water, and then rinsed. The water container should be drained, cleaned and refilled. Steamer door controls should be lightly greased and the door left slightly ajar to allow air to circulate when the steamer is not in use.

Egg recipes

Egg in cocotte (basic recipe)

		4 eggs
25 g	1 oz	butter
		salt, pepper

1. Butter and season 4 egg cocottes.
2. Break an egg carefully into each.
3. Place the cocottes in a sauté pan containing 1 cm ($\frac{1}{2}$ in.) water.
4. Cover with a tight-fitting lid, place on a fierce heat so that the water boils rapidly.
5. Cook for 2 to 3 minutes until the eggs are lightly set, and serve.

Egg cocottes and whole eggs

Eggs in cocotte with cream

1. Proceed as for the basic recipe.
2. Half a minute before the cooking is completed add 1 dessertspoon of cream to each egg and complete the cooking.

Fish recipes

In the recipes given for poached fish (pages 32 – 33) the fish may be cooked by steaming, the sauce made separately and the fish (well drained) coated with the sauce and served. Similarly, in the recipes given for boiled fish (page 23) the fish may be cooked by steaming.

Vegetable recipes

All vegetables cooked by boiling, including potatoes, may also be cooked by steaming, and if modern high pressure steamers are used the vegetables can be cooked more quickly. Provided they are served immediately, vegetables retain a more appetising colour and more goodness (nutritive value). The term 'batch cookery' means the cooking of vegetables in smaller quantities continuously throughout the service. In order to do this some kitchens will have a number of smaller high-pressure steamers rather than 1 large one.

Pudding recipes

Steak pudding *4 portions*

200 g	8 oz	suet paste
400 g	1 lb	prepared stewing beef
		Worcester sauce
		1 tsp chopped parsley
		salt, pepper
		1 dessertspoon flour (white or wholemeal)
50 – 100 g	2 – 4 oz	onion (if required)
125 ml	$\frac{1}{4}$ pt	water (approx)

1. Line a greased $\frac{3}{4}$ litre ($1\frac{1}{2}$ pt) basin with three-quarters of the suet paste and retain one-quarter for the top.
2. Mix all the other ingredients together.
3. Place in the basin with the water to within 1 cm ($1\frac{1}{2}$ in.) of top.
4. Moisten the edge of the suet paste, cover the top and seal firmly.
5. Cover with greased greaseproof paper and kitchen foil.
6. Cook in a steamer for at least $3\frac{1}{2}$ hours and serve.

Extra gravy should be served separately.

Suet paste *4 portions*

200 g	8 oz	flour (white or wholemeal)
		1 level tsp baking-powder
		$\frac{1}{4}$ tsp salt
75 – 100 g	3 – 4 oz	prepared beef suet
125 ml	$\frac{1}{4}$ pt	water (approx)

1. Sieve the flour, salt and baking powder into a basin.
2. Mix in the suet with the flour and make a well in the centre.
3. Add the water and mix to a soft dough.

Steak and kidney pudding

As for steak pudding, with the addition of 50 – 100 g (2 – 4 oz) ox kidney, or 1 or 2 sheep's kidneys with the skin and gristle removed and then cut into neat pieces.

Steamed fruit puddings *6 portions*

Apple, apple and blackberry, rhubarb, rhubarb and apple, etc.

200 g	8 oz	suet paste (see above)
$\frac{3}{4}$ – 1 kg	$1\frac{1}{2}$ – 2 lb	fruit
100 g	4 oz	sugar
		2 tbsp water

1. Grease the basin.
2. Line, using three-quarters of the paste.
3. Add prepared and washed fruit and sugar. Add 1 – 2 cloves in an apple pudding.
4. Add 2 tbsp water.
5. Moisten the edge of the paste.
6. Cover with the remaining quarter of the pastry.
7. Seal firmly.
8. Cover with greased greaseproof paper and foil.
9. Steam for $1\frac{1}{2}$ hours approx.
10. Clean the basin and serve with custard sauce separately.

Steamed jam roll *6 portions*

200 g	8 oz	suet paste (see page 37)
100 g	4 oz	jam

1. Roll out paste into a rectangle 3 × 16 cm (12 × 6 in.) approx.
2. Spread with jam, leaving 1 cm ($\frac{1}{2}$ in.) clear on all edges.
3. Fold over two short sides 1 cm ($\frac{1}{2}$ in.).
4. Roll the pastry from the top.
5. Moisten the bottom edge to seal the roll.
6. Wrap in buttered greaseproof paper and foil. Steam for $1\frac{1}{2}$ to 2 hours.
7. Serve with jam or custard sauce.

Steamed currant, sultana or raisin pudding *6 portions*

100 g	4 oz	flour (white or wholemeal)
10 g	$\frac{1}{2}$ oz	baking-powder
100 g	4 oz	breadcrumbs
100 g	4 oz	suet
100 g	4 oz	fruit
100 g	4 oz	sugar
		pinch salt
		1 egg, size 3
125 ml	$\frac{1}{4}$ pint	milk

1. Mix all the dry ingredients together.
2. Add the liquid and mix.
3. Place in a greased pudding basin or sleeve and steam for $1\frac{1}{2}$ to 2 hours.
4. Serve with custard sauce.

Golden syrup or treacle pudding
6 portions

150 g	6 oz	flour (white or wholemeal)
		pinch salt
10 g	$\frac{1}{2}$ oz	baking-powder
75 g	3 oz	chopped suet
50 g	2 oz	castor sugar
		zest 1 lemon
		1 egg, size 3
125 ml	$\frac{1}{4}$ pint	milk
125 ml	$\frac{1}{4}$ pint	golden syrup or light treacle

1. Sieve the flour, salt and baking-powder into a bowl.
2. Mix the suet, sugar and zest.
3. Mix to a medium dough, incorporating the beaten egg and milk.
4. Pour the syrup into a well-greased basin.
5. Place the mixture on top.
6. Cover securely; steam for $1\frac{1}{2}$ to 2 hours.
7. Turn out and serve with warm syrup containing the lemon juice.

Steamed sponge pudding (basic recipe) *6 portions*

100 g	4 oz	butter or margarine
100 g	4 oz	castor sugar
		2 eggs, size 3
150 g	6 oz	flour (white or wholemeal)
10 g	$\frac{1}{2}$ oz	baking-powder
		few drops of milk
		few drops of vanilla essence

1. Cream the butter or margarine and sugar in a bowl until fluffy and almost white.
2. Gradually add the beaten eggs, mixing vigorously.
3. Sieve the flour and baking-powder.
4. Gradually incorporate into the mixture as lightly as possible, keeping to a dropping consistency by the addition of the milk.
5. Place in a greased pudding basin.
6. Cover securely with greased, greaseproof paper.
7. Steam for 1 to $1\frac{1}{2}$ hours.
8. Turn out and serve with a suitable sauce, e.g. jam (page 16), custard (page 16).

Chocolate sponge pudding

Add 25 g (1 oz) chocolate or cocoa powder in place of 25 g (1 oz) flour – that is 125 g (5 oz) flour, 25 g (1 oz) chocolate to basic recipe (see above). Serve with a chocolate sauce (page 17).

Sultana sponge pudding, currant sponge pudding, raisin sponge pudding

Add 100 g (4 oz) of washed, well-dried fruit to the basic recipe above. Serve with custard sauce (page 16).

Questions – Steaming

1. What is steaming? MOIST HEAT
2. Give 3 examples of how food can be steamed. Plate over saucepan steamer. pressure cooker
3. Why are steamed fish and chicken suitable for invalids?
   light & digestable.
4. Why is pressure steaming economical?
   Less heat – quicker cooking
5. Why must steamed puddings be covered before cooking?
   Prevent penetration of moisture
6. Does food cook more quickly or slowly with a high steam pressure? QUICKLY
7. Anagrams relating to stewing and steaming:

   a) GAVE BEETS 'L' VEGETABLES.
   b) CAP HERE CHEAPER
   c) COAL COME IN ECONOMICAL

Answers can be found on page 152.

7
Stewing

General objectives An understanding and knowledge of stewing.
Specific objectives To be able to define and state the principle of stewing; to explain the reasons for stewing; to demonstrate stewing; to list foods cooked by stewing; to specify the effects of stewing foods; to select suitable equipment and state its care and use; to explain the advantages of stewing; to explain and apply efficiency and safety procedures; to use recipes associated with stewing.

Definition

This is the slow cooking of food in the smallest quantity of liquid (water, stock, wine, beer or sauce), in which the food is cut up and the food and cooking liquid are served together.

Principles of stewing

Cooking may take place on top of the stove (the pan is covered with a lid) or in the oven.

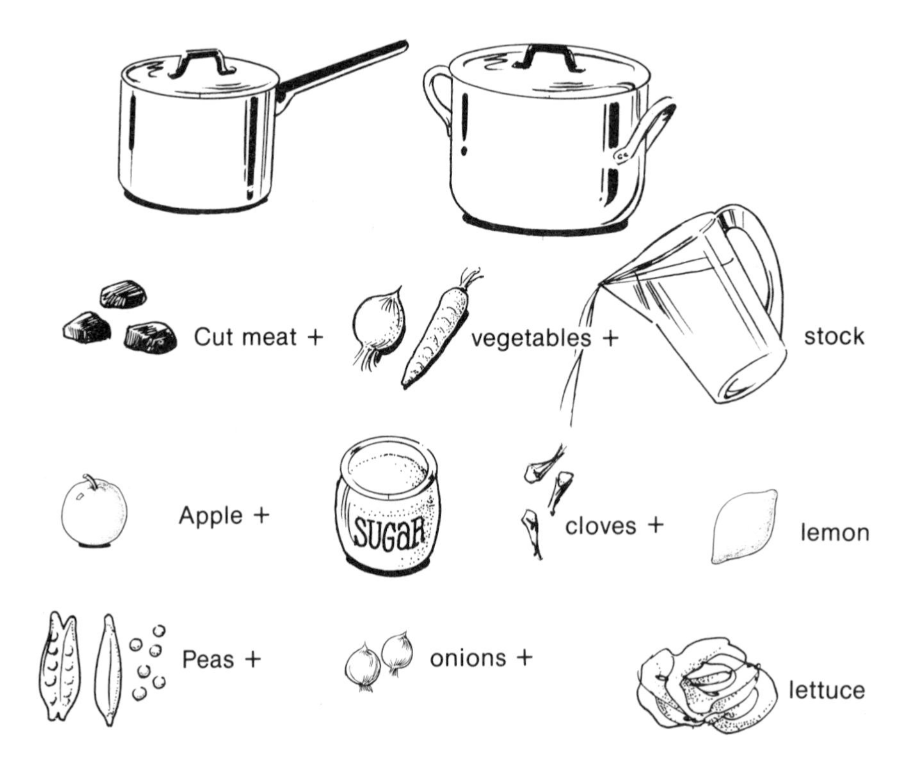

Stewing

a) helps to retain all the flavour and goodness of the ingredients,
b) prevents excess evaporation of the liquid, as the condensation from the heat of the stew changes to steam, and forms liquid on the inside of the lid, which falls back into the stew, keeping it moist and also reducing the risk of burning.

Stews are both economical and nutritious because the cheaper cuts of meat and poultry (unsuitable for roasting and grilling) can be made tender and palatable, that is, tasty to eat, and there is little waste by evaporation. The meat juices which escape from the meat during the cooking are not lost but are present in the liquid which is served with the stew.

Fruits such as apples may be stewed and some varieties of apple will break up into a *purée* when stewed. See also *poaching*.

Stewed foods must not boil rapidly; the liquid must gently simmer to get the best results.

Equipment

Thick bottomed pans with lids should be used. These should be clean, in good repair and hygienically stored when not in use. Pans should be cleaned in hot detergent water, then rinsed and dried before storing.

Meat recipes

Curried lamb or beef *4 portions*

500 g	1 lb 4 oz	stewing lamb or beef
25 g	1 oz	oil
200 g	8 oz	onions
		1 clove garlic
10 g	$\frac{1}{2}$ oz	curry powder
10 g	$\frac{1}{2}$ oz	flour (white or wholemeal)
10 g	$\frac{1}{2}$ oz	tomato purée
$\frac{1}{2}$ litre	1 pt	stock or water
		salt
25 g	1 oz	chopped chutney
5 g	$\frac{1}{4}$ oz	desiccated coconut
10 g	$\frac{1}{2}$ oz	sultanas

1. Trim the meat and cut into even pieces.
2. Season and quickly colour in hot fat or oil.
3. Add the chopped onion and chopped garlic, cover with a lid and sweat for a few minutes.
4. Drain off the surplus fat.
5. Add the curry powder and flour, mix in and cook for a few minutes over a gentle heat.
6. Mix in the tomato purée, and gradually add the hot stock. Stir thoroughly, bring to the boil, season and skim.
7. Allow to simmer and add the rest of the ingredients.
8. Cover with a lid and simmer in the oven or on top of the stove till cooked.
9. Correct the seasoning and consistency, skim off all fat. At this stage a little cream or yoghurt may be added.
10. Serve accompanied with rice, which may be plain boiled or pilaff (see pages 23 and 45).

Other accompaniments to curry

There are many other optional accompaniments to curry, for example grilled Bombay duck and poppadums, which are grilled or deep fried, and served separately. Other accompaniments include the following:

chopped chutney
sultanas
desiccated coconut
slices of lemon
chopped apple
chow-chow
quarters of orange
sliced banana
chopped onions

Brown beef or lamb stew *4 portions*

400 g	1 lb	prepared stewing beef or
500 g	1 lb 4 oz	prepared stewing lamb
25 g	1 oz	dripping or oil
75 g	3 oz	carrots
75 g	3 oz	onions
25 g	1 oz	flour (white or wholemeal)
		1 tbsp tomato purée
750 ml	$1\frac{1}{2}$ pt	brown stock
		bouquet garni
		clove garlic (optional)
		seasoning

1. Remove excess sinew and fat from the meat.
2. Cut into 2 cm (1 in.) pieces and lightly season.
3. Fry quickly in hot fat or oil till lightly browned.
4. Add the *mirepoix* (roughly cut onion and carrot) and continue frying to a golden colour.
5. Add the flour, mix in and singe in the oven or brown on top of the stove for a few minutes.

6. Mix in the tomato purée.
7. Stir in the stock, bring to the boil and skim.
8. Add the bouquet garni, season and cover with a lid and simmer gently till cooked, preferably in the oven, approximately 1½ – 2 hours.
9. When cooked place the meat in a clean pan.
10. Correct the sauce and pass on to the meat.
11. Lightly sprinkle with chopped parsley.

Brown beef or lamb stew with vegetables

As in the previous recipe, with a garnish of vegetables, that is, turned or neatly cut glazed carrots, turnips and button onions, or peas and diamonds of French beans. Button mushrooms may also be used. The vegetables are cooked separately and they may be a) mixed in, b) arranged in groups or c) sprinkled on top of the stew.

Minced beef *4 portions*

50 – 100 g	2 – 4 oz	chopped onion
25 g	1 oz	dripping, butter, margarine or oil
300 g	12 oz	lean minced beef
125 ml	¼ pt	demi-glace, jus-lié or stock
		seasoning

Method 1: using raw minced beef:

1. Sweat the onion in the fat or oil.
2. Add the beef and cook to a light colour.
3. Add the liquid; season.
4. Bring to the boil, skim and simmer gently till cooked, approximately ½ hour.

If using stock, this may be thickened a) by adding 10 g (½ oz) flour after cooking the meat and before adding the stock or b) by finishing with approximately 5 g (¼ oz) of diluted cornflour or fécule.

Method 2: using cooked beef:

Sweat the onion in the fat or oil and add the minced cooked beef. Add the demi-glace or jus-lié, bring to the boil and skim. Season and boil for 10 minutes.

To aid presentation this dish may be served with a border of piped duchess potato which has been previously dried, eggwashed and browned.

Irish stew *4 portions*

500 g	1 lb 4 oz	stewing lamb
		bouquet garni
400 g	1 lb	potatoes
100 g	4 oz	onions
100 g	4 oz	celery
100 g	4 oz	savoy cabbage
100 g	4 oz	leeks
100 g	4 oz	button onions
		parsley

1. Trim the meat and cut into even pieces.
2. Blanch and refresh.
3. Place in a sauteuse or shallow saucepan, cover with water, bring to the boil, season and skim.
4. Add the bouquet garni. Meanwhile turn the potatoes into barrel shapes.
5. Cut the potato trimmings, onion, celery, cabbage and leek into small neat pieces and add to the meat. Simmer for 30 minutes.
6. Add the button onions and simmer for a further 30 minutes.
7. Add the turned potatoes and simmer gently, with a lid on the pan, till cooked. If tough meat is being used allow ½ – 1 hour stewing before adding any vegetables.
8. Correct the seasoning and skim off all fat.
9. Serve sprinkled with chopped parsley.

Vegetable recipes

Peas, French style *4 portions*

1 kg	2 lb	peas (in the pod) or
200 g	½ lb	frozen peas
		12 spring or button onions
		1 small lettuce
25 g	1 oz	butter
		salt
		½ tsp castor sugar

1. Shell and wash the peas and place in a sauteuse.
2. Peel and wash the onions, shred the lettuce and add to the peas with 10 g (½ oz) butter, salt and the sugar.
3. Barely cover with water. Cover with a lid and cook steadily, preferably in the oven, until tender.
4. Correct the seasoning.
5. Blend the other 10 g (½ oz) butter with 5 g (¼ oz) flour and shake into the boiling peas until thoroughly mixed and serve.

Note. When using frozen peas allow the onions almost to cook before adding the peas.

Ratatouille *4 portions*

200 g	$\frac{1}{2}$ lb	baby marrows
200 g	$\frac{1}{2}$ lb	aubergines
200 g	$\frac{1}{2}$ lb	tomatoes
50 ml	$\frac{1}{8}$ pt	oil
50 g	2 oz	onion (finely sliced)
		1 clove garlic
		1 tsp chopped parsley
		salt, pepper

1. Trim off both ends of the marrow and aubergines.
2. Remove the skin using a peeler.
3. Cut into 3 mm ($\frac{1}{8}$ in.) slices.
4. Concassée the tomatoes (peel, remove seeds, roughly chop).
5. Place the oil in a thick-bottomed pan and add the onions.
6. Cover with a lid and allow to cook gently for 5 to 7 minutes without colouring.
7. Add the peeled chopped garlic, the marrow and aubergine slices.
8. Season with salt and mill pepper.
9. Allow to cook gently for 4 to 5 minutes, toss occasionally and keep covered with a lid.
10. Add the tomato and allow to continue cooking gently until all is tender (approximately 20 – 30 minutes).
11. Mix in the parsley, correct the seasoning and serve.

Questions – Stewing

1. Which type of meat is suitable for stewing, the cheaper or the more expensive?
2. It is not always necesary to cover a stew with a lid during cooking – true or false?
3. Stewed foods should cook gently?
   rapidly?
4. Is stewing a slow or fast method of cooking?
5. Is meat for a stew always cut into pieces before being cooked?
6. On the diagram which follows indicate the cuts suitable for stewing.

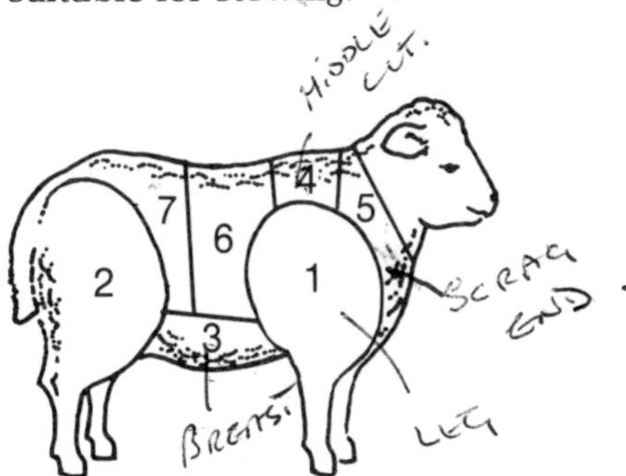

Answers can be found on page 153.

8

Braising

General objectives To have a knowledge and understanding of braising.
Specific objectives To give a definition of and state the principles of braising; to explain the reasons for braising; to demonstrate the practice of braising; to state the foods cooked by braising; to describe the effects of braising on foods; to specify the advantage of braising; to choose suitable equipment and explain its care and use; to state the procedures for efficiency and safety; to use recipes associated with braising; to explain the techniques of braising; e.g. marinading, sealing, tenderising.

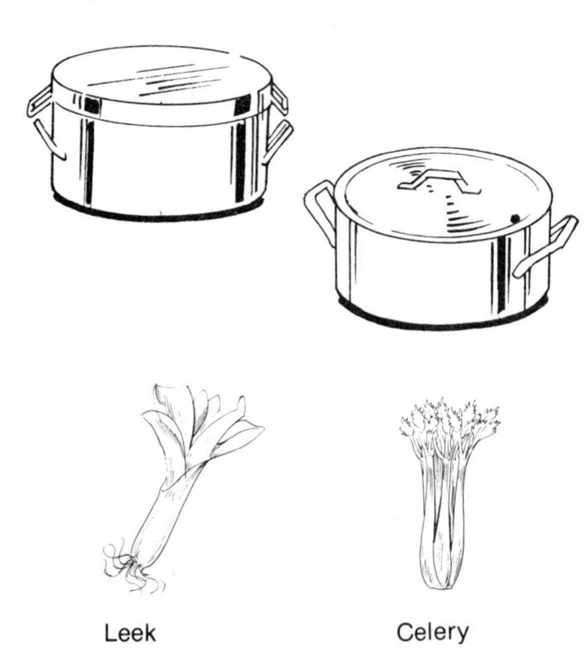

Definition

Braising is a combination of stewing and roasting in a pan with a tight-fitting lid (known as a braising pan) or in an ovenproof dish.

Principles of braising

The lid is essential to minimise evaporation and to enable the food to retain not only its own juices but also the flavour of the commodities added for flavouring, e.g. bacon, ham, vegetables, herbs, etc.

Braising is a slow method of cooking and takes a long time, therefore less tender joints of meat and poultry can be used. When braising non fatty joints such as lean beef or venison the meat is *marinaded* in red wine with vegetables and herbs for a few hours before being cooked. Marinading helps to:

a) tenderise by the action of the acid in the wine, softening the meat fibres,
b) give additional flavour,
c) moisten the joint, which might otherwise be dry because of lack of fat.

Braised meats are *sealed* quickly on all sides by browning in hot, shallow fat either in a pan on the stove or in a hot oven. Sealing the meat in this way not only helps to retain maximum flavour and goodness but also gives an appetising brown colour.

Equipment

Thick-bottomed pans or ovenproof dishes (2 handles for preference) with tight-fitting lids should be used. Because of the long cooking process sauce may stick to the pan. To assist the cleaning it is advisable to soak the pan in cold water. Pans should then be cleaned in hot detergent water, rinsed, dried and stored.

Safety

1. Always use a thick, dry cloth to remove pans from the oven.
2. When the pan is removed from the oven sprinkle a little flour on to the lid as a warning to people that the dish is hot.

Foods cooked by braising

Meats	beef mutton	oxtail ox-liver	hearts
Poultry – older and therefore less tender birds	chicken goose	duck pigeon	partridge
Vegetables	celery onions	cabbage leeks	

Braised rice *4 portions*

Also known as pilaff of rice

50 g	2 oz	butter or oil
25 g	1 oz	chopped onion
100 g	4 oz	rice (long grain)
200 ml	$\frac{3}{8}$ pint approx.	white stock (preferably chicken)

1. Place 25 g (1 oz) butter or oil in a small sauteuse. Add the onion.
2. Cook gently without colouring for 2 to 3 minutes. Add the rice.
3. Cook gently without colouring for 2 to 3 minutes.
4. Add twice the amount of stock to rice.
5. Season, cover with a buttered paper, and bring to the boil.
6. Place in a hot oven (200 – 230°C, Reg. 6 – 8) for approximately 15 minutes until cooked.
7. Remove immediately into a cool pan or dish to stop the rice cooking further.
8. Carefully mix in the remaining butter or oil.
9. Correct the seasoning and serve.

It is usual to use long grain rice for pilaff because the grains are firm, and there is less likelihood of them breaking up and becoming mushy. During cooking the long grain rice absorbs more liquid, loses less starch and retains its shape well as it swells. The short or medium grains may split at the ends and become less distinct in outline.

Meat recipes

Hot pot of lamb or mutton *4 portions*

500 g	1 lb 4 oz	stewing lamb
100 g	4 oz	onions
400 g	1 lb	potatoes
1 litre	2 pt	brown stock
25 g	1 oz	dripping
		chopped parsley

1. Trim the meat and cut into even pieces.
2. Place in a deep ovenproof dish.
3. Season lightly with salt and pepper.
4. Mix the shredded onion and thinly sliced potatoes together.
5. Season and place on top of the meat.
6. Three parts cover with stock.
7. Neatly arrange an overlapping layer of 2 mm-thick ($\frac{1}{12}$ in.) sliced potatoes on top.
8. Add the oil or fat in small pieces.
9. Thoroughly clean the edges of the dish and place to cook in a hot oven (200 – 230°C, Reg. 6 – 8) till lightly coloured.
10. Reduce the heat and allow to simmer gently till cooked, approximately $1\frac{1}{2}$ – 2 hours.
11. Press the potatoes down occasionally during cooking.
12. Serve with the potatoes brushed with oil, butter or margarine, and sprinkle with chopped parsley.

This is a dish to which there are many accepted regional variations.

Braised loin chops or braised chump chops *4 portions*

		4 chops
25 g	1 oz	fat or oil
100 g	4 oz	onion
100 g	4 oz	carrot
25 g	1 oz	flour (white or wholemeal)
		1 tbsp tomato purée
500 ml	1 pt	brown stock
		bouquet garni
		seasoning
		chopped parsley

1. Fry the seasoned chops in a sauté pan quickly on both sides in very hot fat or oil.
2. When turning the chops add the *mirepoix* (onion and carrot).
3. Draw aside, drain off the surplus fat.
4. Add the flour and mix in. Singe in the oven or on top of the stove.
5. Add the tomato purée and the hot stock.
6. Stir with a wooden spoon till thoroughly mixed.
7. Add the bouquet garni, season, skim and allow to simmer. Cover with a lid.
8. Cook, preferably in the oven, skimming off all fat and scum.
9. When cooked transfer chops to a clean pan.

10. Correct the seasoning and consistency of the sauce.
11. Skim off any fat and pass through a fine strainer on to the chops. Serve sprinkled with chopped parsley.

Braised steaks

As for braised chops, using 400 g (1 lb) stewing beef cut into $4\frac{1}{2}$ – 1 cm ($\frac{1}{4}$ – $\frac{1}{2}$ in.) thick steaks and allowing longer cooking time, according to the quality of the meat.

Braised beef *4 portions*

400 g	1 lb	lean beef (topside or thick flank)
25 g	1 oz	fat or oil
100 g	4 oz	carrots
100 g	4 oz	onions
500 ml	1 pt (approx.)	brown stock)
10 g	$\frac{1}{2}$ oz	tomato purée
250 ml	$\frac{1}{2}$ pt	espagnole

Method 1

1. Trim and tie the joint securely.
2. Season and colour quickly on all sides in hot fat to seal the pores.
3. Place into a small braising pan (any pan or casserole with a tight-fitting lid suitable for the oven).
4. Place the joint on the lightly fried, sliced vegetables.
5. Add the stock, which should be two-thirds of the way up the meat; season lightly.
6. Add the bouquet garni and tomato purée and, if available, add a few washed mushroom trimmings.
7. Bring to the boil, skim and cover with a lid and cook in a moderate oven (150 – 180°C, Reg. 3 – 4).
8. After approximately 1 hour cooking remove the meat.
9. Add the espagnole, reboil, skim and strain.
10. Replace the meat. Do not cover, but baste every 30 minutes and continue cooking approximately 2 – $2\frac{1}{2}$ hours in all. Braised beef should be well cooked. Allow approximately 35 minutes per $\frac{1}{2}$ kg (1 lb), plus 35 minutes. To test if cooked, pierce with a trussing needle. This should penetrate the meat easily and there should be no sign of blood.
11. Remove the joint and correct the colour, seasoning and consistency of the sauce.
12. To serve: remove the string and carve into 2 mm-thick ($\frac{1}{12}$ in.) slices across the grain.

Pour some of the sauce over the slices and serve the remainder of the sauce separately.

Suitable garnishes include spring vegetables or noodles.

Method 2

As for method 1, but use for cooking liquor either a) jus-lié or b) half brown stock and half demi-glace, or espagnole.

Method 3

As for method 1, but when the joint and vegetables are browned sprinkle with 25 g (1 oz) flour and singe in the oven, add the tomato purée, stock and bouquet garni, season and complete the recipe.

Braised ox liver and onions *4 portions*

300 g	12 oz	liver
25 g	1 oz	flour (white or wholemeal)
50 g	2 oz	fat or oil
200 g	$\frac{1}{2}$ lb	onions
500 ml	1 pt (approx.)	brown stock

1. Prepare the liver by removing the skin and tubes, then cut into slices.
2. Pass the sliced liver through seasoned flour.
3. Fry on both sides in hot fat or oil.
4. Place in a braising pan or casserole.
5. Fry the sliced onions to a light golden brown, drain and add to the liver.
6. Just cover with the stock.
7. Season and cover with a lid.
8. Simmer gently in the oven till tender – approximately $1\frac{1}{2}$ – 2 hours.
9. Correct the sauce and serve.

Vegetable recipes

Braised cabbage *4 portions*

$\frac{1}{2}$ kg	1 lb	cabbage
100 g	4 oz	carrot
100 g	4 oz	onion
$\frac{1}{4}$ litre	$\frac{1}{2}$ pt	white stock
		bouquet garni
$\frac{1}{8}$ litre	$\frac{1}{4}$ pt	jus-lié
		salt, pepper

1. Quarter the cabbage.
2. Remove the centre stalk and discoloured leaves; wash well.
3. Place in boiling salted water, boil for 5 minutes.
4. Refresh until cold.
5. Take the four best green leaves and lay out flat on the table.
6. Place the remainder of the cabbage on the centre of each and lightly season.
7. Wrap each portion of cabbage in a tea-cloth and shape into a fairly firm ball.
8. Remove from the tea-cloth. Place on a bed of roots.
9. Add the stock half way up the cabbage, and the bouquet garni.
10. Bring to the boil, cover with a lid and cook in the oven approximately 1 hour.
11. Dress the cabbage in the serving dish.
12. Add the cooking liquor to the jus-lié, correct the seasoning and consistency.
13. Pour over the cabbage.

Braised celery *4 portions*

		2 heads of celery
100 g	4 oz	carrots, sliced
100 g	4 oz	onion, sliced
		bouquet garni
$\frac{1}{4}$ litre	$\frac{1}{2}$ pt	white stock
		salt, pepper
50 g	2 oz	fat bacon or suet (optional)
		2 crusts of bread

1. Trim the celery heads and the root, cutting off any outside discoloured stalks and cutting the heads to approximately 15 cm (6 in.) lengths.
2. Wash well under running cold water.
3. Place in a pan of boiling water. Simmer for approximately 10 minutes until limp.
4. Refresh and rewash.
5. Place the sliced vegetables in a sauté pan, sauteuse or casserole.
6. Add the celery heads whole or cut them in halves lengthwise; fold over and place on the bed of roots.
7. Add the bouquet garni, and barely cover with stock; season with salt and pepper.
8. Add the fat bacon or suet, and the crusts of bread. Cover with buttered greaseproof paper and a tight lid and cook gently in a moderate oven (150 – 180°C, Reg. 3 – 4) for $1\frac{1}{2}$ to 3 hours, depending on the size or tenderness of the celery.
9. Remove the celery from the pan, drain well and dress neatly in the serving dish.
10. Add the cooking liquor to an equal amount of jus-lié or demi-glace, reduce, and correct the seasoning and consistency.
11. Mask the celery and finish with chopped parsley.

Braised leeks

$\frac{1}{2}$ kg (1 lb) of leeks will yield approximately 2 portions

1. Cut the roots from the leeks. Remove any discoloured outside leaves and trim the green.
2. Cut through lengthwise and wash well under running water.
3. Tie into a neat bundle.
4. Place in boiling salted water for 5 minutes approx.
5. Place on a bed of roots.
6. Barely cover with stock, add the bouquet garni and season.
7. Cover with a lid and cook until tender – approximately $\frac{1}{2}$ – 1 hour.
8. Remove leeks from pan and fold neatly. Arrange in the serving dish.
9. Meanwhile add jus-lié to the cooking liquor and correct the seasoning and consistency.
10. Pour the sauce over the leeks.

Braised onions

1. Select medium, even-sized onions; allow 2 – 3 portions per $\frac{1}{2}$ kg (1 lb).
2. Peel, wash and cook in boiling salted water for $\frac{1}{2}$ hour.
3. Drain and place in a pan or casserole suitable for placing in the oven.
4. Add a bouquet garni, half cover with stock and a lid and braise gently (150 – 180°C, Reg. 3 – 4) in the oven till tender; drain the onions well.
5. Reduce the cooking liquor with an equal amount of jus-lié or demi-glace. Correct the seasoning and consistency and pass. Mask the onions and sprinkle with chopped parsley.

Fondant potatoes

1. Select small or even-sized, medium potatoes.
2. Wash, peel and rewash.
3. Turn into 8-sided barrel shapes, allowing 2 – 3 per portion, approximately 5 cm (2 in.) long, end diameter $1\frac{1}{2}$ cm ($\frac{3}{4}$ in.), centre diameter $2\frac{1}{2}$ cm ($1\frac{1}{4}$ in.), or cut into neat, even pieces.
4. Brush with melted butter, margarine or oil.
5. Place in a pan suitable for the oven.

6. Half cover with white stock; season with salt and pepper.
7. Cook in a hot oven (200 – 230°C, Reg. 6 – 8), brushing the potatoes frequently with melted butter or margarine.
8. When potatoes are cooked the stock should be completely absorbed.
9. Brush with melted butter or margarine and serve.

Questions – Braising

1. Braising is a combination of roasting and s
2. State three commodities added to beef being braised to give additional flavour.
3. Explain why joints of meat are sealed before braising.
4. Other than meat, name two braised dishes.
5. What is a bed of roots?
6. Specify the kind of meat suitable for braising.
7. In this word search there are 8 words related to the principles of cookery, including *braise*.

    G R I L L M
    B R A I S E
    H C A O P A
    Y R F B A T
    R E M M I S

8. Why is braising a nutritious method of cooking?
9. When carving a braised joint of meat, is it best to cut with the meat grain or against it?

Answers can be found on page 153.

9

Roasting

General objectives To have a knowledge and understanding of roasting.
Specific objectives To define roasting and state the principles of roasting; to explain roasting as a method of cookery; to demonstrate the practice of roasting; to state the foods cooked by roasting; to explain the effects of roasting on foods; to specify the advantages of roasting; to select equipment and state its care and use; to specify efficiency and safety procedures; to use recipes associated with roasting; to explain the techniques of roasting, e.g. basting, carving, convection, pot-roasting.

Definition

Roasting is the cooking of food with the aid of hot fat in the oven.

Principles of roasting

1. Control of oven temperature is essential.
2. Frequent basting, that is using a spoon to pour the hot fat over the item being roasted, is essential:

a) it keeps the food moist,
b) it helps to produce an even and attractive colour,

Roasting

c) it helps to reduce shrinkage,
d) basting should occur every 20 – 30 minutes.

Equipment

Trays used for roasting must be kept clean and in good repair. Trays may need prior soaking, after which they should be washed in hot detergent water, rinsed thoroughly, dried and stored.

Foods suitable for roasting

1. Tender cuts of meat.
2. Young and tender poultry and game.
3. Potatoes and parsnips.

Safety

1. Care must be taken not to be burned by contact with the oven, shelves or hot fat. Arms need to be protected by sleeves, and a sound, thick cloth used to handle dishes.
2. Extra care is needed with large dishes or trays. They need one hand on the front and one on the side to balance the weight.

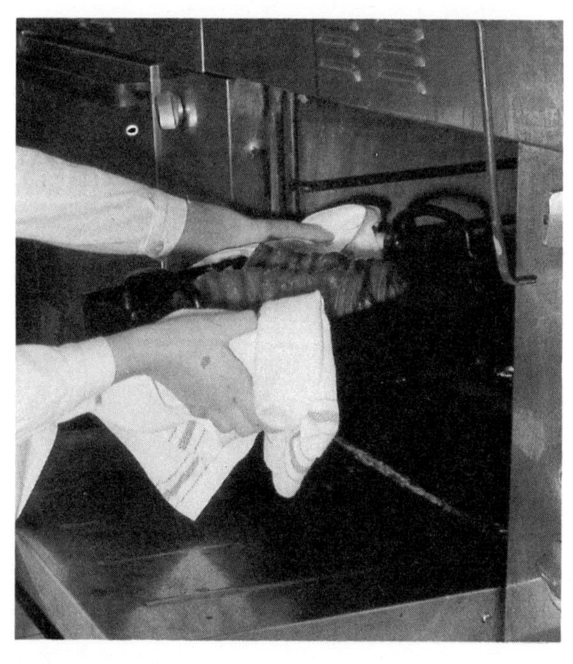

Removing a dish from the oven

3. Gas ovens may have a pilot light, which lights the main gas jets. It is very important to check that the pilot light has ignited the gas supply when the oven is turned on, otherwise there may be an explosion.

Hygiene

Ovens, oven shelves and all equipment used in roasting must be kept clean. A good roast cook keeps a clean oven; a dirty oven could affect the flavour of food being cooked.

Foods cooked by roasting

Meat

Preparation – beef, lamb, mutton, veal, pork.

1. Only good quality tender meat is roasted.
2. Joints are prepared by:
   a) removing bones which may interfere with carving,
   b) trimming excess fat and sinew,
   c) tying where necessary to keep the joint compact and in shape,
   d) covering with fat to protect the lean meat.
3. The meat is placed on a trivet or bones in the roasting tray, so that the joint does not fry in the fat in the tray.
4. The meat is then placed in a pre-heated oven for about 10 minutes:
   a) to seal the outside of the meat so that the juices are prevented from issuing from the meat,
   b) to enable cooking to commence immediately.

   The heat is then reduced.
5. The regulo or heat control should be used to increase or decrease heat during the cooking process.
6. Frequent basting should take place until the meat is cooked.
7. Cooking time depends on the kind of meat, its quality, weight, thickness and shape.

	Approximate cooking times	Degree of cooking
Beef	15 minutes per $\frac{1}{2}$ kg (1 lb) plus 15 mins	Underdone
Lamb	20 minutes per $\frac{1}{2}$ kg (1 lb) plus 20 mins	Cooked through
Mutton	20 minutes per $\frac{1}{2}$ kg (1 lb) plus 20 mins	Cooked through
Veal	25 minutes per $\frac{1}{2}$ kg (1 lb) plus 20 mins	Cooked through
Pork	25 minutes per $\frac{1}{2}$ kg (1 lb) plus 25 mins	Thoroughly cooked

8. The hottest part of the oven is usually at the top.
9. Convection ovens produce an even heat throughout with the aid of a fan, which is inside the oven.
10. To achieve even cooking and colouring it is necessary to turn the dish round as required.
11. If excessive spluttering noises occur in the oven the roasting is cooking too quickly.
12. The degree of cooking is indicated by pressure of the finger on the joint – the firmer the meat feels the more well cooked the joint will be.
13. Meat thermometers inserted into the centre of the meat can also be used to indicate when the meat is cooked.

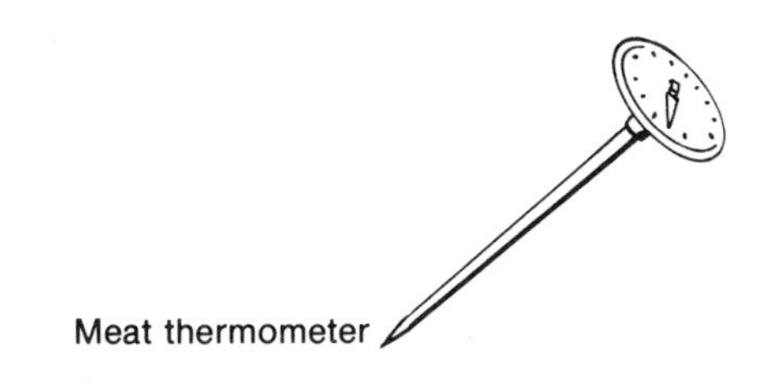
Meat thermometer

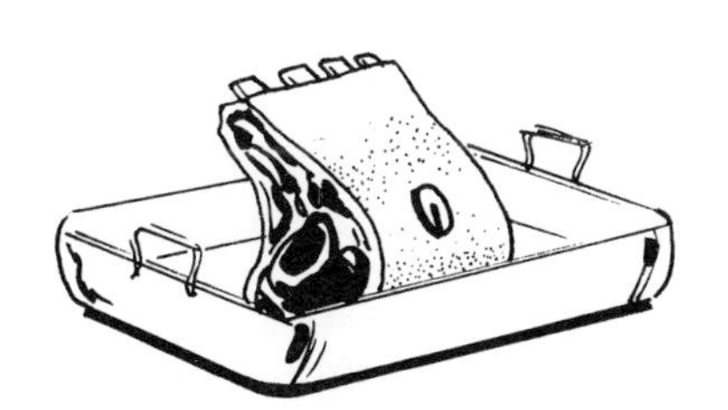

14. When cooked, remove meat from the oven and allow to stand for 15 minutes before carving across the grain. This allows the meat to set, so making carving easier, and gives maximum portion yield.

Poultry and game

Poultry, e.g. chicken, duck, turkey, geese, and game, e.g. venison, hare, pheasant and partridge, may be roasted.

1. Poultry is prepared by removing the wish bone to make carving easier.
2. Poultry is *trussed* to keep the bird in shape.
3. To enable the bird to cook evenly it is cooked on its side for one-third of the time, turned on to the other leg for one-third of the time and the cooking and final colouring are completed with the breast uppermost.
4. Basting is essential during the cooking.
5. To test if cooked, insert a fork into the leg and hold over a dish; the juice issuing from the bird should not show any signs of blood.
6. Time required for roasting depends on quality and size. Due to bone structure, heat penetrates from within the carcass as well as from the outside. As a guide, allow 15 – 20 minutes per pound.
7. Before serving, allow to stand for some 15 minutes before carving or dissecting.
8. Carve across the grain to produce the best texture for eating.

Vegetables

Roast potatoes and parsnips
Washed, peeled potatoes are cut to an even size, placed in a roasting tray with hot fat and cooked in a hot oven until cooked and golden brown. During cooking the potatoes are turned to produce an even colour. Parsnips are cooked in the same way.

Pot roasting

Pot roasting is the method of cooking in an oven in a casserole or pan with a lid, using butter for basting.

1. Only good quality meats, poultry or game are cooked in this way.
2. The food is cooked on a bed of roots (thick slices of onion and carrots).
3. When cooked the joint is removed and the remaining vegetables and juices used to make the sauce or gravy.
4. The advantage of this method is that most of the goodness and flavour are retained in the meat and in the sauce or gravy.

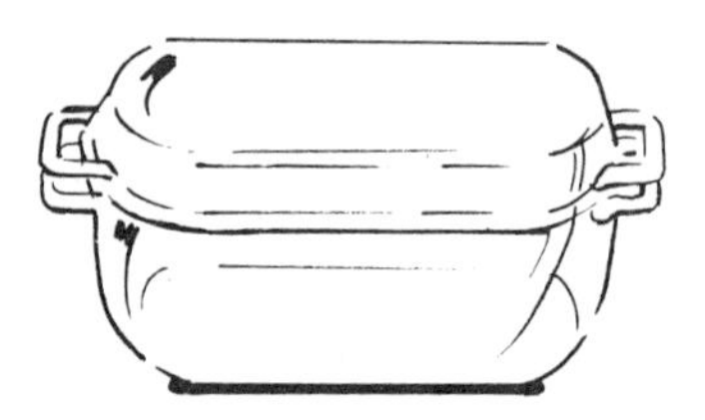

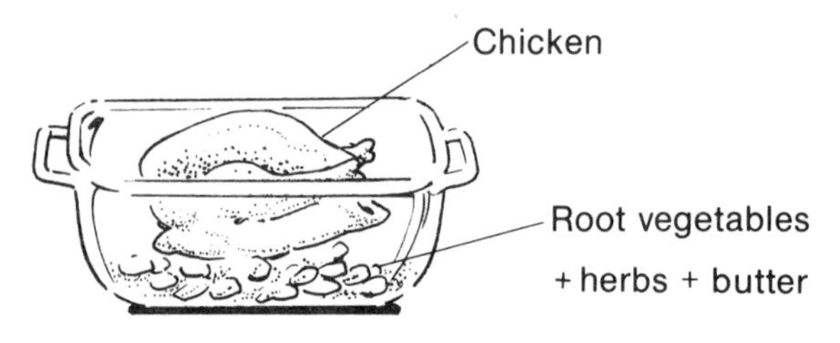

Pot roasting

Roasting of lamb and mutton

See page 135.

Allow approximately 150 g (6 oz) meat on the bone per portion (legs, shoulders, saddle or loin, best end and breast).

Preparation of joints

Shoulder
Clean and trim knucklebone to leave approximately 3 cm ($1\frac{1}{2}$ in.) of clean bone.
Boning Remove the blade bone and upper arm bone (see below), and tie with string. The shoulder may be stuffed (see page 54) before tying.

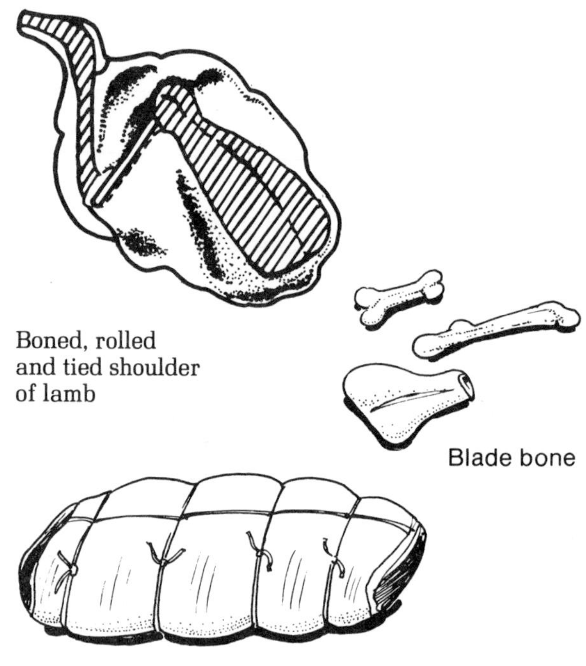

Boned, rolled and tied shoulder of lamb

Legs
Remove the pelvic or aitchbone. Trim the knuckle cleaning 3 cm ($1\frac{1}{2}$ in.) bone. Trim off excess fat and tie with string if necessary.

Accompaniments

Beef	roast gravy	Yorkshire pudding	horseradish sauce
Lamb	roast gravy	mint sauce	redcurrant jelly
Pork	roast gravy	apple sauce	sage and onion stuffing
Chicken	roast gravy	bread sauce	game chips, watercress

Best end

1. Cut either side of the backbone and divide from the inside, removing the complete chine bone.
2. Skin from head to tail and from breast to back.
3. Remove the sinew and the tip of the blade bone.
4. Complete the preparation of the rib bones as indicated in the diagram below.

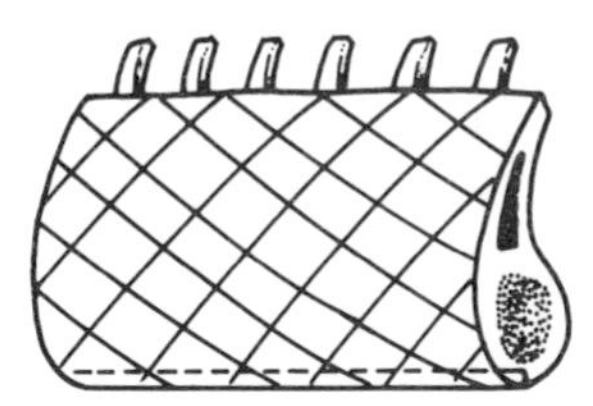

Best end

5. Clean the sinew from between the rib bones and trim the bones.
6. Score the fat neatly to approximately 2 mm ($\frac{1}{12}$ in.) deep as shown.

The overall length of the rib bones to be trimmed to two and a half times the length of the nut of meat.

Loin

Skin, remove excess fat and sinew, remove the pelvic bone and tie with string.

Roast loin, boned and stuffed

Remove the skin, excess fat and sinew. Bone-out. The fillet may then be replaced, and tied up. When stuffed, bone-out, season, stuff and tie with string.

1. The joints are seasoned with salt and placed on a trivet or on bones in a roasting tray.
2. Place a little dripping on top and cook in a hot oven (230 – 250°C, Reg. 6 – 8).
3. Baste frequently and reduce the heat gradually when necessary, as for example in the case of large joints.
4. Roasting time, approximately 20 minutes per $\frac{1}{2}$ kg (1 lb) and 20 minutes over.
5. To test if cooked, place on a tray and press firmly in order to see if the juices released contain any blood.
6. In general, all joints should be cooked through, that is to say not left underdone (unless particularly requested pink).
7. Allow to stand for approximately 15 to 20 minutes before carving; if this is not done, the meat will tend to shrink and curl.

Roast gravy

1. Place the roasting tray on the stove over a gentle heat to allow the sediment to settle.
2. Carefully strain off the fat, leaving the sediment in the tray.
3. Return the tray to the stove and brown carefully. Deglaze with good brown stock.
4. Allow to simmer for a few minutes.
5. Correct the seasoning and colour, then strain and skim.

In some establishments the gravy served with stuffed joints and also pork and veal is slightly thickened with diluted cornflour, fécule or arrowroot.

Carving

Roast leg

Holding the bone, carve with a sharp knife at an angle of 45° and take off each slice as it is cut. Continue in this manner along the joint, turning it from side to side as the slices get wider.

Shoulder

To obtain reasonable sized slices of meat, carve the flesh side, not the skin side, of the joint. When you have obtained the slices it is then necessary to carve round the bones. Due to the awkward shape of the bone structure, the shoulder may be boned-out, rolled and tied before cooking to facilitate carving.

Roast loin

Boned-out – cut in slices across the joint. When stuffed cut slightly thicker.

Roast best end

Divide into cutlets by cutting between bone.

Service

When carved, serve a little gravy over the slices as well as a sauce-boat of gravy. Mint sauce is served with roast lamb, and redcurrant jelly should be available. With roast mutton, redcurrant jelly and/or onion sauce is served.

Mint sauce *8 portions* 125 ml ($\frac{1}{4}$ pt)

		2 – 3 tbsp mint
		1 dessertspoon castor sugar
125 ml	$\frac{1}{4}$ pint	vinegar

1. Chop the washed, picked mint with the sugar.
2. Place in a china basin and add the vinegar.
3. If the vinegar is too sharp, dilute with a little water.

Served with roast lamb.

Stuffing for lamb

This is used for stuffing joints, e.g. loin, shoulder, breast.

50 g	2 oz	chopped suet (optional)
50 g	2 oz	chopped onions cooked in a little fat or oil without colour
		1 egg yolk or small egg
100 g	4 oz	white breadcrumbs
		pinch powdered thyme
		pinch chopped parsley
		salt, pepper

Combine all the ingredients together.

Roasting of beef (see page 134)

Suitable joints

First class – sirloin, wing ribs, fore-ribs.
Second class – topside, middle-ribs.

1. Season the joints with salt and place on a trivet or on bones in a roasting tray.
2. Place a little dripping or oil on top and cook in a hot oven (200 – 230°C, Reg. 6 – 8).
3. Baste frequently and reduce the heat gradually when necessary, as for example in the case of large joints.
4. Roasting time approximately 15 minutes per $\frac{1}{2}$ kilo (1 lb) and 15 minutes over.
5. To test if cooked, place on a tray and press firmly in order to see if the juices released contain any blood.
6. Beef should be underdone, and a little blood should show in the juice which issues when the meat is pressed.
7. On removing the joint from the oven, rest it for 15 minutes, then carve in thin slices against the grain.

Serve the slices neatly, and moisten with a little gravy. Garnish with Yorkshire pudding (allowing 25 g (1 oz) flour per portion) and watercress. Serve separately sauce-boats of gravy and horseradish sauce.

Horseradish sauce *8 portions*

25 – 30 g	1 – 1$\frac{1}{2}$ oz	grated horseradish
$\frac{1}{8}$ litre	$\frac{1}{4}$ pt	lightly whipped cream or yoghurt
		1 tbsp vinegar
		pepper, salt

Wash, peel and rewash the horseradish and grate finely, then mix all the ingredients together.

Yorkshire pudding *4 – 6 portions*

100 g	4 oz	flour
		salt
		1 egg, size 3
250 ml	$\frac{1}{2}$ pt	milk or milk and water
25 g	1 oz	dripping from the roasting meat

Sieve flour and salt into a basin, and make a well in the centre. Break in the egg, add half the liquid and whisk to a smooth mixture, gradually adding the rest of the liquid, and allow to rest.

Select a shallow pan 15 cm (6 in.) in diameter. Add 25 g (1 oz) dripping from the joint and heat in the oven. Pour in the mixture and cook in a hot oven (200 – 230°C, Reg. 6 – 8) for approximately 15 minutes.

Roasting of pork (see page 136)

Preparation of joints

Leg
Remove the pelvic or aitchbone, and trim and score the rind neatly. That is to say, with a sharp-pointed knife, make a series of 3 mm ($\frac{1}{2}$ in.) deep incisions approximately 2 cm (1 in.) apart all over the skin of the joint. Trim and clean the knuckle bone.

Loin (on the bone)
Saw down the chine bone (backbone) in order to facilitate carving; trim excess fat and sinew, and score the rind in the direction in which the joint will be carved. Season and secure with string.

Loin (boned-out)
Remove the fillet and bone-out carefully. Trim off excess fat and sinew, score the rind and beat the

flap. Season, replace the fillet, roll up and secure with string.

This joint is sometimes stuffed (see below).

Spare rib
Remove excess fat, bone and sinew, and trim neatly.

Belly
Remove all the small rib bones, season with salt, pepper and chopped sage, roll and secure with string. This joint may be stuffed.

Shoulder
This is usually boned-out, excess fat and sinew removed, seasoned, scored and rolled, and secured with string. This joint may be stuffed or may be divided into two smaller joints.

1. Season the prepared joint of pork.
2. Lightly brush the skin with oil in order to make the crackling crisp.
3. Place on a trivet in a roasting tin, with a little dripping or oil on top.
4. Start to cook in a hot oven (230 – 250°C), basting frequently.
5. Gradually reduce the heat, allowing approximately 25 minutes per $\frac{1}{2}$ kg (1 lb) and 25 minutes over. Pork must always be well cooked.
6. When the meat is cooked remove from the pan and prepare a roast gravy from the sediment in the usual way.
7. Serve the joint accompanied by roast gravy, apple sauce, and sage and onion stuffing. If to be carved, proceed as for roast lamb (see page 53).

Sage and onion stuffing for pork
4 portions

50 g	2 oz	chopped onion
50 g	2 oz	pork dripping
100 g	4 oz	white breadcrumbs
		pinch chopped parsley
		good pinch powdered sage
		salt, pepper

1. Cook the onion in the dripping without colour.
2. Combine all the ingredients, place in a greased dish and heat through in the oven.

Apple sauce $\frac{1}{4}$ litre ($\frac{1}{2}$ pint) *4 – 6 portions*

400 g	1 lb	cooking apples
25 g	1 oz	sugar
25 g	1 oz	margarine or butter

1. Peel, core and wash the apples.
2. Place, with the sugar and margarine or butter, in a little water in a saucepan with a tight-fitting lid.
3. Cook to a purée.
4. Liquidise or pass through a sieve.

Roasting of chicken (see page 137)

Cleaning

1. Remove any small feathers, using a small knife.
2. Singe in order to remove any hairs – take care not to scorch the skin.
3. Split the neck by gripping firmly and making a lengthwise incision on the underside. Cut off the neck as close to the body as possible.
4. Cut off the head.
5. Remove the crop and loosen intestines and lungs with forefinger.
6. Cut out vent and wipe clean.
7. Loosen intestines with forefinger.
8. Draw out the innards being careful not to break the gall-blader.
9. Wipe vent end if necessary.
10. Split and clean the gizzard.

Trussing

1. To facilitate carving remove the wishbone.
2. Place the bird on its back.
3. Hold the legs back firmly.
4. Insert the trussing needle through the bird, midway between the leg joints.
5. Turn on to its side.
6. Pierce the winglet, the skin of the neck, the skin of the carcass and the other winglet.
7. Tie ends of string securely.
8. Secure the legs by inserting the needle through the carcass and over the legs; take care not to pierce the breast.

Roast chicken *4 portions*

$1\frac{1}{4}$ – $1\frac{1}{2}$ kg	$2\frac{1}{2}$ – 3 lb	1 chicken
50 g	2 oz	fat or oil
125 ml	$\frac{1}{4}$ pint	brown stock
25 g	1 oz	game chips
		1 bunch watercress
125 ml	$\frac{1}{4}$ pt	bread sauce

1. Lightly season the chicken inside and out with salt.
2. Place on its side in a roasting tin.
3. Cover with the fat or oil.

4. Place in hot oven (200 – 230°C, Reg. 6 – 8), approximately 20 – 25 minutes.
5. Turn on to the other leg.
6. Cook for a further 20 – 25 minutes approx.
7. Baste frequently.
8. To test if cooked, pierce with a fork between the drumstick and thigh and hold over a plate. The juice issuing from the chicken should not show any sign of blood.
9. Prepare roast gravy with the stock and the sediment in the roasting tray.
10. If to be served whole, serve on a flat dish with game chips in front and the watercress at the back of the bird.
11. If served in portions, remove the legs and divide each into 2. Cut off the wings so that the breast can be divided into 2, giving 4 equal pieces. Each portion then consists of a piece of leg and a wing or piece of breast.

Roast gravy and bread sauce are served separately. Always remove trussing string from the bird before serving.

Bread sauce $\frac{1}{4}$ litre ($\frac{1}{2}$ pint) 4 – 6 *portions*

375 ml	$\frac{3}{4}$ pt	milk
		small onion studded with a clove
25 g	1 oz	breadcrumbs
		salt, cayenne
10 g	$\frac{1}{2}$ oz	butter or margarine

1. Infuse the simmering milk with the studded onion for 15 minutes.
2. Remove the onion and mix in the crumbs.
3. Simmer 2 – 3 minutes.
4. Season and correct the consistency.
5. Add the butter on top of the sauce to prevent a skin forming.
6. Mix well when serving.

Roast potatoes

1. Wash, peel and rewash the potatoes.
2. Cut into even-sized pieces; allow 3 – 4 pieces per portion.
3. Heat a good measure of dripping or oil in a roasting tray.
4. Add the well dried potatoes and lightly brown on all sides.
5. Season with salt and cook in a hot oven (200 – 230°C, Reg. 6 – 8).
6. Turn the potatoes over after approximately 30 minutes.
7. Cook to a golden brown. Drain and serve.

The cooking time is approximately 1 hour.

Questions – Roasting

1. Roasting is cooking in the oven with the aid of what? FAT
2. Name two vegetables which can be roasted. POTS PARSNIP
3. Explain the term *basting*. SPOON FAT OVER
4. What kind of meats are suitable for roasting? TENDER MEAT
5. Why is the oven pre-heated before adding the meat? SEAL PORES
6. Which of the following are suitable for roasting:

   best end of lamb, ✓
   ox-tail,
   sirloin of beef, ✓
   leg of pork? ✓
7. When meat is roasting how can one tell if it is cooking too quickly? NOISE OF FAT SPLATTERING
8. Match the following:

Roast beef	Mint sauce
Roast lamb	Horseradish sauce
Roast pork	Bread sauce
Roast chicken	Cranberry sauce
Roast turkey	Apple sauce
9. How is it possible to decide how long to cook meat, and whether it is cooked sufficiently?
10. Explain pot roasting.
11. Indicate on the following diagrams those parts of the lamb and beef which are suitable for roasting.

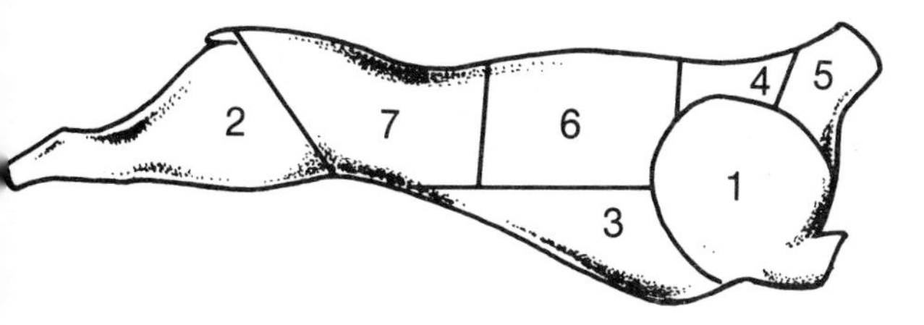

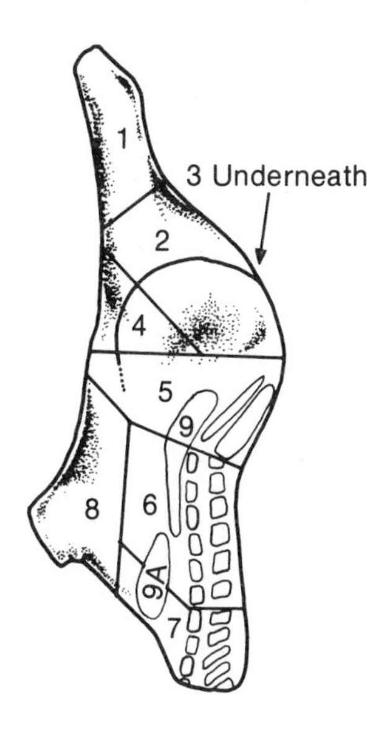

Answers can be found on page 153.

10
Grilling

General objectives To have a knowledge and understanding of grilling.
Specific objectives To state the definition and the principles of grilling; to explain the reasons for grilling foods; to demonstrate the practices of grilling; to list foods that are grilled; to specify the effects of grilling; to describe the advantages of grilling; to explain the techniques of grilling, e.g. charring, scoring (fish), glazing, gratinating.

Definition

Grilling is the method of cooking which uses direct, intense heat.

Principles of grilling

1. It is a fast method of cooking and is only suitable for tender foods which cook quickly.
2. Because of the speed of cooking the goodness in the food is not lost.
3. Due to *charring* or colouring, the food gains flavour.
4. To prevent the food burning a little oil, butter or margarine is used to moisten the surface.
5. Half-way through the grilling process the food is turned, so that both sides are cooked.
6. Extra thick foods, such as large trout or herring, may be partially grilled; they may then be finished in the oven to cook the centre of the food.
7. When using solid fuel grills, the centre and back of the grill will be the hottest.

Equipment

Salamander and grill bars must be kept clean and lightly greased before, during and after use. The salamander drip tray should also be cleaned after use.

Safety

1. Tongs, a fish slice or large palette knife should be used to turn foods.
2. When using trays under a salamander, they should have a rim or edge to prevent any hot liquid being spilled.

Foods cooked by grilling

Meat

Beef steaks – rump, sirloin, fillet
Lamb – loin chops, chump chops, cutlets
Pork – chops
Poultry – chicken legs, half chicken, whole split chicken
Kebabs, bacon, sausage, kidneys, liver, mixed grill

1. Steaks are cooked to the customer's preference – underdone, medium or well done.
2. The degree of cooking will depend on:

   a) the control of heat,
   b) the length of cooking time,
   c) the quality of the meat and

d) thickness of the food being grilled.

3. Criss-cross grill bar marks improve appearance.
4. Half-way through the cooking time the meat is turned.
5. Pressure of the finger on the meat indicates the degree of cooking – the firmer the feel or resistance the more well cooked the meat will be.

Under-fired grill

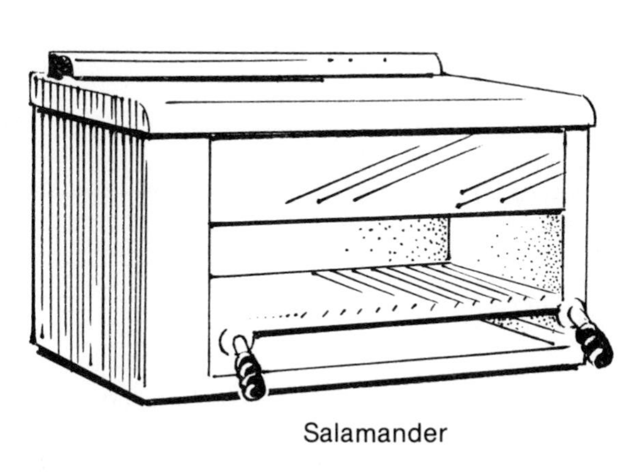

Salamander

6. Pork and sausages must not be underdone – they must always be thoroughly cooked.
7. Lamb, liver, kidney and chicken are cooked through but not overcooked, as they would dry out and become tough.
8. Kebabs and sausages are turned several times and brushed with fat to ensure even cooking.
9. When cooking mixed grills, items taking the longest time to cook are grilled first.
10. Grilled meats may be served with watercress, parsley butter and fried potatoes.
11. Grills are suitable for all meals.

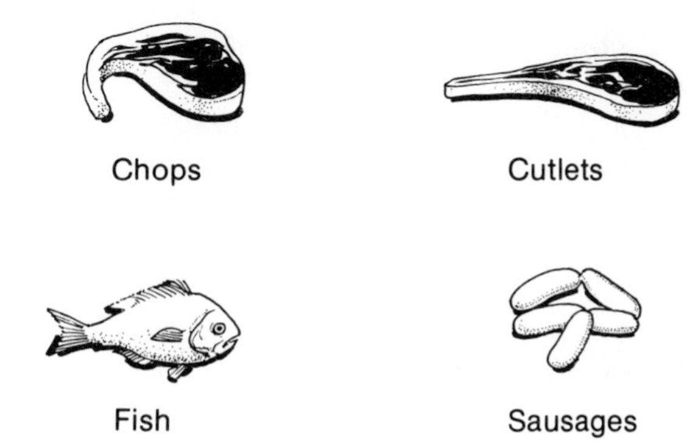

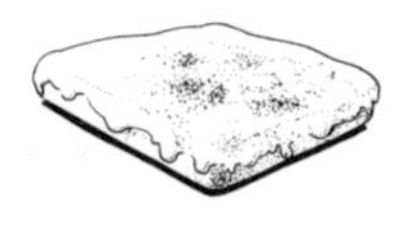

Welsh rarebit

Grilling

Fish

Whole fish – herring, mackerel, trout, plaice
Cuts of fish:
on the bone – cod, salmon, plaice
filleted – plaice, cod, haddock

1. Fish must be fresh and thoroughly cleaned.
2. Due to its delicate texture, it must be handled with care.
3. Before grilling, fish must be washed and dried.
4. A coating is always necessary to protect the fish from burning. Either:
   a) brush the fish with oil, melted butter or margarine, or
   b) pass the fish through seasoned flour, and brush with oil.
5. Fish is usually placed on a greased rimmed tray and grilled under the salamander.
6. Half-way through cooking the fish is carefully turned and the cooking completed.
7. The length of time required depends on the type and size of the fish being grilled.
8. To enable the heat to penetrate whole, round fish they are scored – incisions are cut part way through the fish.

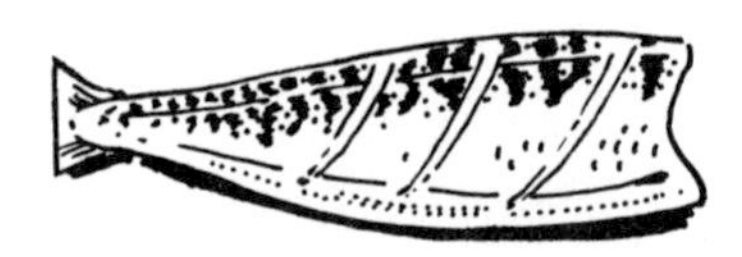

Scoring fish

9. Large fish may need to have the cooking finished in the oven.
10. It is usual to serve lemon, picked parsley and parsley butter with grilled fish.

Vegetables

Tomatoes and mushrooms may be grilled.

1. Vegetables are brushed with oil, melted butter or margarine before grilling.
2. They are placed on a rimmed tray and grilled under the salamander.
3. Tomatoes may be halved or grilled whole.

Barbecue

Cooking outdoors, usually using charcoal grills, is quite popular. All foods suitable for grilling, as well as items such as hamburgers, can be used.

Glazing

A salamander or overhead grill may be used to finish items to give colour and gloss, for example fish dishes with a sauce containing cream and yolk of egg.

Gratinating

Some dishes are finished with grated cheese or breadcrumbs, and coloured under the salamander, e.g. macaroni cheese, cauliflower cheese.

Toasting

Items such as bread, teacakes, scones and buns may be toasted.

1. Toasted bread or toast can be produced under a salamander or domestic grill or in a toaster.
2. Toast can be served on its own, with butter and jam or marmalade.

3. Toast can be the base for poached eggs, scrambled egg, sardines, baked beans and other savouries.

Grilled fish

Grilled cod or salmon steaks

1. Wash the steaks well and drain.
2. Pass through seasoned flour.
3. Brush with melted butter, margarine or oil.
4. Place on a greased baking tray.
5. Cook on both sides under the salamander, brushing occasionally with fat.
6. To test if cooked, carefully remove the centre bone.
7. Garnish with a slice of lemon and picked parsley; serve a suitable sauce or butter separately (e.g. parsley butter).

Parsley butter *4 portions*

50 g	2 oz	butter
		juice of $\frac{1}{4}$ lemon
		$\frac{1}{4}$ tsp chopped parsley
		salt, pepper

1. Combine all the ingredients.
2. Shape into a roll 2 cm (1 in.) in diameter.
3. Place in wet greaseproof paper.
4. Harden in the refrigerator.
5. Cut into $\frac{1}{2}$ cm ($\frac{1}{4}$ in.) slices.

Parsley butter may be served with grilled meats and fish, and with fried fish.

Grilled herring

1. Remove the scales from the fish with the back of a knife.
2. Remove the head, clean out the intestines, trim off all fins, take care not to damage the roe, and trim the tail.
3. Wash and drain well.
4. Make three incisions 2 mm ($\frac{1}{12}$ in.) deep on either side of the fish.
5. Pass through seasoned flour.
6. Brush with melted butter, margarine or oil, and place on a greased baking tray.
7. Grill on both sides, taking care not to burn the tails.
8. Garnish with a slice of lemon and picked parsley.
9. Serve with a sauceboat of mustard sauce (see page 14).

Fillets of grilled plaice

1. Fillet the plaice and remove the black skin.
2. Wash well and drain.
3. Pass through seasoned flour and shake off all surplus flour.
4. Place on a greased baking tray, skinned side down.
5. Brush with melted butter, margarine or oil.
6. Grill on both sides under the salamander.
7. Serve with a slice of lemon, picked parsley and suitable sauce or butter.

Anchovy butter *4 portions*

50 g	2 oz	butter
		salt, pepper
		few drops of anchovy essence

1. Combine all the ingredients.
2. Shape into a roll 2 cm (1 in.) in diameter.
3. Place in wet greaseproof paper.
4. Harden in the refrigerator.
5. Cut into $\frac{1}{2}$ cm ($\frac{1}{4}$ in.) slices.

Grilled meat

Brochette of lamb Also known as shish kebab

Prime meat must be used, the ideal cuts being the nut of the lean meat of the loin and best end. Other meats which may be used are beef, pork, liver, kidney, bacon, ham, sausage, chicken. Tomato, pineapple and apple may also be used.

Brochette of lamb

1. Cut the meat into pieces, season and place on a skewer with peeled, washed mushrooms and two halves of bay leaf to each skewer. Slices of onion and red or green pepper may also be included.
2. Season, brush with melted oil or fat and grill gently, turning and brushing with fat until the meat is cooked. Brochettes are usually served on a pilaff of rice (see page 45).

Further variety in flavour may also be given by marinading the skewered meats in oil, lemon juice, spices and herbs for 1 to 2 hours before cooking.

Preparation of chops

Loin chops

Skin the loin, remove the excess fat and sinew, then cut into chops approximately 100 – 150 g (4 – 6 oz) in weight. Some loin chops may have a piece of kidney skewered in the centre.

Chump chops

These are cut from the chump end of the loin. Cut into approximately 150 g (6 oz) chops, trimming where necessary.

Grilled loin or chump chops

1. Season with salt and milled pepper.
2. Brush with oil or fat, and place on hot greased grill bars or on a greased baking tray.
3. Cook quickly for the first 2 to 3 minutes on each side, in order to seal the pores of the meat.
4. Continue cooking steadily, allowing approximately 12 – 15 minutes in all.
5. Remove the skewer before serving.
6. Garnish with picked watercress and fried potatoes.

Parsley butter may also be served.

Preparation of cutlets

Prepare best end as for roasting, excluding the scoring, and divide evenly between the bones, or the cutlets can be cut from the best end and prepared separately. A double cutlet consists of 2 bones, therefore a 6 bone best end yields 6 single or 3 double cutlets.

Grilled cutlets

1. Lightly season the prepared cutlets with salt and pepper (preferably from the pepper mill).
2. Brush with oil or fat.
3. When cooked on the bars of the grill, place the prepared cutlets on the pre-heated bars, which have been greased.
4. Cook for approximately 5 minutes, turn and complete the cooking.
5. When cooked under the salamander place on a greased tray, cook for approximately 5 minutes, turn and complete the cooking.
6. Serve garnished with fried potatoes and watercress. Parsley butter may also be served.

Mixed grill

4 sausages	4 rashers streaky bacon
4 cutlets	watercress
4 kidneys	straw potatoes
4 tomatoes	parsley butter
4 mushrooms	

These are the usually accepted items for a mixed grill, but there are many variations to this list, e.g. steaks, liver.

In economical catering a Welsh rarebit and fried egg may be used in place of more expensive items.

Grill in the order given and dress neatly on the serving dish. Garnish with fried potatoes and watercress and a slice of parsley butter on each kidney.

Grilled kidneys

1. Prepare the kidneys by removing the skin, cutting three-quarters of the way through lengthwise, and skewer.
2. Lightly season the prepared kidneys.
3. Brush with melted butter, margarine or oil.
4. Place on pre-heated grill bars or on a greased baking tray.
5. Grill fairly quickly on both sides, approximately 5 – 10 minutes depending on size.
6. Serve with parsley butter, picked watercress and fried potatoes.

Grilled pork chop

Season and grill until cooked through and serve with picked watercress and fried potatoes. Offer a suitable sauce separately, e.g. apple sauce (see page 55).

Grilled gammon steaks

Brush the rashers lightly with oil or fat on both sides and cook on greased, pre-heated grill bars on both sides for approximately 5 to 10 minutes in all. Serve with watercress and any other food as indicated, e.g. tomatoes, mushrooms, eggs. If a sauce is required, serve any sharp demi-glace sauce.

Grilled back or streaky rashers

Remove the rind and bone from the rashers and arrange on a baking tray and grill on both sides under the salamander.

Grilled chicken

Preparation

1. Remove the wishbone.
2. Cut off the claws at the first joint.
3. Place bird on its back.
4. Insert a large knife through the neck end and out of the vent.
5. Cut through the backbone.
6. Open out.
7. Lightly season the prepared chicken with salt and mill pepper.
8. Brush with oil, melted butter or margarine and place on pre-heated greased grill bars or on a flat baking tray under a salamander.
9. Brush frequently with melted fat during cooking and allow approximately 15 – 20 minutes each side.
10. Test if cooked by piercing the drumstick with a skewer or trussing needle; there should be no sign of blood issuing from the leg.
11. Serve garnished with picked watercress and offer a suitable sauce separately.

Grilled chicken may be served with streaky bacon, tomatoes and mushrooms

Grilled mushrooms *4 portions*

200 g	8 oz	grilling mushrooms
		salt, pepper
50 g	2 oz	butter or fat

1. Peel and remove the stalks and wash well.
2. Place on a tray and lightly season with salt and pepper.
3. Brush with oil or melted fat and grill on both sides for approximately 3 to 4 minutes. and serve.

Grilled tomatoes

Allow 1 or 2 per portion, according to size
$\frac{1}{2}$ kg (1 lb) will yield approx. 3 – 4 portions

1. Wash the tomatoes, and remove the eyes with a small knife.
2. Place on a greased, seasoned baking tray.
3. Make an incision 2 mm ($\frac{1}{12}$ in.) cross-shape on the opposite side to the eye and peel back the four corners.
4. Brush with melted fat and oil and season with salt and pepper.
5. Grill under a moderately hot salamander.
6. Garnish with picked parsley, and serve.
7. Large tomatoes can be halved and grilled cut side up.

Grilled beef

Beef steaks are cut from the rump, sirloin or fillet.

Rump is trimmed of excess fat and all sinew and then cut into slices approximately $1\frac{1}{2}$ cm ($\frac{3}{4}$ in.) thick. The slices are then cut into steaks of the required weight.

Sirloin – the fillet is removed, the sirloin boned-out and after excess fat, sinew and gristle have been removed the sirloin is cut into one of the following:

a) minute steaks – 1 cm ($\frac{1}{2}$ in.) slices, flattened with a meat bat dipped in water, making them as thin as possible.
b) sirloin steaks – 1 cm ($\frac{1}{2}$ in.) slices, approximate weight 150 g (6 oz).
c) double sirloin steaks – 2 cm (1 in.) slices approximate weight 250 – 300 g (10 – 12 oz).
d) porterhouse and T-bone steaks – complete slices and sawn through the sirloin, including bone and fillet. All sirloin steaks are also known as entrecôte steaks.

Fillet – after fat and sinew is removed is cut into one of the following:

a) double fillet steak – also known as Chateaubriand, which is cut from the head or thick part of the fillet 3 – 10 cm ($1\frac{1}{2}$ – 4 in.), weight 300 g – 1 kg ($\frac{3}{4}$ – 2 lb).
b) fillet steak – cut $1\frac{1}{2}$ – 2 cm ($\frac{3}{4}$ – 1 in.) thick, weight 100 – 150 g (4 – 6 oz).
c) tournedos – cut 2 – 4 cm (1 – $1\frac{1}{2}$ in). thick, weight 100 g (4 oz).

Cooking

1. All steaks are lightly seasoned with salt and milled pepper, and brushed with oil on both sides.
2. Place steaks on pre-heated grill bars.
3. Turn steaks over half-way through cooking.
4. Brush occasionally with oil.
5. Cook to the degree ordered by the customer.

Degrees of cooking grilled meats
Rare or blue
Underdone
Just done or pink
Well done

Test with finger pressure – the springiness or resilience of the meat, together with the amount of blood issuing from it, indicates the degree to which the steak is cooked. This calls for experience, but if the meat is placed on a plate and tested, then the more underdone the steak the greater the springiness and the more blood will be shown on the plate.

Serve garnished with watercress, deep-fried potato, and parsley butter.

Questions – Grilling

1. Explain what you understand by grilling as a method of cookery.
2. Name 3 kinds of food which may be grilled. Give an example of each.
3. What is a salamander?
4. Explain why certain foods are turned half-way through grilling.
5. List the items which make a mixed grill.
6. Which is the food that is not grilled: pork chop, lamb cutlet, beef steak, ox kidney? Explain why.
7. In this word search there are at least 10 words, 4 of which related to grilling. Can you find them?

   C L O C K
   U H O R A
   T D O V E
   L P D P T
   E E L O S
   T T G T G

8. Find out the purchasing cost of a 100 g (4 oz) lamb chop and a 150 g (6 oz) piece of cod on the bone. How much would a 150 g (6 oz) grilled steak cost in a restaurant?
9. State 3 sources of heat used for grilling.

Answers can be found on page 154.

11
Frying

General objectives To understand and know the principles of shallow and deep frying.
Specific objectives To be able to define shallow and deep frying; to explain the reasons for frying; to demonstrate the ability to shallow and deep fry; to state foods cooked by frying; to describe the effects of frying; to list the advantages of frying; to select equipment, and state its care and use; to fry efficiently and apply safety procedures; to use recipes associated with frying; to explain blue haze, flash point, coating, meunière, friture, spider.

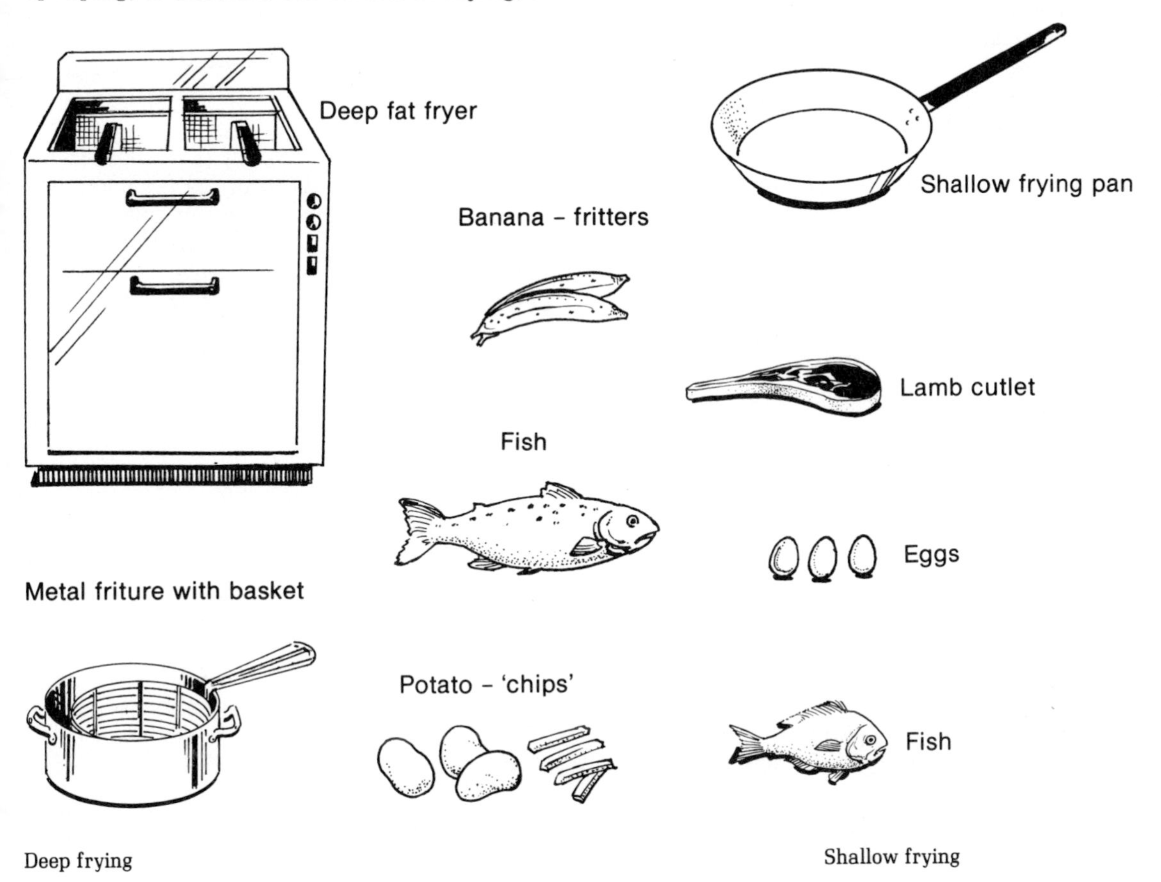

Deep frying

Shallow frying

Definition

Frying is a fast method of cooking and may be either:

a) *shallow frying* in a small amount of fat, as in a frying-pan, or
b) *deep-frying* in a large amount of deep fat, as in a deep fryer.

More accidents are caused during the process of frying than when cooking by any other method.

To fry foods successfully a good cook must:

a) know and apply the rules of safety,
b) develop an attitude to safety, so that at all times the observance of these rules becomes second nature.

Principles of frying

1. To cook food to an attractive brown colour, crisp where appropriate, producing a variety of textures.
2. To make food digestible, increase flavour and enjoyable to eat.

Advantages

1. Speed – foods can be cooked quickly.
2. Colour – appetising brown colours are produced.
3. Texture – a variety of textures result from shallow and deep frying.
4. Smell – some fried foods can stimulate the palate, e.g. bacon, onion.

Equipment

Care of deep fat fryers

1. Change fat periodically as required.
2. Clean daily after use, according to manufacturer's instructions, e.g.:

    a) turn off heat;
    b) drain and strain fat;
    c) close stopcock, fill fryer with hot detergent water and boil 10 – 15 minutes;
    d) drain off water, refill with clean water, add $\frac{1}{8}$ litre of vinegar to 5 litres of water, reboil 10 – 15 minutes;
    e) drain off, dry the fryer, close stopcock, refill with clean fat.

Care of shallow fryers

Frying pans Clean thoroughly after each use by:

a) using kitchen cloth or paper and a little salt as an abrasive if necessary,
b) storing upside down on racks or hanging on hooks.

Sauté pans To clean:

a) wash in hot detergent water, rinse in hot clean water and dry,
b) store on racks or hang on hooks.

Griddle plates To clean:

a) warm the plate and scrape off food particles,
b) clean the surface with pumice or griddle stone,
c) clean with hot detergent water,
d) rinse with clean water and wipe dry,
e) lightly grease griddle surface.

Flash point

When frying, food is added to the fat when a slight blue haze appears or, in the case of a deep fat fryer, when the temperature gauge reaches the required temperature.

The fat must never be allowed to get so hot that smoke rises from it, as the next thing to happen is the fat bursting into flames (this is known as the 'flash point'). *Heat control* is therefore essential:

1. For safety.
2. In the cooking process because:

    a) too little heat will cause the food to absorb fat and be greasy.
    b) too much heat will cause the food to be over-coloured and not cooked.

The competent cook will:

a) assess the quality, size and shape of the food to be fried,
b) ensure that it is cooked to the correct degree,
c) check that it has a pleasing colour,
d) check that it is not greasy.

Coatings

In order to prevent the fat being absorbed, which would cause the food to be greasy and also to break up, most foods are coated in either:

a) flour, egg and breadcrumbs,
b) milk and flour,
c) batter.

All foods *must* be dried before being added to the fat, otherwise the moisture will cause the hot fat to spit and may cause a severe burn. As frying is a quick method of cooking, it is unsuitable for tough meat or poultry.

Shallow frying

This is cooking in shallow fat or oil in a frying pan, sauté pan or on a griddle. As frying takes only a short time, careful attention must be given throughout the cooking process, and foods must not be left unattended, otherwise they will burn.

Eggs and bacon

Chicken breast sauté

Foods suitable for shallow frying

Eggs, bacon, sausages, hamburgers, small, tender cuts of meat, liver, kidneys and poultry, small whole fish (up to 400 g, 1 lb), slices and fillets of fish, vegetables, pancakes.

Heat control is essential to achieve satisfactory results:

1. The fat must *always* be hot before food is placed in the pan, otherwise it may stick to the pan and break up.
2. The *temperature* of the fat must be maintained, so that the food 'fries' and does not 'boil' in the fat.
3. The *presentation* side of the food should always be fried first because it will be cooked in clean fat and therefore have a better appearance.
4. All food should be turned and cooked on both sides.

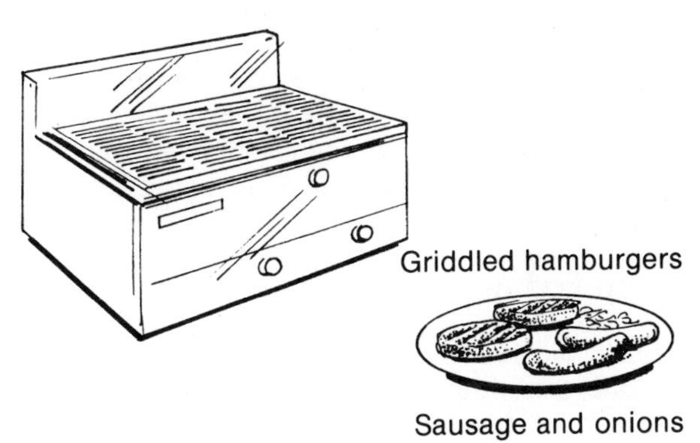

Griddled hamburgers

Sausage and onions

Griddle plate – lightly greased and can be used for hamburgers, sausages, chops, steaks, bacon, eggs, scotch pancakes, onions.

Fish – small fish, cuts or fillets of fish may be passed through milk and seasoned flour, or flour, egg and breadcrumbs before shallow-frying. Round fish such as herring, trout, mackerel are given 3 light cuts (scored) on either side in order to help the heat penetrate through. Round fish are also cooked slowly because of their thickness. A popular method of serving fried fish is to finish the cooked fish with *nut-brown* butter, lemon juice, and chopped parsley. This is then called *meunière*.

Type of fat or oil	Approximate flash point °C	Smoke point °C	Recommended frying temperature °C
Finest vegetable oil	324	220	180
Finest vegetable fat	321	220	180
High class vegetable oil	324	204	180
Pure vegetable fat	318	216	175
Pure vegetable oil	330	216	175
Finest maize oil	224	215	180
Finest fat	321	202	180
Finest dripping	300	165	175
Finest olive oil	271	150	175

Eggs – for frying, eggs are carefully cracked and placed (so as not to break the yolks) in hot fat or oil, and then fried gently until set. The yolk should be soft and hot fat can, if required, be splashed from the pan over the yolk in order to heat and cook it. Before serving, drain off any surplus fat, unless the egg is fried in butter.

Vegetables – potatoes cut thinly can be shallow fried from raw, more often they are boiled or steamed in their skins, peeled, sliced and fried; they are then known as *sauté* potatoes. Mushrooms, egg plant and tomatoes are fried from raw. Cooked cauliflower and sprouts may be lightly fried after being boiled and well drained.

Deep frying

This is cooking in a deep pan (known as a *friture*) containing oil which enables the food being cooked to be immersed completely, as, for example, 'fish and chips'. As deep frying has been the cause of many accidents, these rules must always be followed to ensure safety and also to achieve good results.

1. The friture should not be more than one-half to three-quarters full.
2. Oil must never be allowed to become so hot that it smokes.
3. Normal cooking temperature is 175 – 195°C (350 – 380°F).
4. Do not fry too much food at a time, because the temperature will drop and cause the food to absorb fat and become soggy.
5. Allow oil to recover its heat before adding the next batch of food.
6. A frying basket and spider must always be to hand as a safety measure.
7. Wet foods, such as potatoes, must be well dried before frying.
8. Oil needs to be strained after use.
9. Certain foods are coated with flour, egg and crumbs, batter or pastry. This coating should not be damaged in the cooking as it is used for protection, as follows:
   a) to prevent the escape of goodness from the food,
   b) to prevent food absorbing oil,
   c) to protect the surface of food from intense heat,
   d) to modify too rapid penetration of heat.
10. When adding food to the friture carefully place it in away from you to avoid being splashed by hot fat.

Meat and poultry – made-up dishes, using cooked meats and poultry thickened with a sauce and egg yolks, are shaped into croquettes, cutlets or rissoles, coated with pastry, batter or flour, egg and breadcrumbs and deep fried. Cut pieces of raw chicken, e.g. drumstick, thigh or breast, are coated and fried, as in Kentucky fried chicken.

Fish – whole, in cuts, pieces or fillets must always be coated with either a) milk and flour b) flour, egg and breadcrumbs or c) batter before being deep fried. The fish should be well drained and free from fat or oil before being served.

Serving – deep-fried fish is usually served with a piece of lemon and a sharp tasting sauce, e.g. tartar sauce.

Vegetables – potatoes are cut in various shapes and sizes and deep fried raw. Large size cuts may require pre-cooking (*blanching*) before final cooking to ensure they are cooked through.

Boiled or steamed potato, mashed and mixed with egg yolks and butter, is known as duchess potato mixture, and can be moulded into shapes, coated in flour, egg and breadcrumbs and deep fried.

Egg plant (aubergine) and baby marrow (courgette) are sliced and floured; cauliflower sprigs are passed through batter.

Fruits – apples, bananas and pineapple, when peeled, sliced, coated in batter and deep fried, are known as fritters.

Choux paste – mixed with grated cheese and deep fried in walnut-shaped pieces are known as cheese fritters.

Recipes for shallow frying

Scrambled eggs (basic recipe) *4 portions*

		6 – 8 eggs
		salt, pepper
50 g	2 oz	butter

1. Break the eggs in a basin, lightly season with salt and pepper and thoroughly mix with a whisk.
2. Melt 25 g (1 oz) butter in a thick-bottomed pan, add the eggs and cook over a gentle heat, stirring continuously until the eggs are lightly cooked.
3. Remove from the heat, correct the seasoning and mix in the remaining 25 g (1 oz) butter.
4. Serve in individual egg dishes.

Scrambled eggs should be cooked to a thick, creamy consistency, therefore do not cook too quickly or for too long.

Scrambled eggs on toast

As above, serving each portion on a slice of freshly buttered toast, with the crust removed.

Scrambled eggs with tomatoes

400 g	1 lb	tomatoes
25 g	1 oz	chopped onion
25 g	1 oz	fat or oil

1. Prepare, cook and serve the eggs as for the basic method.
2. Prepare a cooked tomato concassée (see page 26).
3. To serve, place a spoonful of tomato in the centre of each dish of egg and a little chopped parsley on the top of the tomato.

Scrambled eggs with mushrooms

200 g	8 oz	button mushrooms
25 g	1 oz	butter or oil
		chopped parsley

1. Prepare, cook and serve the eggs as for the basic method.
2. Peel, wash and slice the mushrooms.
3. Toss in the butter in a frying pan until cooked; drain off any liquid.
4. Dress neatly on top of the eggs with a little parsley.

Omelet (basic recipe)

1. Allow 2 – 3 eggs per portion.
2. Break the eggs into a basin, season lightly with salt and pepper.
3. Beat well with a fork or whisk until the yolks and whites are thoroughly combined and no streaks of white can be seen.
4. Heat the omelet pan.
5. Wipe thoroughly clean with a dry cloth.
6. Add 10 g ($\frac{1}{2}$ oz) butter or oil.
7. Heat until foaming but not brown.
8. Add the eggs and cook quickly, moving the mixture continuously with a fork until lightly set.
9. Remove from the heat.
10. Half fold the mixture over at right angles to the handle.
11. Tap the bottom of the pan to bring up the edge of the omelet.
12. Tilt the pan completely over the serving dish or plate to allow the omelet to fall carefully into the centre of the dish.
13. Neaten the shape if necessary, and serve immediately.

Omelet with mixed herbs

Add a pinch of chopped parsley, chervil and chives to the mixture and proceed as for basic omelet (see above).

Mushroom omelet

1. 25 – 50 g (1 – 2 oz) button mushrooms per portion.
2. Wash and slice the mushrooms.
3. Cook in a frying pan in a little butter or oil, season with salt and pepper; drain off any liquid.
4. Add to the butter in the hot pan and proceed as for basic omelet (see above).

Cheese omelet

1. Allow 25 g (1 oz) grated cheese per portion.
2. Proceed as for basic omelet.
3. Before folding, add the cheese.
4. Fold and serve as for basic omelet.

Jam omelet

1. Allow 25 g (1 oz) sugar, and 1 tbsp jam per portion.
2. Proceed as for basic omelet, without pepper or salt.
3. Add the previously warmed jam before folding.
4. Turn out on to the dish or plate.
5. Sprinkle liberally with icing sugar.
6. Brand with a criss-cross pattern, using a red-hot poker and serve.

Fried eggs

1. Allow 1 or 2 eggs per portion.
2. Melt a little fat in a frying pan.
3. Add the eggs and season lightly.
4. Cook gently until lightly set.
5. Serve on a plate or flat dish.

To prepare an excellent fried egg it is essential to use a high quality egg and to maintain a controlled, low heat.

Fried eggs and bacon

1. Allow 2 – 3 rashers per portion.
2. Remove the rind and any bone from the rashers.
3. Fry the bacon in a little fat or oil or grill on a flat tray under the salamander on both sides.
4. Dress the bacon neatly around the fried egg.

Shallow fried fish

Known as fish *meunière*

Many fish, whole or filleted, may be cooked by this method, e.g. sole, fillets of plaice, trout, brill, cod, turbot, herring, scampi, etc.

1. Prepare and clean the fish; wash and drain.
2. Pass through seasoned flour; shake off all surplus flour.
3. Shallow fry on both sides, presentation side first, in hot clarified butter, margarine or oil.
4. Dress neatly on a serving dish.
5. Peel a lemon, removing the yellow and white skin.
6. Cut the lemon into slices and place one slice on each portion.
7. Squeeze some lemon juice on the fish.
8. Allow 10 – 25 g ($\frac{1}{2}$ – 1 oz) butter per portion and colour in a clean frying pan to the nut-brown stage.
9. Pour over the fish.
10. Sprinkle with chopped parsley and serve.

Meat recipes

Fried crumbed lamb cutlets

1. Pass prepared cutlets through seasoned flour, eggwash and fresh white breadcrumbs.
2. Shake off surplus crumbs and pat firm with a palette knife.
3. Shallow fry in hot clarified fat or oil for the first few minutes, then allow to cook gently.
4. Turn, and continue cooking until a golden brown.
5. To test if cooked, press firmly, no sign of blood should appear.

Finish with a cordon of jus-lié around the dish. Nut-brown butter may be served over the cutlets.

Sautéed kidneys *4 portions*

		8 sheep's kidneys
50 g	2 oz	butter or oil
250 ml	$\frac{1}{2}$ pt	demi-glace

1. Skin and halve the kidneys.
2. Remove the sinews.
3. Cut each half into 3 or 5 pieces.
4. Season lightly.
5. Fry quickly in a frying pan, using the butter or oil, for approximately 4 to 5 minutes.
6. Place in a colander to drain.
7. Add to the finished sauce. Correct the seasoning.
8. Do not reboil before serving.

Hamburg or Vienna steak *4 portions*

25 g	1 oz	finely chopped onion
10 g	$\frac{1}{2}$ oz	fat or oil

200 g	½ lb	lean minced beef
		1 small egg
100 g	4 oz	breadcrumbs
		salt, pepper
		2 tbsp cold water (approx)

1. Cook the onions in the fat or oil without colour.
2. Add to the rest of the ingredients and mix in well.
3. Divide into 4 even pieces and using a little flour make into balls, flatten and shape round.
4. Shallow fry in hot fat or oil on both sides, reducing the heat after the first few minutes, making certain the steaks are cooked right through.
5. Serve with a demi-glace based sauce. The steaks may be garnished with French fried onions (see page 75) and sometimes with a fried egg.

Hamburger American style

The hamburger was originally made using 200 g (8 oz) of minced beef per portion, moulded into a round flat shape and cooked on both sides on a lightly greased hot griddle or pan. The hamburger should not be pricked while cooking as the juices would seep out, leaving a dry product. In its simplest form, when cooked it is placed between two halves of a freshly toasted round, flat bun.

There are many variations in the seasonings and ingredients which may be added to the minced beef, and many garnishes and sauces may accompany the hamburger. The bun may be plain or seeded (sesame seed).

Pork escalopes

Pork escalopes are usually cut from prime cuts of meat in the leg. They may be cut into 75 – 100 g (3 – 4 oz) slices, flattened with a meat bat. They may be used plain or crumbed and served as for veal escalope (see below).

Calf's liver and bacon *4 portions*

300 g	12 oz	liver
		seasoned flour
50 g	2 oz	oil or fat for frying
50 g	2 oz	streaky bacon
125 ml	¼ pint	jus-lié

1. Skin the liver and remove the gristle.
2. Cut into thin slices on the slant.
3. Pass the slices of liver through seasoned flour.
4. Shake off the excess flour.
5. Quickly fry on both sides in hot fat.
6. Remove the rind and bone from the bacon and grill on both sides.
7. Serve the liver and bacon with a cordon of jus-lié, and a sauceboat of jus-lié separately.

Escalope of veal *4 portions*

400 g	1 lb	nut or cushion of veal
25 g	1 oz	seasoned flour
		1 egg
50 g	2 oz	breadcrumbs
		for frying
50 g	2 oz	oil
50 g	2 oz	butter
50 g	2 oz	nut-brown butter

1. Trim and remove all sinew from the veal.
2. Cut into four even slices and bat out thinly, using a little water.
3. Flour, egg and crumb.
4. Mark with a palette knife.
5. Place the escalopes into shallow, hot oil or fat and cook quickly for a few minutes on each side.
6. Place on the plate or serving dish.
7. Pour over 50 g (2 oz) (nut-brown) butter.
8. Finish with a cordon of jus-lié (page 16), and serve.

Escalope of veal with spaghetti and tomato sauce

Known as *Napolitaine*

Cook and serve the escalopes as for the recipe above and garnish with spaghetti napolitaine (see page 22), allowing 10 g (½ oz) spaghetti per portion.

Sauté of chicken (basic recipe)

4 portions

1¼ – 1½ kg	2½ – 3 lb	1 chicken
250 ml	½ pt	jus-lié or demi-glace
		salt, pepper
50 g	2 oz	butter or oil
		chopped parsley

To prepare the chicken for sauté

1. Remove the feet at the first joint.
2. Remove the legs from the carcass.
3. Cut each leg in 2 at the joint.
4. Remove the wishbone. Remove winglets and trim.
5. Remove the wings carefully, leaving two equal portions on the breast.

6. Remove the breast and cut in two.
7. Place the oil or butter in a sauté pan on a fairly hot stove.
8. Lightly season the pieces of chicken and place in the pan in the following order: drumsticks, thighs, wings, winglets and breast.
9. Cook to a golden brown on both sides.
10. Cook with a lid and cook on the stove or in the oven until tender.
11. Dress neatly in the serving dish.
12. Drain off all fat from the sauté pan.
13. Return to the heat and add the jus-lié or demi-glace.
14. Simmer for 3 to 4 minutes.
15. Correct the seasoning and skim.
16. Pass through a fine strainer on to the chicken.
17. Sprinkle with chopped parsley and serve.

Note. The chicken giblets and carcass should always be used in the making of the jus-lié or demi-glace.

Cuts of chicken for sauté and pies
The pieces of cut chicken are named as follows:

1 Wing
2 Breast
Leg: **3** Thigh, **4** Drumstick
5 Winglet
6 Carcass

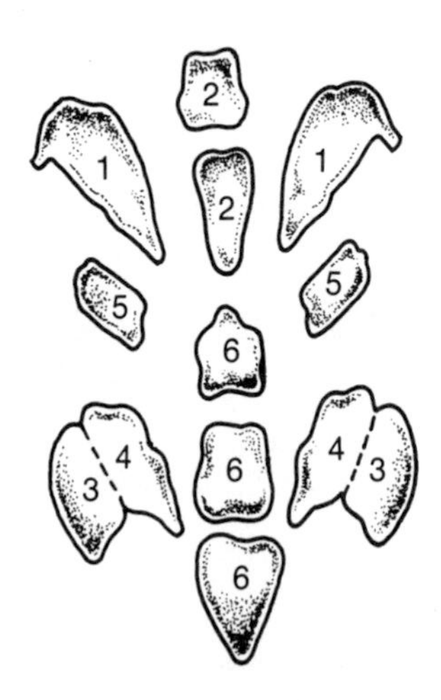

Chicken sauté chasseur *4 portions*

50 g	2 oz	butter or oil
$1\frac{1}{4} - 1\frac{1}{2}$ kg	$2\frac{1}{2} - 3$ lb	1 chicken cut for sauté
10 g	$\frac{1}{2}$ oz	chopped shallot
100 g	4 oz	button mushrooms
		3 tbsp dry white wine
250 ml	$\frac{1}{2}$ pt	jus-lié or demi-glace
200 g	8 oz	tomatoes
		chopped parsley and tarragon

1. Place the butter or oil in a sauté pan on a fairly hot stove.
2. Season the pieces of chicken and place in the pan in the following order: drumsticks, thighs, wings, winglets and breast.
3. Cook to a golden brown on both sides.
4. Cover with a lid and cook on the stove or in the oven until tender. Dress neatly in serving dish.
5. Add the shallots to the sauté pan, cover with a lid, cook on a gentle heat for 1 to 2 minutes without colour.
6. Add washed, sliced mushrooms, cover with a lid, cook gently 3 – 4 minutes without colour.
7. Drain off fat.
8. Add white wine and reduce by half.
9. Add the demi-glace or jus-lié.
10. Add the tomato concassée.
11. Simmer for 5 minutes.
12. Correct the seasoning.
13. Pour over the chicken.
14. Sprinkle with chopped parsley and tarragon, and serve.

Brussels sprouts fried in butter

1. Cook and drain the brussels sprouts.
2. Melt 25 – 50 g (1 – 2 oz) butter in a frying pan.
3. When foaming, add the sprouts and toss lightly, browning slightly, and serve. 400 g (1 lb) of cooked sprouts yields 4 portions.

Cauliflower fried in butter

1. Cut the cooked cauliflower into 4 portions.
2. Lightly colour on all sides in 25 – 50 g (1 – 2 oz) butter.

Fried onions $\frac{1}{2}$ kg (1 lb) will yield approximately 2 portions

1. Peel and wash the onions, cut in halves, slice finely.
2. Cook slowly in 25 – 50 g (1 – 2 oz) fat or oil in a frying pan, turning frequently until tender and nicely browned. Season with salt and pepper, and serve.

Sauté potatoes

1 lb cooked potatoes *3 – 4 portions*

1. Select medium even-sized potatoes.
2. Scrub well.
3. Plain boil or cook in the steamer.
4. Cool slightly and peel.
5. Cut into approximately 3 mm ($\frac{1}{8}$ in.) slices.
6. Toss in hot shallow fat in a frying pan until lightly coloured; season with salt.
7. Serve lightly sprinkled with chopped parsley.

Sauté potatoes with onions

Known as *lyonnaise*

1. Allow $\frac{1}{4}$ kg (8 oz) onion to $\frac{1}{2}$ kg (1 lb) potatoes.
2. Cook the onions as for fried onion.
3. Prepare sauté potatoes as for previous recipe.
4. Combine the two and toss together.
5. Serve as for sauté potatoes.

Pancakes with lemon *4 portions*

100 g	4 oz	flour (white or wholemeal)
		pinch of salt
		1 egg
$\frac{1}{4}$ litre	$\frac{1}{2}$ pt	milk
10 g	$\frac{1}{2}$ oz	melted butter or margarine
50 g	2 oz	lard or oil
50 g	2 oz	sugar

1. Sieve the flour and salt into a bowl, make a well in the centre.
2. Add the egg and milk, gradually incorporating the flour from the sides. Whisk to a smooth batter.
3. Mix in the melted butter, allow to stand.
4. Heat the pancake pan, clean thoroughly.
5. Add 5 g ($\frac{1}{4}$ oz) lard or oil and heat until smoking.
6. Add enough mixture just to cover the bottom of the pan thinly.
7. Cook for a few seconds until brown.
8. Turn and cook on the other side.
9. Turn on to a plate.
10. Sprinkle with sugar.
11. Fold in half, then again.

When making a batch of pancakes it is best to keep them all flat one on top of the other on a plate. Sprinkle sugar between each. Fold them all when ready for service, sprinkle again with sugar and on the serving dish or plate. Garnish with quarters of lemon free from pips. Serve very hot, two per portion.

Pancakes with jam

Mixture as for recipe above.

50 g	2 oz	warm jam
25 g	1 oz	sugar

1. Prepare pancakes as above.
2. Spread each with warm jam.
3. Roll like a swiss roll; trim the ends.
4. Dredge with castor sugar and serve.

Pancakes with apple

Cook as for recipe above and spread with a purée of apple, then roll up, sprinkle with castor sugar.

Recipes for deep-frying

Scotch eggs

		4 hard-boiled eggs
300 g	12 oz	sausage meat
25 g	1 oz	flour (white or wholemeal)
		1 beaten egg
50 g	2 oz	breadcrumbs

1. Completely cover each egg with sausage meat.
2. Pass through flour, egg and breadcrumbs.
3. Shake off surplus crumbs.
4. Deep fry to a golden brown in moderately hot fat.
5. Drain well, cut in halves and serve hot or cold.
6. *Hot*: serve, garnish with fried or sprig parsley and a suitable sauce, e.g. tomato (see page 16). *Cold*: garnish with salad in season and a sauceboat of salad dressing (see page 100).

Frying batters *approx. 6 – 8 portions*

Method 1

200 g	8 oz	flour (white or wholemeal)
		salt
10 g	$\frac{3}{8}$ oz	yeast
250 ml	$\frac{1}{2}$ pt	water or milk

1. Sift the flour and salt into a basin.
2. Dissolve the yeast in a little of the water.
3. Make a well in the flour.
4. Add the yeast and the liquid.
5. Gradually incorporate the flour and beat to a smooth mixture.
6. Allow to rest for at least 1 hour before using.

Method 2

200 g	8 oz	flour (white or wholemeal)
		salt
		1 egg
250 ml	$\frac{1}{2}$ pt	water or milk
		2 tbsp oil

1. Sift the flour and salt into a basin.
2. Make a well.
3. Add the egg and the liquid.
4. Gradually incorporate the flour; beat to a smooth mixture.
5. Mix in the oil.
6. Allow to rest before using.

Method 3

200 g	8 oz	flour (white or wholemeal)
		salt
		1 level tsp baking-powder
250 ml	$\frac{1}{2}$ pt	water or milk

1. Sift the flour, salt and baking-powder into a basin.
2. Make a well in the centre.
3. Incorporate the liquid to a smooth paste.

Fried fish

Allow 100 – 150 g (4 – 6 oz) per portion off the bone.

1. Wash and drain the fish portions well.
2. Flour and batter, or flour, egg and crumb.
3. Deep fry in hot fat, 185°C.
4. Drain well.
5. Serve with quarters of lemon and tartar sauce.

Tartar sauce $\frac{1}{4}$ litre ($\frac{1}{4}$ pint)

8 portions approx.

250 ml	$\frac{1}{2}$ pint	mayonnaise
25 g	1 oz	chopped capers
50 g	2 oz	chopped gherkins
		chopped parsley

Combine all the ingredients. Tartar sauce is usually served with deep fried fish.

Flour, egg and crumbing

Fish cakes *4 portions*

200 g	8 oz	cooked fish (free from skin and bones)
200 g	8 oz	mashed potatoes
		1 egg
		salt, pepper
25 g	1 oz	flour (white or wholemeal)
		1 egg
50 g	1 oz	breadcrumbs

1. Combine the fish, potatoes and egg, and season.
2. Divide into 4 or 8 pieces.
3. Mould into balls.
4. Pass through flour, egg and breadcrumbs.
5. Flatten slightly; neaten with a palette knife.
6. Deep fry in hot fat (185 °C) for 2 to 3 minutes.
7. Serve garnished with fried or picked parsley.
8. Accompany with a suitable sauce, e.g. tomato sauce.

French fried onions

1. Peel and wash the onions.
2. Cut into 2 mm ($\frac{1}{12}$ in.) thick slices, against the grain.
3. Separate into rings.
4. Pass through milk and seasoned flour.
5. Shake off the surplus.
6. Deep fry in hot fat (185 °C).
7. Drain well, season lightly and serve.

Croquette potatoes

1. Duchess mixture, moulded into cylinder shapes 5 × 2 cm (2 × 1 in.).
2. Pass through flour, eggwash and breadcrumbs.
3. Reshape with a palette knife and deep fry in hot, deep fat (185 °C) in a frying basket.
4. When a golden colour drain well and serve.

Crisps

1. Wash, peel and rewash the potatoes.
2. Cut into thin slices on a mandolin.
3. Wash well and dry in a cloth.
4. Cook in hot, deep fat (185 °C) until golden brown and crisp.
5. Drain well and lightly season with salt.

These potatoes are not usually served as a potato by themselves, but as a garnish and are for serving in bars and at cocktail parties.

Fried or chipped potatoes

1. Prepare, wash and trim potatoes.
2. Cut into slices 1 cm ($\frac{1}{2}$ in.) thick and 5 cm (2 in.) long.
3. Cut the slices into strips 5 × 1 × 1 cm (2 × $\frac{1}{2}$ × $\frac{1}{2}$ in.).
4. Wash well and dry in a cloth.
5. Cook in a frying basket without colour in moderately hot fat (165 °C).
6. Drain and place on kitchen paper on trays till required.
7. When required place in a frying basket and cook in hot fat (185 °C) till crisp and golden.
8. Drain well, lightly season with salt and serve.

Apple fritters *4 portions*

400 g	1 lb	cooking apples
150 g		frying batter (6 oz flour) (pages 73 – 74)
125 ml	$\frac{1}{4}$ pt	apricot jam sauce (page 16)

1. Peel and core the apples and cut into $\frac{1}{2}$ cm thick ($\frac{1}{4}$ in.) rings.
2. Pass through flour and shake off the surplus.
3. Dip into frying batter.
4. Lift out with the fingers and place in fairly hot, deep fat (185 °C).
5. Cook approximately 5 minutes on each side.
6. Drain well, dust with icing sugar and glaze under the salamander.
7. Serve with hot apricot sauce.

Banana fritters *4 portions*

		4 bananas
150 g		frying batter (6 oz flour)
125 ml	$\frac{1}{4}$ pt	apricot sauce

Peel and cut the bananas in half lengthwise, then in half across. Cook and serve as for apple fritters.

Doughnuts

1. Take the basic bun dough (see page 91) and divide into 8 pieces.
2. Mould into balls.
3. Press a floured thumb into each.
4. Place a little jam in each hole.
5. Mould carefully to seal the hole.
6. Cover, and allow to prove on a well floured tray.
7. Deep fry in moderately hot fat (175 °C), approximately 12 – 15 minutes.
8. Lift out of the fat, drain and roll in a tray containing castor sugar mixed with a little cinnamon.

Questions – Frying

1. Briefly explain why extra care is necessary when deep frying.

2. What may happen after fat starts to smoke?

3. When shallow frying fish fillets which side is cooked first? Explain why.

4. Which of the following are used as a coating when deep frying fish? Give reasons for your choice.

   a) batter b) egg and crumbs c) oil and crumbs d) milk and flour.

5. Complete 1 to 6 to produce 1 down.
   1. Essential on the road and when deep frying.
   2. Fritter fruit.
   3. Used for frying (French).
   4. Not shallow.
   5. Also used for shopping.
   6. Colour of fried food.

1 Down

1					S	A	F	E	T	Y
2				A	P	P	L	E		
3			F	R	I	T	U	R	E	
4					D	E	E	P		
5	B	A	S	K	E	T				
6				B	R	O	W	N		

6. Which is the odd one out and why?

   Fried potatoes Apple fritters
   Fish cakes Pancakes ✓

7. Name these items:

a) b)

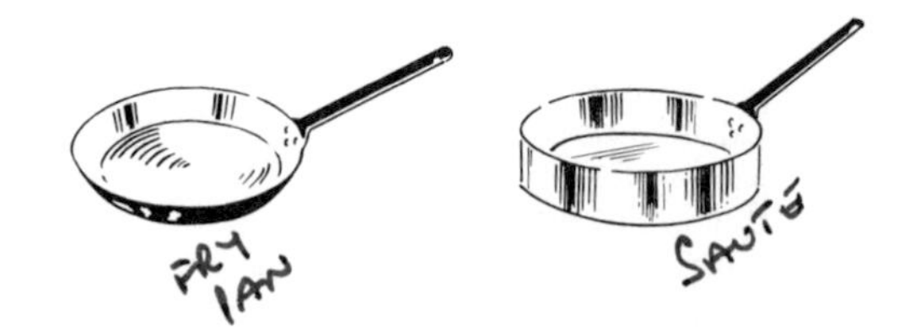

c) d)

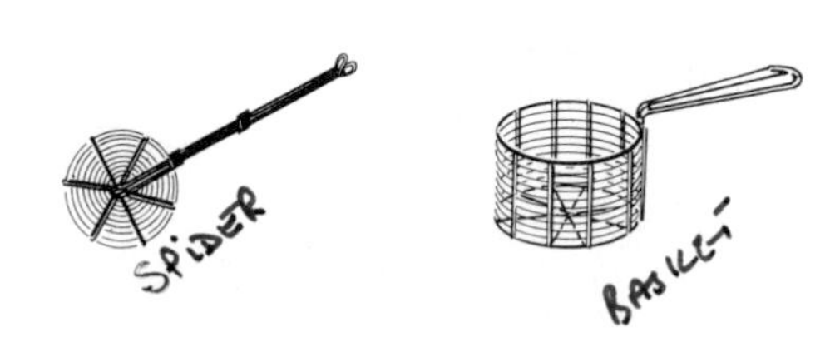

8. State the 2 main differences between deep and shallow frying.

9. State 6 important points of safety to apply when deep frying.

10. Explain the term *sauté* and give 2 examples of dishes of this kind.

Answers can be found on page 154.

12
Baking

General objectives To have a knowledge and understanding of baking.
Specific objectives To define baking as a principle of cookery; to explain the reasons for baking; to demonstrate the method of cooking food in ovens; to list foods cooked by baking; to state the effects of baking; to describe the advantages of baking; to explain specific baking terms – temperature control, recipe ratio and balance, pre-heated oven, oven position, bain-marie; to select equipment and state its care and use; to use recipes associated with baking; to explain and apply efficiency and safety procedures.

Definition

Baking is the principle of cooking in a dry heat inside an oven.

Principles of baking

Baking is mainly applied to bread, cakes and pastry dishes and foods of a sweet and savoury nature. Potatoes and fish may also be baked. The dry heat is modified by the steam produced from the water content of the food being baked; otherwise the food would burn.

Bakers and pastry cooks use this method of cooking for most of their work and a good pastry cook is one who fully understands the specialist ovens, the equipment, the ingredients and the importance of temperature control.

Accuracy in following recipes, and careful attention to weighing and measuring in baking practice, is vital.

Hygiene is essential, as with all cookery, but particularly with baking as certain ingredients, e.g. milk, cream, custard, eggs, which are used in many baked pastry items have potential food poisoning effects which could be hazardous to health.

Equipment

For all ovens (kitchen, baker's or convection, etc.) to be efficient they must be regularly serviced and cleaned. To clean ovens:

1. Clean when warm.
2. Clean oven shelves and all sides by using hot detergent water and a mild abrasive, pad or powder, if necessary.
3. If oven does not become clean by the above method, carefully use special oven cleaners, after which thoroughly rinse with clean hot water and dry.
4. Baking sheets should be cleaned by scraping, dry-wiped and lightly greased. They are only washed when absolutely necessary to lessen the possibility of food sticking to the tray.
5. To clean non-stick surfaces use clean kitchen cloth or paper. Do not use metal scrapers or abrasives.

Flavours and *smells* – fish, meat, poultry, onions and herbs are used in many baked goods, e.g. pies, pastries, flans, and care must be taken that no flavour or smell of these is allowed to contact any sweet dish.

Oven temperature control – this is of crucial importance in baking, as is timing. The experienced pastry cook or baker is often able to smell, by the aroma that comes from the oven, when baked food is almost cooked.

Colour – the correct degree of colour of baked items is essential, so that the food looks appetising. How a pie, tart, pastry or any baked food looks is vital because the customer should be attracted to it by its appearance.

Pre-heating the oven – that is, ensuring that the oven is switched on in sufficient time so that the oven temperature is raised to the degree of heat stated in the recipe before the item to be baked is placed into the oven. This is necessary to enable the food to start cooking at once.

Cold oven – goods to be baked must never be placed in a cold oven, as the fat will melt and the goods lose shape and be spoiled.

Oven positioning – baked foods should not only be placed in the oven when the temperature or regulo number is as stated in the recipe but also placed in either the top, middle or bottom, according to the instructions. With experience it is possible to learn to know and understand ovens, and knowledge gained can be used for the timing and suitable positioning of items in the oven.

Even coloration – to obtain even, all-round colour it is often necessary to turn the dish or tray in the oven. Ovens with in-built fans, known as convection ovens, give an overall, even heat because the effect of the fan is to spread the heat evenly throughout the oven. Positioning and turning trays are, therefore, not necessary.

Bain-marie – certain dishes are placed in a tray containing 2 – 5 cm (1 – 2 in.) water and cooked in the oven, e.g. cream caramel, bread and butter pudding. This tray of water, which should not be allowed to boil, is known as a bain-marie and its purpose is to prevent direct heat, which would cause the egg custard mixture to cook too quickly on the outside before the centre of the custard was set. This would spoil the finished dish because the outside would be overcooked.

Baked potatoes – it should be noted that baked potatoes can be cooked in foil or without foil. Without foil the potato skin retains the steam and the appearance and texture of the skin will be different – it will look baked and have a brown, crispy skin.

Baking

Egg in cocotte (basic recipe)

		4 eggs
25 g	1 oz	butter
		salt, pepper

1. Butter and lightly season 4 egg cocottes.
2. Break an egg carefully into each.
3. Place the cocottes in a sauté pan containing 1 cm ($\frac{1}{2}$ in.) water.
4. Cover with a tight-fitting lid, place on a fierce heat or in oven so that the water boils rapidly.
5. Cook for 2 to 3 minutes until the eggs are lightly set, and serve.

Egg in cocotte with cream

1. Proceed as for the basic recipe.
2. Half a minute before the cooking is completed add 1 dessertspoon of cream to each egg and complete the cooking.

Eggs in the dish (sur le plat)

1. Butter and season an egg dish.
2. Add 1 – 2 eggs.
3. Lightly season with salt and pepper.
4. Allow to cook gently on the side of the stove and finish under the salamander or in a hot oven. The yolk should be soft.
5. Serve the egg on a dish paper on a silver dish.

Eggs in a dish with bacon

1. Allow 1 – 2 rashers of bacon per portion.
2. Grill or fry the bacon.
3. Cut each rasher in half.
4. Place in the bottom of a buttered, seasoned egg dish.
5. Break the eggs on top of the bacon.
6. Cook and serve as for the previous recipe.

Fish pie *4 portions*

250 ml	$\frac{1}{2}$ pt	béchamel (thin) (page 13)
200 ml	8 oz	fish (cooked), free from skin and bone
50 g	2 oz	cooked, diced mushrooms
		1 chopped, hard-boiled egg
		chopped parsley
		salt, pepper
200 g	8 oz	mashed or duchess potato

1. Bring the béchamel to the boil.
2. Add the fish, mushrooms, egg and parsley. Correct the seasoning.
3. Place in a buttered pie-dish.
4. Place or pipe the potato on top.
5. Brush with eggwash or milk.
6. Brown in a hot oven or under the salamander and serve.

Shepherd's pie or cottage pie *4 portions*

100 g	4 oz	chopped onion
35 g	$1\frac{1}{2}$ oz	fat or oil
400 g	1 lb	cooked lamb or mutton
125 – 250 ml	$\frac{1}{4}$ – $\frac{1}{2}$ pt	jus-lié or demi-glace
400 g	1 lb	mashed potato
25 – 50 g	1 – 2 oz	butter or margarine
		milk
		salt, pepper

1. Cook the onion in the fat or oil without colouring.
2. Add the minced cooked meat, from which all fat and gristle has been removed.
3. Season and add sufficient sauce to bind.
4. Bring to the boil, simmer 10 – 15 minutes.
5. Place in a pie or earthenware dish.
6. Prepare the mashed potatoes and arrange neatly on top.
7. Brush with milk or eggwash.
8. Colour lightly under the salamander or in a hot oven, and serve accompanied with a sauceboat of jus-lié.

Note. This dish may be prepared with cooked beef. When using reheated meats care must be taken to heat thoroughly.

Cornish pasties *4 portions*

200 g	$\frac{1}{2}$ lb	short paste (page 82)	
100 g	4 oz	finely diced potato (raw)	filling
100 g	4 oz	raw meat (cut small)	filling
50 g	2 oz	chopped onion	filling
		salt, pepper	

1. Roll out the short paste 3 mm ($\frac{1}{8}$ in.) thick and cut into rounds 12 cm (5 in.) diameter.
2. Mix the filling together, moisten with a little water and place in the rounds in piles. Eggwash the edges of the pastry.
3. Fold in half and seal, flute the edge and brush with eggwash.
4. Cook in a moderate oven (180 – 200°C, Reg. 4), $\frac{3}{4}$ – 1 hour.
5. Serve with a suitable sauce separately, e.g. demi-glace.

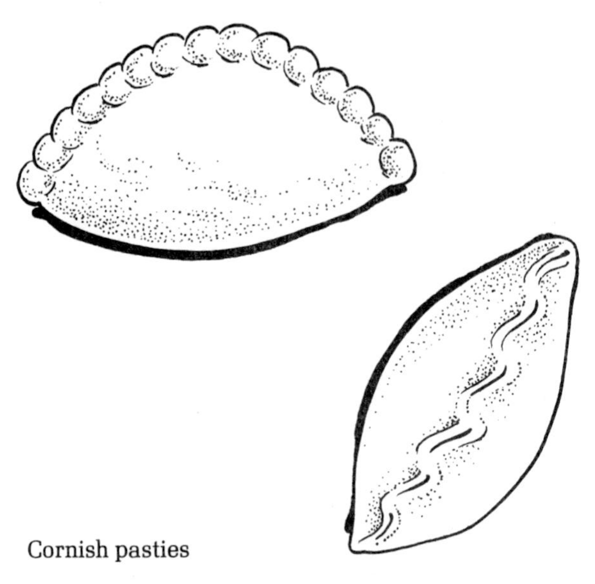

Cornish pasties

Lamb chop, toad in the hole *4 portions*

Other foods used in this way include cutlets, steak and sausages.

		4 lamb chops
50 g	2 oz	dripping

Yorkshire pudding mixture using 100g (4 oz) flour (page 54)

1. Neatly arrange the seasoned chops in a suitable-size roasting tray or shallow earthenware dish with the dripping.
2. Place in a hot oven (200 – 230°C, Reg. 6 – 8) for approximately 5 minutes or until the meat has set.
3. Pour the Yorkshire pudding mixture over the meat.
4. Return to the hot oven until the meat is cooked and the Yorkshire pudding is golden brown, approximately 30 minutes.
5. When cooked in an earthenware dish, clean the edges and serve.
6. In both cases serve with a sauceboat of jus-lié (see page 16) or demi-glace (see page 15).

Note. Any thick slices of cooked meat such as corned beef, luncheon meat, etc., may be prepared toad in the hole. Place the dripping in the tray, heat and add the meat and pour over the mixture, and cook in a hot oven for approximately 20 minutes.

Steak pie *4 portions*

400 g	1 lb	prepared stewing beef
25 g	1 oz	flour
		salt, pepper
25 – 50 g	1 – 2 oz	fat
125 ml	$\frac{1}{4}$ pint	water or brown stock
50 – 100 g	2 – 4 oz	chopped onion (optional)
		few drops Worcester sauce
		1 tsp chopped parsley
100 g	4 oz	puff or short paste

1. Cut the meat and mix with 25 g flour, salt and pepper.
2. Quickly fry off the meat in 25 – 50 g fat or oil until nicely browned.
3. Drain off any excess fat.
4. Place the meat in a pan.
5. Gradually add brown stock and stir to the boil (a little extra stock will be required).
6. Add onion (if required), Worcester sauce and parsley.
7. Cover pan with a lid and allow to simmer gently until tender, $1\frac{1}{2}$ – 2 hrs.
8. Pour into pie-dish, allow to cool and cover with pastry.
9. Eggwash, decorate, rest if possible and bake the pie in a hot oven (220°C, Reg. 7) for 30 – 45 minutes or until pastry is cooked and golden brown.

Steak and kidney pie

As for steak pie, with the addition of 50 – 100 g (2 – 4 oz) ox kidney or 1 or 2 sheep's kidneys, with skin and gristle removed and cut into neat pieces.

Chicken pie *4 portions*

$1\frac{1}{4}$ – $1\frac{1}{2}$ kg	$2\frac{1}{2}$ – 3 lb	1 chicken
		salt, pepper
100 g	$\frac{1}{4}$ lb	streaky bacon
100 g	4 oz	button mushrooms
		1 chopped onion
		pinch of chopped parsley
		1 hard-boiled egg (chopped)
$\frac{1}{4}$ litre	$\frac{1}{2}$ pt	chicken stock (approx)
200 g	8 oz	puff paste (page 86)

1. Cut the chicken as for sauté (see page 72) or bone-out completely and cut into pieces 4 × 1 cm ($1\frac{1}{2}$ × $\frac{1}{2}$ in.).
2. Season lightly with salt and pepper.
3. Wrap each piece in thin streaky bacon.
4. Place in a pie-dish.
5. Add the washed, sliced mushrooms.
6. Add the remainder of the ingredients.
7. Add sufficient cold stock to barely cover the chicken.
8. Cover with pastry, allow to rest.

9. Eggwash and place in a hot oven (220°C, Reg. 7) for 10 to 15 minutes.
10. Reduce heat to 190°C, Reg. 5 for 15 minutes.
11. Reduce heat to 160°C, Reg. 3 for 15 minutes.
12. Reduce heat to 150°C, Reg. 2 to complete cooking.

Baked jacket potatoes

1. Select good-sized potatoes and allow 1 per portion.
2. Scrub well, make a 2 mm ($\frac{1}{12}$ in.) deep incision round the potato.
3. Place on a bed of salt on a tray in a hot oven (230°C, Reg. 8) for approximately 1 hour. Turn the potatoes over after 30 minutes.
4. Test by holding the potato in a cloth and squeezing gently; if cooked it should feel soft.

Baked jacket potatoes with cheese

		4 large potatoes
75 g	3 oz	butter
25 g	1 oz	grated cheese

1. Bake the potatoes as for previous recipe.
2. Cut the potatoes in halves lengthwise.
3. Remove the potato from the skin, using a spoon.
4. Place the potato in a basin.
5. Add 50 g (2 oz) butter, season lightly with salt and pepper.
6. Mix lightly with a fork.
7. Refill the potato skin with the mixture.
8. Place on a baking sheet.
9. Sprinkle with grated cheese and the remaining 25 g (1 oz) melted butter.
10. Place in the oven (200°C, Reg. 6) until golden brown and serve.

Baked apple *4 portions*

		4 medium-sized cooking apples
50 g	2 oz	sugar or honey
	1 oz	4 cloves
25 g	1 oz	butter (optional)
60 ml	$\frac{1}{8}$ pt	water

1. Core the apples and make an incision 2 mm ($\frac{1}{12}$ in.) deep round the centre of each. Wash well.
2. Place in a roasting tin or ovenproof dish.
3. Fill the centre with sugar and add a clove.
4. Place 5 g ($\frac{1}{4}$ oz) butter on each.
5. Add the water.
6. Bake in a moderate oven (200°C, Reg. 6), 15 – 20 minutes approx.
7. Turn the apples over carefully.
8. Return to the oven until cooked, approximately 40 minutes in all.
9. Serve with a little of the cooking liquor, and custard separately.

Stuffed baked apple

Proceed as for baked apples, but fill the centre with washed sultanas.

Baked rice pudding *4 portions*

50 g	2 oz	rice (short grain)
50 g	2 oz	sugar
$\frac{1}{2}$ litre	1 pt	milk
10 g	$\frac{1}{2}$ oz	butter (optional)
		2 – 3 drops vanilla essence
		grated nutmeg

1. Wash the rice, place in a pie-dish.
2. Add the sugar and milk; mix well.
3. Add the butter, essence and nutmeg.
4. Place on a baking sheet, clean the rim of the pie-dish.
5. Bake in a moderate oven (180 – 200°C, Reg. 4 – 6) until the milk starts simmering.
6. Reduce the heat and allow the pudding to cook slowly, allowing approx $1\frac{1}{2}$ – 2 hours in all.

Baked egg custard *4 portions*

		3 eggs, size 3
50 g	2 oz	sugar
		2 – 3 drops vanilla essence
$\frac{1}{2}$ litre	1 pt	milk
		grated nutmeg

1. Whisk the eggs, sugar and essence in a bowl.
2. Pour on the warmed milk, whisking continuously.
3. Pass through a fine strainer into a pie-dish.
4. Add a little grated nutmeg. Wipe the edge of the pie-dish clean.
5. Stand in a roasting tray half-full of water and cook slowly at 160°C, Reg. 3 for approximately 45 minutes to 1 hour.
6. Clean the edges of the pie-dish and serve.

Bread and butter pudding *4 portions*

25 g	1 oz	sultanas
		2 thinly cut slices of well-buttered bread
		3 eggs, size 3
50 g	2 oz	sugar
		2 – 3 drops vanilla essence
$\frac{1}{2}$ litre	1 pt	milk

1. Wash the sultanas and place in a pie-dish.
2. Remove the crusts from the bread and cut each slice into four triangles; neatly arrange overlapping in the pie-dish.
3. Prepare an egg custard as in the previous recipe.
4. Strain on to the bread; dust lightly with castor sugar.
5. Cook and serve, as in the previous recipe.

Cream caramel *6 portions*

Caramel

125 ml	$\frac{1}{4}$ pt	water
100 g	4 oz	sugar
$\frac{1}{2}$ litre	1 pt	milk
		4 eggs, size 3
50 g	2 oz	sugar
		3 – 4 drops vanilla essence

1. Prepare the caramel by placing three-quarters of the water in a thick-bottomed pan, adding the sugar and allowing to boil gently, without shaking or stirring the contents of the pan.
2. When the sugar has cooked to a golden brown caramel colour, add the remaining quarter of the water, reboil until the sugar and water mix, then pour into the bottom of 6 dariole moulds.
3. Prepare the cream by warming the milk and whisking on to the beaten eggs, sugar and essence.
4. Strain and pour into the prepared moulds.
5. Place in a roasting tin half-full of water.
6. Cook at 160°C, Reg. 3 for approximately 30 minutes.
7. When thoroughly cold, loosen the edges of the cream caramels with the fingers, shake firmly to loosen and turn out on to the serving dish.
8. Pour any caramel remaining in the mould around the creams.

Pastes

Short pastry

200 g	8 oz	flour (white or wholemeal or half of each)
		pinch salt
50 g	2 oz	butter or margarine
50 g	2 oz	lard or oil
		2 – 3 tbsp water (approx.)

1. Sieve the flour and salt.
2. Rub in the fat to a sandy texture.
3. Make a well in the centre.
4. Add sufficient water to make a fairly firm paste.
5. Handle as little and as lightly as possible.

The amount of water used varies according to: the type of flour, e.g. a very fine, soft flour is more absorbent; the degree of heat, e.g.

Rubbing flour into fat

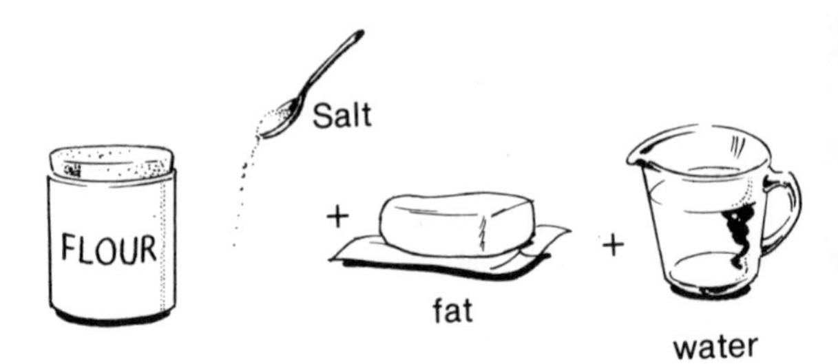

prolonged contact with hot hands, and weather conditions.

Uses: fruit pies, Cornish pasties, etc.

Possible reasons for faults in short pastry

1. *Hard*	too much water too little fat fat rubbed in insufficiently too much handling and rolling overbaking
2. *Soft – crumbly*	too little water too much fat
3. *Blistered*	too little water water added unevenly fat not rubbed in evenly
4. *Soggy*	too much water

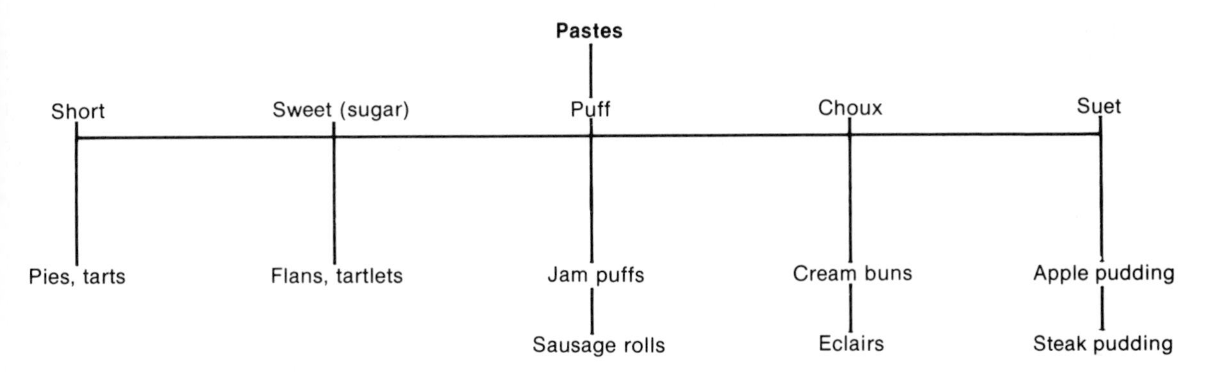

	too cool an oven
	baked for an insufficient time
5. *Shrunken*	too much handling and rolling
	pastry stretched while handling

Fruit pies

Apple, blackberry, blackberry and apple, cherry, rhubarb, gooseberry, damson, damson and apple, raspberry and redcurrant, etc.

Preparation of fruit for pies

Apples	peel, quarter, core, cut in slices
Cherries	remove the stalks, wash
Blackberries	remove the stalks, wash
Gooseberries	remove the stalks and tails, wash
Damsons	pick and wash
Raspberries	remove stalks and wash
Redcurrants	remove stalks and wash
Rhubarb	remove leaves and root, remove tough strings, cut into 2 cm (1 in.) pieces, wash

Fruit pie *4 portions*

400 g	1 lb	fruit
100 g	4 oz	sugar
		2 tbsp water

short paste, using 150 g (6 oz) flour

1. Prepare the fruit; wash and place half in a $\frac{1}{2}$ litre (1 pt) pie-dish.
2. Add the sugar and water and the remainder of the fruit.
3. Place a clove in the apple pie.
4. Roll out the pastry $\frac{1}{2}$ cm ($\frac{1}{4}$ in.) thick to the shape of the pie-dish; allow to relax. Edge the rim of the pie-dish with a strip of the pastry. Damp the rim first.
5. Damp the edge of pastry.
6. Carefully lay the pastry on the dish without stretching it, and firmly seal the rim of the pie.
7. Cut off any surplus pastry, and notch the edge.
8. Brush with milk and sprinkle with castor sugar.
9. Place the pie on a baking sheet and bake in a hot oven (220°C, Reg. 7) for approximately 10 minutes.
10. Reduce the heat or transfer to a cooler part of the oven and continue cooking for a further 30 minutes (approx). If the pastry colours too quickly, cover with a sheet of greaseproof paper or foil.
11. To serve, clean the pie-dish, and serve $\frac{1}{4}$ litre ($\frac{1}{2}$ pt) custard.

Jam tart *4 portions*

short or sugar paste, using 100 g (4 oz) flour
2 tbsp jam

1. Prepare short paste; mould into a ball.
2. Roll out into a 3 mm thick ($\frac{1}{8}$ in.) round.
3. Place carefully on a greased ovenproof plate.
4. Cut off any surplus pastry.
5. Neaten the edges.
6. Prick the bottom several times with a fork.
7. Spread on the jam to within 1 cm ($\frac{1}{2}$ in.) of the edge.
8. Roll out any surplus pastry, cut into $\frac{1}{2}$ cm ($\frac{1}{4}$ in.) strips and decorate the top.
9. Place on a baking sheet and bake in a hot oven (230°C, Reg. 8) for approximately 20 minutes.

A jam tart may also be made in a shallow flan ring.

Baked apple dumplings *4 portions*

200 g	(8 oz flour)	short paste
100 g	(4 oz each)	4 small cooking apples
		4 cloves
50 g	2 oz	sugar (white or unrefined)

1. Roll out pastry 3 mm ($\frac{1}{8}$ in.) thick into a square.
2. Cut into 4 even squares.
3. Damp the edges.
4. Place a whole peeled, cored and washed apple in the centre of each square.
5. Pierce the apple with a clove.
6. Fill the centre with sugar.
7. Fold over the pastry to completely seal the apple, without breaking the pastry.
8. Roll out any debris of pastry and cut neat 2 cm (1 in.) fancy rounds and place one on top of each apple.
9. Egg or milk wash, and place on a lightly greased baking sheet.
10. Bake at 200°C, Reg. 6 for approximately 30 minutes.
11. Serve with custard.

Sugar or sweet pastry

		1 egg, size 3
50 g	2 oz	sugar
125 g	5 oz	margarine or butter
200 g	8 oz	flour (soft)
		pinch salt

Method 1
1. Taking care not to over soften, cream the egg and sugar.
2. Add the margarine and mix for a few seconds.
3. Gradually incorporate the sieved flour and salt.
4. Mix lightly until smooth.
5. Allow to rest in a cool place before using.

Method 2
1. Sieve the flour and salt.
2. Lightly rub in the margarine to a sandy texture.
3. Make a well in the centre.
4. Add the sugar and beaten egg.
5. Mix the sugar and egg until dissolved.
6. Gradually incorporate the flour and margarine and lightly mix to a smooth paste.

Uses: flans, fruit tartlets.

Flans

Basic preparation: allow 25 g (1 oz) flour per portion and prepare sugar pastry (see above).

1. Grease the flan ring and baking sheet.
2. Roll out the pastry 2 cm (1 in.) larger than the flan ring.
3. Place the flan ring on the baking sheet.
4. Carefully place the pastry on the flan ring, by rolling it loosely over the rolling-pin, picking up, and unrolling it over the flan ring.
5. Press the pastry into shape without stretching it, being careful to exclude any air.
6. Allow a $\frac{1}{2}$ cm ($\frac{1}{4}$ in.) ridge of pastry on top of the flan ring.
7. Cut off the surplus paste by rolling the pin firmly across the top of the flan ring.
8. Mould the edge with thumb and forefinger.
9. Decorate a) with pastry tweezers or b) with thumb and forefingers, squeezing the pastry neatly to form a corrugated pattern.

Apple flan *4 portions*

100 g	(4 oz flour)	sugar paste
400 g	1 lb	cooking apples
50 g	2 oz	sugar
		2 tbsp apricot glaze

Flan ring and apple flan

1. Line flan ring as above. Pierce the bottom several times with a fork.
2. Keep the best-shaped apple and make the remainder into a purée (see page 85).
3. When cool place in the flan case.
4. Peel, quarter and wash the remaining apple.
5. Cut into neat, thin slices and lay carefully on the apple purée, overlapping each slice. Ensure that each slice points to the centre of the flan, then

no difficulty should be encountered in joining the pattern up neatly.

6. Sprinkle a little sugar on the apple slices and bake the flan in the oven (200 – 220°C, Reg. 6 – 7) for approximately 30 to 40 minutes.
7. When the flan is almost cooked, remove the flan ring carefully, and return the flan to the oven to complete the cooking. Mask with apricot glaze.

Apricot glaze

Prepare by boiling apricot jam with a little water and passing it through a strainer. Glaze should be used hot.

Apple meringue flan

Cook as for apple flan, without arranging sliced apples. Pipe with meringue (see page 89), using two egg whites. Return to moderately hot oven to cook and colour meringue, approximately 5 minutes.

Apple purée *4 portions*

400 g	1 lb	cooking apples
10 g	$\frac{1}{2}$ oz	butter or margarine
50 g	2 oz	sugar
		clove and/or lemon juice (optional)

Peel, core and slice the apples. Place the butter or margarine in a thick-bottomed pan, heat until melted, add the apples and sugar, cover with a lid and cook gently until soft. Drain off any excess liquid and pass through a sieve or liquidise.

Fruit tartlets

These are made from the same pastry and the same fruits as the fruit flans. The ingredients are the same. The tartlets are made by rolling out the pastry 3 mm ($\frac{1}{8}$ in.) thick and cutting out rounds with a fluted cutter and neatly placing them in greased tartlet moulds. Depending on the fruit used, they may sometimes be cooked blind, e.g. strawberries, raspberries.

Jam tartlets *4 portions*

100 g	4 oz	sugar paste
50 g	2 oz	jam

1. Prepare the tartlets as above.
2. Prick the bottom with a fork.
3. Add a little jam to each.
4. Place on a baking sheet.
5. Bake in the oven at 200 – 220°C, Reg. 6 – 7 for 20 to 30 minutes.

Soft fruit and tinned fruit flans

For soft fruit (e.g. strawberry, raspberry, banana) and tinned fruits (e.g. pear, peach, pineapple, cherry) the flan case is lined in the same way, the bottom pierced and then cooked 'blind', i.e. tear a piece of paper 2 cm (1 in.) larger in diameter than the flan ring, place it carefully in the flan case.

Fill the centre with dried peas, beans or small pieces of stale bread. Bake in the oven at 220°C, Reg. 7 for approximately 30 minutes. Remove the flan ring, paper and beans before the flan is cooked through, eggwash and return to the oven to complete the cooking. Add pastry cream and sliced or whole drained fruit. Mask with glaze. The glaze may be made with the fruit juice, thickened with arrowroot, approximately 10 g ($\frac{1}{2}$ oz) to $\frac{1}{4}$ litre ($\frac{1}{2}$ pt).

Pastry cream

		4 egg yolks
100 g	4 oz	castor sugar
50 g	2 oz	flour (white)
$\frac{1}{2}$ litre	1 pt	milk
		vanilla

1. Whisk the egg yolks and sugar in a bowl until almost white.
2. Mix in the flour.
3. Boil the milk in a thick-bottomed pan.
4. Whisk on to the yolks, sugar and flour and mix well.
5. Return to the cleaned pan; stir to the boil.
6. Add a few drops of vanilla.
7. Remove from the heat and pour into a basin.
8. Sprinkle the top with a little castor sugar to prevent a skin forming.

Mincemeat tart

200 g	using 8 oz flour	sugar paste (page 84)
200 g	8 oz	mincemeat

1. Roll out half the pastry 3 mm ($\frac{1}{8}$ in.) thick into a neat round and place on a greased plate.
2. Prick the bottom several times with a fork.
3. Add the mincemeat.
4. Moisten the edges.
5. Roll out the other half of the pastry to a neat round and place on top.
6. Seal firmly, trim off excess pastry and mould the edges.
7. Brush with milk and sprinkle with castor sugar.

8. Place on a baking sheet and bake in the oven at 200 – 220°C, Reg. 6 – 7 for approximately 40 minutes.
9. Remove from the plate carefully and serve.

Puff pastry

200 g	8 oz	white flour (strong)
		salt
200 g	8 oz	margarine or butter
125 ml	$\frac{1}{4}$ pt	ice-cold water
		few drops of lemon juice

1. Sieve the flour and salt.
2. Rub in 50 g (2 oz) butter or margarine.
3. Make a well in the centre.
4. Add the water, and lemon juice (which makes the gluten more elastic), and knead well into a smooth dough in the shape of a ball.
5. Relax the dough in a cool place for approximately 30 minutes.
6. Cut a cross half-way through the dough and pull out the corners to form a star shape.
7. Roll out the points of the star square, leaving the centre thick.
8. Knead the remaining 150 g (6 oz) of butter or margarine to the same texture as the dough. This is most important – if the fat is too soft it will melt and ooze out, if too hard it will break through the paste when being rolled.
9. Place the butter or margarine on the centre square, which is 4 times thicker than the flaps.
10. Fold over the flaps.
11. Roll out approximately 30 × 15 cm (1 × $\frac{1}{2}$ ft), cover with a cloth and rest for 5 to 10 minutes in a cool place.
12. Roll out approximately 60 × 20 cm (2 × $\frac{2}{3}$ ft), fold both ends to the centre and fold in half again to form a square. This is 1 double turn.
13. Allow it to rest in a cool place for approximately 20 minutes.
14. Half-turn the paste to the right or the left.
15. Give 1 more double turn, allow to rest for 20 minutes.
16. Give 2 more double turns, allowing to rest between each.
17. Allow to rest before using.

Making puff paste

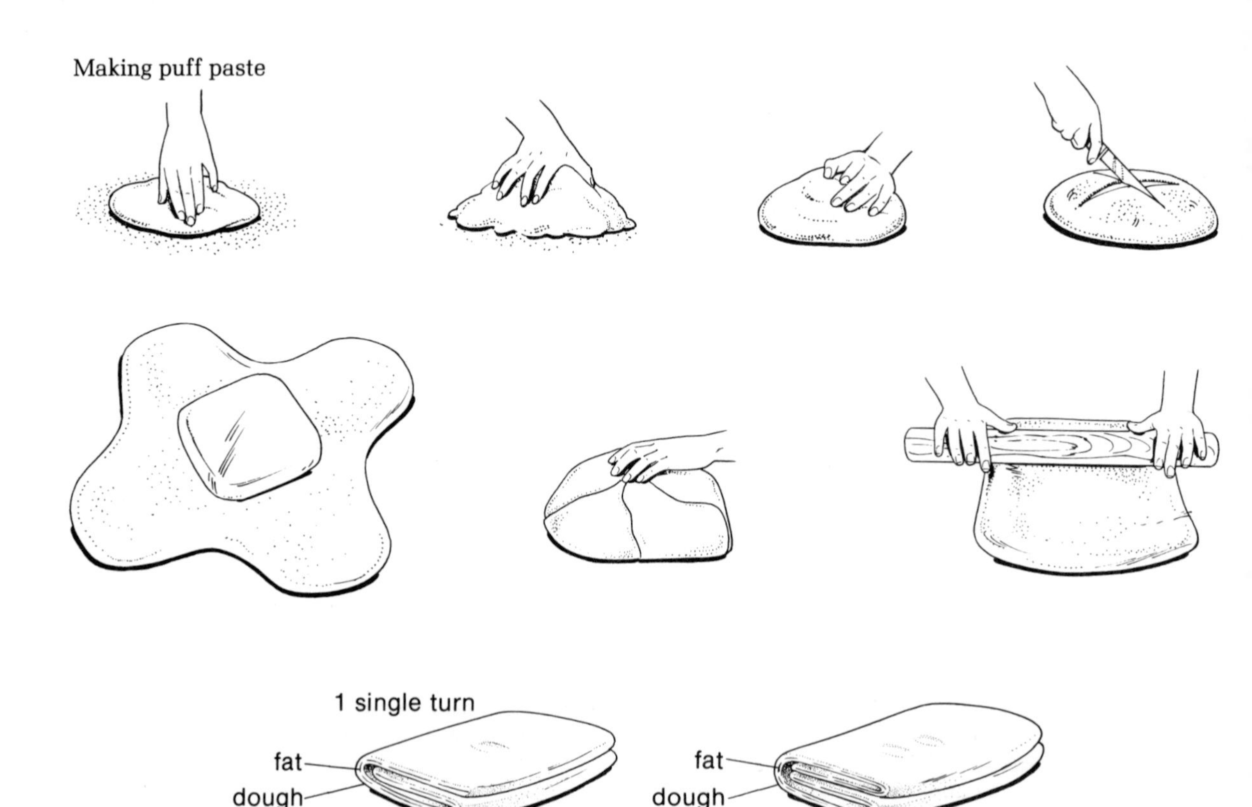

Care must be taken when rolling out the paste to keep the ends and sides square.

The lightness of puff pastry is mainly due to the air which is trapped when folding the pastry during preparation. The addition of lemon juice (acid) is to strengthen the gluten in the flour, thus helping to make a stronger dough, so that there is less likelihood of the fat oozing out. The rise is caused by the fat separating layers of paste and air during rolling. When heat is applied in the oven, steam is produced, causing the layers to rise and give the characteristic flaky formation.

Uses: meat pies, sausage rolls, jam-puffs, etc.

Possible reasons for faults in puff pastry

1. *Not flaky*	Fat too warm, thus preventing the fat and paste remaining in layers. Excessively heavy use of rolling pin.
2. *Fat oozes out*	Fat too soft. Dough too soft. Edges not sealed. Uneven folding and rolling. Oven too cool.
3. *Hard*	Too much water. Flour not brushed off between rollings. Overhandling.
4. *Shrunken*	Insufficient resting between rolling. Overstretching.
5. *Soggy*	Underbaked. Oven too hot.
6. *Uneven rise*	Uneven distribution of fat. Sides and corners not straight. Uneven folding and rolling.

Sausage rolls *yield: 12 rolls*

200 g	8 oz flour	puff pastry
400 g	1 lb	sausage meat

1. Roll out pastry 3 mm ($\frac{1}{8}$ in.) thick into a strip 10 cm (4 in.) wide.
2. Make sausage meat into a roll 2 cm (1 in.) in diameter.
3. Place on the pastry.
4. Moisten the edges of the pastry.
5. Fold over and seal.
6. Cut into 8 cm (3 in.) lengths.
7. Mark the edge with the back of a knife.
8. Brush with eggwash.
9. Place on to a greased, dampened baking sheet.
10. Bake in the oven (220 – 230°C, Reg. 7 – 8) for approximately 20 minutes.

Cream horns *yield: 16 horns*

200 g	8 oz flour	puff pastry
50 g	2 oz	jam
50 g	2 oz	castor sugar
		few drops vanilla essence
$\frac{1}{2}$ litre	1 pt	cream

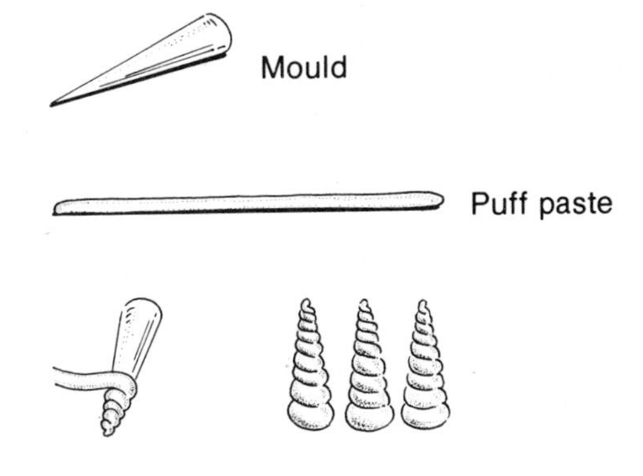

Making cream horns

1. Roll out the pastry 2 mm ($\frac{1}{2}$ in.) thick, 30 cm (1 ft) long.
2. Cut into $1\frac{1}{2}$ cm wide ($\frac{3}{4}$ in.) strips.
3. Moisten one side of the strip.
4. Wind carefully round lightly greased horn moulds, starting at the point and carefully overlapping each round slightly.
5. Brush with eggwash on one side and place on a greased baking sheet.
6. Bake in the oven at 220 – 230°C, Reg. 7 – 8 for approximately 20 minutes.
7. Sprinkle with icing sugar and return to a hot oven for a few seconds to glaze.
8. Remove carefully from the mould and allow to cool.
9. Place a little jam in the bottom of each.
10. Add the sugar and essence to the cream and whip stiffly.
11. Place in a piping bag with a star tube, and pipe a neat rose into each horn.

Jam turnovers *yield: 12 turnovers*

200 g	8 oz flour	puff pastry
200 g	8 oz	jam

1. Roll out pastry 2 mm ($\frac{1}{12}$ in.) thick.
2. Cut with a fancy cutter into 8 cm diameter (4 in.) rounds.
3. Roll out slightly oval 12 × 10 cm (5 × 4 in.).
4. Moisten the edges.
5. Place a little jam in the centre of each.
6. Fold over and seal firmly.
7. Brush with egg white and dip in castor sugar.
8. Place sugar side up on a greased baking sheet.
9. Bake in a hot oven (220 – 230°C, Reg. 7 – 8), approximately 15 – 20 minutes.

Scones *yield: 8 scones*

200 g	8 oz	flour (white or wholemeal)
10 g	$\frac{1}{2}$ oz	baking-powder
		salt
50 g	2 oz	butter or margarine
25 – 50 g	1 – 2 oz	castor sugar
95 ml	$\frac{3}{16}$ pt (approx.)	milk or water

1. Sieve the flour, baking-powder and salt.
2. Rub in the fat to a sandy texture.
3. Make a well in the centre.
4. Add the sugar and the liquid.
5. Dissolve the sugar in the liquid.
6. Gradually incorporate the flour; mix lightly.
7. Roll out two rounds 1 cm ($\frac{1}{2}$ in.) thick.
8. Place on a greased baking sheet.
9. Cut a cross half-way through the rounds with a large knife.
10. Milk wash and bake in the oven at 200 – 220°C, Reg. 6 – 7 for 15 to 20 minutes.

The comparatively small amount of fat, rapid mixing to a soft dough, and quick and light handling are essentials to produce a light scone.

Fruit scones

Add 50 g (2 oz) washed and dried sultanas to the scone mixture.

Choux paste

$\frac{1}{4}$ litre	$\frac{1}{2}$ pt	water
		pinch of sugar
100 g	4 oz	butter, margarine or oil
125 g	5 oz	flour (white)
		pinch of salt
		4 eggs (approx.), size 3

1. Bring the water, sugar and fat to the boil in a saucepan.
2. Remove from heat.
3. Add the sieved flour and salt and mix in with a wooden spoon.
4. Return to a moderate heat and stir continuously until the mixture leaves the side of the pan.
5. Remove from the heat and allow to cool.
6. Gradually add the beaten eggs, mixing well.
7. The paste should be of dropping consistency.

Uses: éclairs, cream buns, profiteroles, etc.

Possible reasons for faults in choux paste

1. *Greasy and heavy*	Basic mixture overcooked.
2. *Soft – not aerated*	Flour insufficiently beaten in the mixture. Oven too cool. Underbaked.

Chocolate éclairs *yield: 12 éclairs*

125 ml	$\frac{1}{4}$ pt	choux paste
$\frac{1}{4}$ litre	$\frac{1}{2}$ pt	whipped cream
100 g	4 oz	fondant
25 g	1 oz	chocolate couverture

1. Place the choux paste into a piping bag with 1 cm ($\frac{1}{2}$ in.) plain tube.
2. Pipe into 8 cm (3 in.) lengths on to a lightly greased baking sheet.
3. Bake in a moderate oven (220 – 230°C, Reg. 7 – 8), approximately 30 minutes.
4. Allow to cool.
5. Slit down one side with a sharp knife.
6. Fill with sweetened, vanilla-flavoured whipped cream, using a piping bag and small tube.
7. Warm the fondant, add the finely cut chocolate, allow to melt slowly, and adjust the consistency with a little sugar and water syrup if necessary. Do not overheat or the fondant will lose its shine.
8. Glaze the éclairs by dipping them in the fondant; remove the surplus with the finger.
9. Allow to set and serve.

Coffee éclairs

Add a few drops of coffee essence instead of chocolate to the fondant.

Cream buns *yield: 8 buns*

125 ml	$\frac{1}{4}$ pt	choux paste
25 g	1 oz	chopped almonds
$\frac{1}{4}$ litre	$\frac{1}{2}$ pt	whipped cream

1. Place the choux paste into a piping bag with a 1 cm ($\frac{1}{2}$ in.) plain tube.
2. Pipe out on to a lightly greased baking sheet into pieces the size of a walnut.
3. Sprinkle each with chopped almonds.
4. Cook, cool, split and fill as for éclairs.
5. Sprinkle with icing sugar and serve.

Profiteroles

These are small choux paste buns, which can be made in a variety of sizes:

a) pea size – for consommé garnish,
b) double pea size (stuffed) for garnish,
c) half-cream bun size – filled with cream and served with chocolate sauce.

Profiteroles and chocolate sauce

		choux paste ($\frac{1}{4}$ pt water)
$\frac{1}{4}$ litre	$\frac{1}{2}$ pt	whipped, sweetened, vanilla-flavoured cream
$\frac{1}{4}$ litre	$\frac{1}{2}$ pt	chocolate sauce (page 17)

1. Proceed as for cream buns (see above), pipe out half the size and omit the almonds.
2. Fill with cream and dredge with icing sugar.
3. Dress neatly on a doily on a silver flat dish and serve with a sauceboat of cold chocolate sauce.

Trifle *6 – 8 portions*

Victoria sandwich (see page 90)

25 g	1 oz	jam
		1 tin fruit (pears, peaches, pineapple)
35 g	$1\frac{1}{2}$ oz	custard powder
375 ml	$\frac{3}{4}$ pt	milk
50 g	2 oz	castor sugar
125 ml	$\frac{1}{4}$ pt	cream (optional)
$\frac{1}{4}$ litre	$\frac{1}{2}$ pt	whipped sweetened cream
25 g	1 oz	angelica
25 g	1 oz	glacé cherries

1. Cut the sponge in half sideways, spread with jam and cut into dice.
2. Place in a glass bowl and soak with fruit syrup.
3. 60 – 125 ml ($\frac{1}{8}$ – $\frac{1}{4}$ pt) of sherry may be added.
4. Cut the fruit into small pieces and add to the sponge.
5. Dilute the custard powder in a basin with some of the milk; add the sugar.
6. Boil the remainder of the milk, pour a little on the custard powder, mix well, return to the saucepan and over a low heat stir to the boil.
7. Add the cream and pour on to the sponge.
8. Leave to cool.
9. Decorate with whipped cream, angelica and cherries, and serve.

Meringue

		4 egg whites
200 g	8 oz	castor sugar

1. Whip the egg whites stiffly.
2. Sprinkle on the sugar and carefully mix in.
3. Place in a piping bag with a large plain tube and pipe on to greaseproof paper on a baking sheet.
4. Bake in the slowest oven possible or in a hot plate (90 – 100°C, Reg. $\frac{1}{4}$). The aim is to cook the meringues without *any* colour.

To gain maximum efficiency when whipping egg whites the following points should be observed:

a) eggs should be fresh;
b) when separating yolks from whites no speck of egg yolk must be allowed to remain in the white – egg yolk contains fat, the presence of which can prevent the white being correctly whipped;
c) the bowl and whisk must be scrupulously clean, dry and free from any grease.

Piping meringue

Sponge cake

Possible reasons for faults in sponges

1. *Close texture*	Underbeating. Too much flour. Oven too cool or too hot.
2. *Holey texture*	Flour insufficiently folded in. Tin unevenly filled.
3. *Cracked crust*	Oven too hot.
4. *Sunken*	Oven too hot. Tin removed during cooking.
5. *White spots on surface*	Insufficient beating.

Creaming method

Victoria sandwich

100 g	4 oz	castor sugar
100 g	4 oz	flour (white)
		$\frac{1}{2}$ level tsp baking-powder
100 g	4 oz	butter or margarine
		2 eggs, size 3

1. Cream the fat and sugar until soft and fluffy.
2. Gradually add the beaten eggs.
3. Lightly mix in the sieved flour and the baking-powder.
4. Divide into two 18 cm (7 in.) greased sponge tins.
5. Bake in a hot oven (220°C, Reg. 7), approximately 12 – 15 minutes.
6. Turn out on to a wire rack to cool.
7. Spread one half with jam and place the other half on top.
8. Dust with icing sugar.

Bread rolls *yield: 8 rolls*

200 g	8 oz	flour (strong)
5 g	$\frac{3}{8}$ oz	yeast
125 ml	$\frac{1}{4}$ pt	liquid (half water, half milk)
		$\frac{1}{4}$ tsp castor sugar
10 g	$\frac{1}{2}$ oz	butter or margarine
		salt.

1. Sieve the flour into a bowl and warm in the oven or above the stove.
2. Cream the yeast in a small basin with a quarter of the liquid.
3. Make a well in the centre of the flour and add the dissolved yeast.
4. Sprinkle over a little of the flour, cover with a cloth, leave in a warm place until the yeast ferments (bubbles).
5. Add the remainder of the liquid (warm), sugar, fat and salt.
6. Knead firmly until smooth and free from stickiness.
7. Return to the basin, cover with a cloth and leave in a warm place until double its size (this is called proving the dough).
8. Knock back to its original size.
9. Divide into 8 even pieces.
10. Mould into desired shapes.
11. Place on a floured baking sheet.
12. Cover with a cloth.
13. Leave in a warm place to prove (double in size).
14. Brush carefully with eggwash.
15. Bake in a hot oven (220°C, Reg. 7), approximately 10 minutes.

At all times extreme heat must be avoided, as the yeast will be killed and the dough spoiled.

Possible reasons for faults using yeast doughs

1. *Close texture*	Insufficiently proved. Insufficiently kneaded. Insufficient yeast.

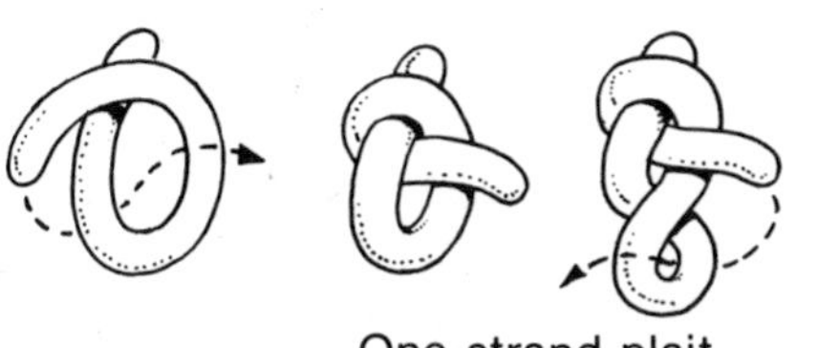
One-strand plait

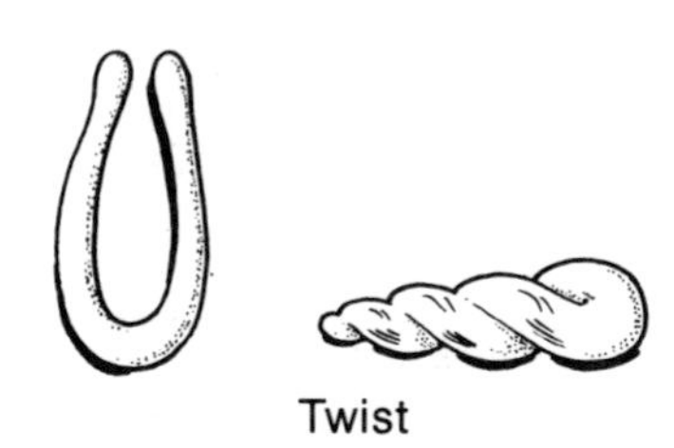
Twist

Knot

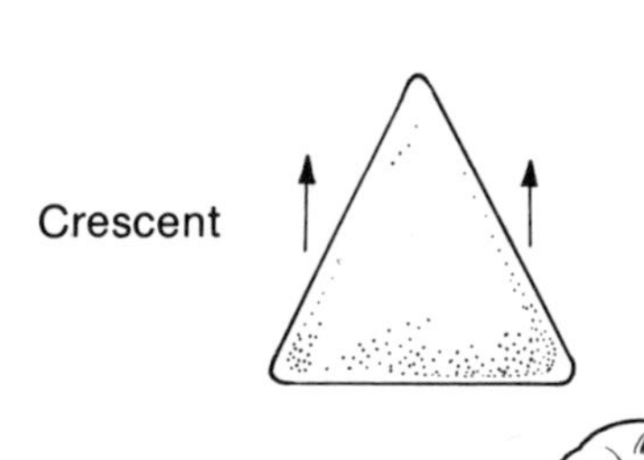

Bread rolls

	Oven too hot. Too much water. Too little water.
2. *Uneven texture*	Insufficient kneading. Oven too cool. Overproving.
3. *Coarse texture*	Too much water. Too much salt.

Bun dough (basic mixture) *yield: 8 buns*

200 g	½ lb	flour (strong)
		pinch of salt
5 g	⅜ oz	yeast
125 ml	¼ pt (approx.)	milk and water
25 g	1 oz	castor sugar
		1 egg, size 3
50 g	2 oz	butter or margarine

1. Sieve the flour and salt into a bowl and warm.
2. Dissolve the yeast in a basin with a little of the liquid.
3. Make a well in the centre of the flour.
4. Add the dissolved yeast, sprinkle with a little flour, cover with a cloth, leave in a warm place until the yeast ferments (bubbles).
5. Add the sugar, beaten egg, butter or margarine and remainder of the liquid. Knead well to form a soft, slack dough, knead until smooth and free from stickiness.
6. Keep covered and allow to prove in a warm place.
7. Use as required.

Bun wash

100 g	4 oz	sugar
125 ml	¼ pt	water

Boil together until the consistency of a thick syrup.

Fruit buns

1. Add 50 g (2 oz) washed, dried fruit (currants, sultanas) and a little mixed spice to the basic mixture.
2. Mould into 8 round balls.
3. Place on a lightly greased baking sheet.
4. Cover with a cloth; allow to prove.
5. Bake in a hot oven (220°C, Reg. 7), approximately 15 – 20 minutes.
6. Brush liberally with bun wash as soon as cooked.

Hot cross buns

1. Proceed as for fruit buns, using a little more spice.
2. When moulded make a cross with the back of a knife, or make a slack mixture of flour and water and pipe on crosses using a greaseproof paper cornet.
3. Allow to prove, and finish as for fruit buns.

Small cakes (basic recipe)

100 g	4 oz	margarine
100 g	4 oz	castor sugar
		2 eggs, size 3
100 g	4 oz	flour (white)
		½ level tsp baking-powder

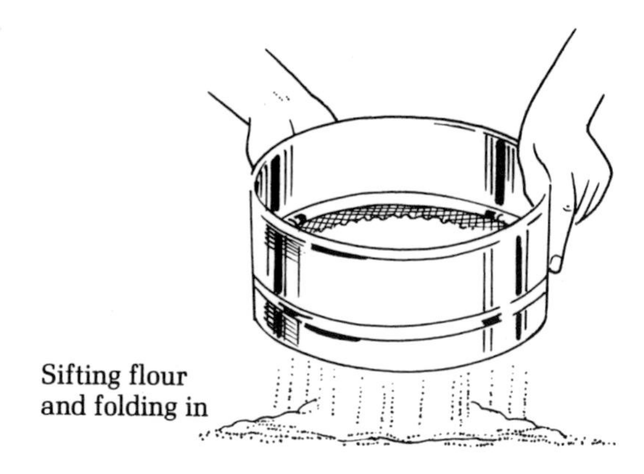

Sifting flour and folding in

1. Beat the margarine in a mixing bowl.
2. Add the sugar. Cream together until light and creamy.
3. Add the eggs one at a time.
4. Beat in thoroughly.
5. Add the sieved flour, fold in gently with a metal spoon.
6. Spoon into paper cases or small greased cake tins, yield 18 – 24.
7. Cook in a pre-heated oven at 200°C, Reg. 6 for 20 – 25 minutes.

Queen cakes – fold in 50 – 75 g (2 – 3 oz) dried fruit after adding the flour.

Cherry cakes – add 50 g (2 oz) glacé cherries after adding the flour.

Cheese and ham savoury flan or quiche

100 g	4 oz	rough puff, puff or short pastry
50 g	2 oz	chopped ham
25 g	1 oz	grated cheese
		1 egg, size 3
125 ml	$\frac{1}{4}$ pt	milk
		cayenne, salt

1. Lightly grease four good-size barquette or tartlet moulds.
2. Line thinly with pastry.
3. Prick the bottoms of the paste two or three times with a fork.
4. Cook in a hot oven (230°C, Reg. 8) for 3 to 4 minutes or until the pastry is lightly set.
5. Remove from the oven, press the pastry down if it has tended to rise.
6. Add the chopped ham and grated cheese.
7. Mix the egg, milk, salt and cayenne thoroughly.
8. Strain into the barquettes.
9. Return to a moderate oven (200°C, Reg. 6) and bake gently till nicely browned and set, approximately 15 – 20 minutes.

Savoury flan

Line a 15 cm (6 in.) flan-ring with short paste and proceed as in the previous recipe, or vary the filling by using lightly fried lardons of bacon (in place of ham), chopped cooked onion and chopped parsley. A variety of savoury flans can be made by using imagination and by experimenting with different combinations of food, e.g. Stilton and onion, salmon and cucumber, sliced sausage and tomato, etc.

Questions – Baking

1. Baking is cooking in ——— heat.

2. Match the following:

choux paste	apple flans
short paste	jam puffs
puff paste	chocolate éclairs
sweet paste	meat pies

3. Complete the required words or figures which indicate the oven temperature or heat:

a)	slow	=	. . . . °F or . . . . °C
b)	regulo 6 – 8	=	. . . . oven
c)	moderately hot	=	regulo . . . . .

4. Yeast is a raising agent used for:

a) scones c) apple turnovers
b) currant buns d) Yorkshire pudding

5. Which two of the following statements are correct?
   a) the creaming method is used for scones
   b) the rubbing in method is used for rock cakes
   c) queen cakes are produced by creaming method

6. 1. Short and sweet.
   2. Hot in the oven – tyres need this.
   3. CONES (anagram).
   4. Needed between puff pastry turns and served in prisons?
   5. Millionaires drive them.
   6. Pancakes don't require this – bread does.

1	P				
2	A				
3	S				
4	T				
5	R				
6	Y				

7. What causes these items to rise?

   puff pastry goods
   bread rolls
   small cakes

8. Name three raising agents.

9. Give two examples of use from each of the following pastes: a) puff b) sweet and c) choux.

10. Which are true?
    a) meringue is made with whites of egg
    b) puff pastry is cooked in a hot oven
    c) yeast is used in scones
    d) cream caramels are cooked in a bain-marie
    e) baked potatoes require fat when cooking them

Answers can be found on page 155.

13

Microwave cookery

General objectives To have a knowledge and understanding of the principle of microwave ovens.

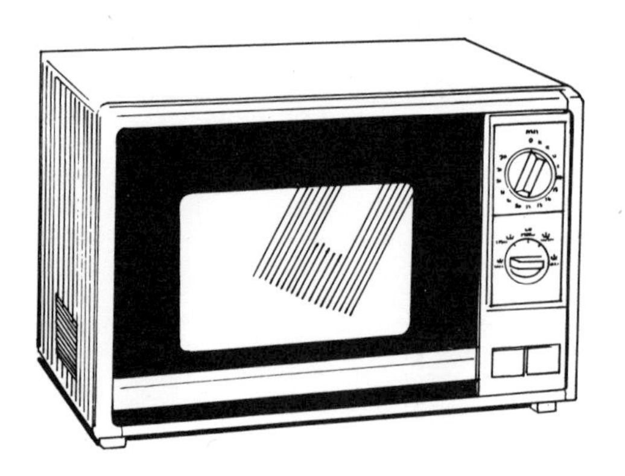

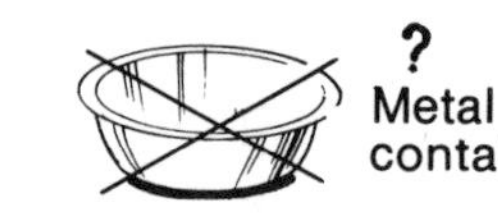

Microwave

Specific objectives To define microwave energy; to explain how food is cooked by microwave; to specify the uses of microwave cookery; to state the advantages of microwave cookery; to state the disadvantages of microwave cookery; to describe the care and use of equipment; to explain efficiency and safety procedures.

Advantages

1. Cooking time is much less – one-quarter to one-fifth of normal time.
2. As it is so quick, there can be saving on fuel.
3. From the food hygiene aspect it is safe for reheating foods, because the whole dish of food is heated through at the same time.
4. It is useful for defrosting small amounts of frozen food.

Average cooking times (in minutes)

Item	Conventional oven	Microwave oven
400 g (1 lb) fish	10	4
Baked potato	60	5
Meat casserole	120	45
2 lamb chops	7	5
2 sausages	10	2
Sponge pudding	60	4

Disadvantages

1. Only small amounts of food can be cooked, defrosted or reheated at a time.

2. Most microwave ovens do not colour foods, but there are some ovens that have a built-in colouring unit.
3. Microwaves can penetrate food only to a depth of 4 cm ($1\frac{1}{2}$ in.).

Definition of microwave energy

Microwave energy is a high frequency power similar to the energy which carries television signals from the broadcasting transmitter to the receiver, but it operates at much higher frequencies. In a television set the *cathode ray tube* is used; in a microwave oven it is a tube called a *magnetron* which generates the microwaves. When the oven is switched on the invisible microwaves enter the oven and pass through the food. The oven is lined with metal and because microwaves are reflected by metal they are reflected back into the food.

Microwaves

1. Microwaves are *reflected* by metal.
2. Microwaves are *transmitted* through glass, ceramics, paper and types of plastic (therefore foods are only placed in containers made from these materials.
3. Microwaves are *absorbed* by food.

How food is cooked

When your hands are cold, if you rub them together quickly heat is generated by the friction. Food is composed of small particles known as molecules and when microwaves pass through the food they rub together quickly or agitate the molecules, causing friction and heat which cooks the food.

Safety

The seal round the door to the oven must always be intact – on no account should a microwave oven be used if the seal is not perfect.

Points to note

1. Large, thick items of food cannot be cooked by this method.
2. The air in the oven does not get hot; only the food gets hot.
3. The containers used should always be glass, ceramic, plastic or paper. Metal will damage the magnetron in certain types of oven.
4. It is not possible to produce a crisp outside to the food, nor does the food colour, other than in microwave ovens with a browning element.
5. Large quantities of food may best be cooked in a conventional oven, e.g. it may be more convenient to cook a large number of baked potatoes in a conventional oven for $1\frac{1}{2}$ hours than 6 potatoes at a time for 6 minutes in a microwave.

Cleaning

1. Comply with manufacturers instructions.
2. Wash oven interior, doors and seals with hot detergent water; rinse and dry.
3. Do not use scouring pads or abrasives.
4. If there is an air filter it should be washed regularly.

Questions – Microwave cookery

1. Why is the use of a microwave oven economical?
2. State 3 kinds of material from which containers can be made for use in a microwave oven.
3. A microwave must not be used if the s... is not perfect.
4. Suggest 2 good uses of the microwave oven.
5. Give 2 examples of cookery when a microwave oven is not suitable.

Answers can be found on page 155.

14

Cook-freeze/cook-chill

Cook-freeze and cook-chill systems, and also vacuum cooking, are found in use in more and more places, especially in situations where there is little time or space to prepare the food to a high standard.

Cook-freeze system

Definition

This is a system in which:

1. Food is prepared in a large centralised kitchen. The food is then portioned, frozen, packed, stored in a deep freeze and distributed to various outlets;
2. The various outlets receive the frozen food which is stored in deep freeze units, then thawed, re-heated and served as required.

Advantages of the system:

a) A more even day's work for skilled cooks, free from the pressure and stress of service time experienced in many kitchens;
b) The nutritional content of foods is more likely to be retained as food is not kept hot for long periods of time before being frozen;
c) Food production planning is easier and food wastage should be cut down or eliminated;
d) Unskilled operators can supervise the thawing, re-heating and serving of meals at the various outlets.

Points to note

1. The highest standards of food and personal hygiene are essential at all stages, otherwise there will be dangers of contamination which can result in sickness, severe illness and, in some cases, death;
2. Certain commodities and recipes may need adjustment if they are to be successfully frozen. This is specialised food technology knowledge and must only be dealt with by qualified personnel.

Cook-chill system

Definition

This is a system of food preparation and cooking followed by fast chilling, retaining the food at 0 to 3°C then reheating immediately before being served.

Advantages:

a) When the regenerated food is served it is as appetising as when first cooked;
b) Skilled staff are used for the preparation, less skilled staff for reheating the foods;
c) Economic use of kitchen facilities — a regenerative kitchen is not so expensive to instal as a normal kitchen;
d) The system is suitable for bulk production and service in outlets.

Points to note:

1. Foods must be quickly cooled to 0 to 3°C in under 90 minutes;
2. When chilled, foods must be maintained below 3°C until reheated;
3. Maximum time from production to consumption is 5 days;
4. Strict temperature control is essential to prevent growth of bacteria which could be a risk to health, even leading to death;
5. The highest standards of personal and food hygiene are essential.

The system

Preparation and Cooking

↓

Chilling

↓

Storing

↓

Distribution

↓

Regeneration and service

Vacuum cooking

Definition

This is a method of cooking in which food is sealed in vacuum-sealed plastic pouches and cooked in a temperature-controlled convection steam cooker.

Raw food products, e.g. cuts of fish, poultry or meat, are placed with any required cut vegetables, herbs, spices, stock or wine into individual or multi-portion pouches, air is extracted to leave a vacuum and the pouches sealed. At this stage the pouches will keep perfectly fresh for several days if stored in a refrigerator.

The pouches of food may also be cooked and chilled to 10°C and, if kept in refrigerators, they can be stored for several days provided that the cooking, chilling and storage process has not taken longer than two hours. When required for service the pouches are either placed in boiling water or in a pressureless steam oven.

Advantages:

1. A good mise-en-place can be made of a variety of dishes giving opportunities to widen menu choice;
2. The preparation of pouches can be carried out during slacker periods of time, thereby helping to even-out the work-load over the day;
3. The flavour of all ingredients is retained within the pouches, which should improve food quality;
4. Portion control becomes easier.

15
Cold dishes

Hors-d'oeuvre

The choice of a wide variety of foods, combination of foods and recipes is available for preparation and service as hors d'oeuvre. Hors-d'oeuvre can be divided into three categories:

a) single cold food items, e.g. smoked salmon, pâté, melon, etc.,
b) a selection of well seasoned cold dishes,
c) well seasoned hot dishes.

Hors-d'oeuvre may be served for luncheon, dinner or supper and the wide choice, colour appeal and versatility of the dishes makes many items and combination of items suitable for snacks, salads and light meals.

Grapefruit

These are halved, the segments are individually cut with a small knife, then they are chilled. Serve with a maraschino cherry in the centre.

The common practice of sprinkling with castor sugar is incorrect, as some customers prefer their grapefruit without sugar.

Serve half a grapefruit per portion in a coupe.

Florida cocktail

This is a mixture of grapefruit, orange and pineapple segments.

Fruit cocktail Allow $\frac{1}{2}$ kg (1 lb) unprepared fruit for 4 portions

This is a mixture of fruits such as apples, pears, pineapples, grapes, cherries, etc., washed, peeled and cut into neat segments or dice and added to a syrup (100 g (4 oz) sugar to $\frac{1}{4}$ litre ($\frac{1}{2}$ pt) water) and the juice of half a lemon. Neatly place in cocktail glasses and chill.

Chilled melon Approximately $\frac{1}{2}$ a honeydew or cantaloup melon for 4 portions

Cut the melon in half, remove the pips and cut into thick slices. Cut a piece of the skin so that the slice will stand firm.

Avocado pear Allow $\frac{1}{2}$ a pear per portion

The pears must be ripe (test by pressing gently – the pear should give slightly).

1. Cut in half lengthwise.
2. Remove the stone.
3. Serve garnished with lettuce, accompanied by vinaigrette (see page 100) or variations to vinaigrette.

Avocado pears are sometimes filled with shrimps or crabmeat bound with a shellfish cocktail sauce or other similar fillings, and may be served hot or cold, using a variety of fillings and sauces.

Soused herring or mackerel

		2 herrings or mackerel
		salt, pepper
25 g	1 oz	carrots
25 g	1 oz	button onions
		$\frac{1}{2}$ bay leaf
		6 peppercorns
60 ml	$\frac{1}{8}$ pint	vinegar
		sprig of thyme

1. Clean, scale and fillet the fish.
2. Wash fillets, season lightly with salt and pepper.
3. Roll up with the skin outside.
4. Place in an ovenproof dish.
5. Peel and wash the carrot and onion.
6. Cut into neat thin rings.
7. Blanch for 2 to 3 minutes and refresh.
8. Add to the fish with the remainder of the ingredients.
9. Cover with greaseproof paper and cook in a moderate oven for 15 to 20 minutes.
10. Allow to cool; place in a dish with the onion and carrot.
11. Garnish with picked parsley and serve.

Egg mayonnaise

To cook hard-boiled eggs:

1. Place the eggs in boiling water.
2. Reboil and simmer for 8 to 10 minutes. Refresh until cold.

If eggs are overcooked a blackish ring will form around the yolk.

As part of a selection for hors-d'oeuvre – cut the hard-boiled eggs in quarters or slices and coat with mayonnaise.

As an individual hors-d'oeuvre – allow 1 hard-boiled egg per portion, cut in half and dress on a leaf of lettuce, coat with mayonnaise, garnish with quarters of tomatoes, slices of cucumber and serve.

As a main dish – allow 2 hard-boiled eggs per portion, cut in halves, dress on a plate and coat with mayonnaise sauce. Surround with a portion of lettuce, tomato, cucumber, potato salad, vegetable salad, beetroot or coleslaw.

Fish mayonnaise – shrimp, prawn, crab, or any cooked, flaked fish

As an hors-d'oeuvre, allow 25 – 35 g (1 – 1½ oz) prepared fish per portion.

		1 lettuce
100 – 150 g	4 – 6 oz	prepared fish
125 ml	¼ pt	mayonnaise sauce
		capers, anchovies
		parsley for decoration

1. Shred the lettuce finely and place in a ravier.
2. Add the fish.
3. Coat with mayonnaise sauce.
4. Decorate as desired.

This may also be served as a main course, in which case the amount of fish is doubled and the other ingredients are slightly increased.

Vegetable salad (sometimes known as Russian salad)

100 g	4 oz	carrots
50 g	2 oz	turnips
50 g	2 oz	French beans
50 g	2 oz	peas
		1 tbsp vinaigrette
60 ml	⅛ pint	mayonnaise
		salt, pepper

1. Peel and wash the carrots and turnips.
2. Cut into ½ cm (¼ in.) dice or batons.
3. Cook separately in salted water.
4. Refresh and drain well.
5. Top and tail the beans.
6. Cut in ½ cm (¼ in.) dice, cook and refresh.
7. Cook the peas and refresh.
8. Mix all the well drained vegetables with vinaigrette and then mayonnaise.
9. Correct the seasoning and serve.

Meat salad

200 g	8 oz	cooked lean meat
25 g	1 oz	gherkins
50 g	2 oz	cooked French beans
50 g	2 oz	tomatoes
5 g	¼ oz	chopped onion or chives
		chopped parsley
60 ml		1 tbsp vinaigrette

1. Cut the meat and gherkin in ½ cm (¼ in.) dice.
2. Cut the beans into ½ cm (¼ in.) dice.
3. Skin the tomatoes and remove the seeds.
4. Cut into ½ cm (¼ in.) dice.
5. Mix with the remainder of the ingredients.
6. Correct the seasoning.
7. Decorate with lettuce leaves, tomatoes and fans of gherkins and serve.

Well cooked braised or boiled meat is ideal for this salad.

Rice salad

100 g	4 oz	2 tomatoes
100 g	4 oz	cooked rice

50 g	2 oz	peas (cooked)
		1 tbsp vinaigrette
		salt, pepper

1. Skin and remove seeds from tomatoes.
2. Cut into ½ cm (¼ in.) dice.
3. Mix with the rice and peas.
4. Add the vinaigrette, correct the seasoning and serve.

Haricot bean salad

200 g	8 oz	haricot beans (cooked)
		1 tbsp vinaigrette
		chopped parsley
10 g	½ oz	chopped onion or chives
		salt, pepper

Combine all the ingredients, correct the seasoning and serve.

Coleslaw /

200 g	8 oz	white cabbage or Chinese leaves
50 g	2 oz	carrot
25 g	1 oz	onion
125 ml	¼ pt	mayonnaise

1. Trim off the outside leaves of the cabbage.
2. Cut into quarters.
3. Remove the centre stalk.
4. Wash the cabbage, shred finely and drain well.
5. Mix with a fine julienne of raw carrot and shredded raw onion.
6. Bind with mayonnaise sauce.

To modify the strong flavour of the raw onion it can be blanched for 1 to 2 minutes and refreshed before adding to the mixture.

Salad dressings

1. Vinaigrette
2. Mayonnaise
3. Acidulated cream

These dressings may be varied by the addition of other ingredients.

Vinaigrette (or French dressing)

3 – 6 tbsp olive or other good quality oil, according to taste
1 tbsp French mustard
1 tbsp vinegar
salt, mill pepper

Combine all the ingredients.

Variations on vinaigrette

a) English mustard in place of French mustard;
b) chopped herbs (chives, parsley, tarragon, etc.);
c) chopped, hard-boiled egg;
d) lemon juice in place of vinegar (lemon dressing);
e) malt, wine, cider, tarragon and raspberry are examples of some of the many vinegars.

Mayonnaise ¼ litre (½ pint)

		2 egg yolks
		2 tsp vinegar
		salt, ground white pepper
		⅛ tsp mustard
250 ml	½ pint	good quality oil
		1 tsp boiling water

1. Place yolks, vinegar and seasoning in a bowl and whisk well.
2. Slowly add the oil, whisking continuously.
3. Whisk in the boiling water.
4. Correct seasoning.

Acidulated cream /

juice of ¼ lemon
4 tbsp cream

Gently stir the juice into the cream at the last moment before serving.

Salads

A large number and variety of foods and combination of foods can be prepared and served as salads. Good, clean, well presented dishes of salad are always popular both as an accompaniment to other hot and cold foods and as dishes in their own right. They can be served for lunch, tea, high tea, dinner, supper and as light meals.

Salads may be divided into two sections:

a) simple salads – using 1 ingredient;

b) mixed salads – using more than 1 ingredient.

A dressing should always be offered with any salad.

Beetroot salad

200 g	8 oz	cooked beetroot
		chopped parsley
10 g	$\frac{1}{2}$ oz	chopped onion or chive (optional)
		1 tbsp vinaigrette

Combine all the ingredients and serve.

Celery

Trim off the green part and wash well. Remove any discoloured outer stalks. Cut into thin strips, serve crisp.

Curled chicory (also known as curled endive)

Thoroughly wash and trim off the stalk. Drain well and use as required.

Cucumber salad

$\frac{1}{2}$ cucumber
1 tbsp vinaigrette
chopped parsley

1. Peel and slice the cucumber.
2. Sprinkle with vinaigrette and parsley, and serve.

Mustard and cress

Trim off the stalk ends of the cress. Wash well and lift out of water so as to leave the seed cases behind. Drain well and serve.

Watercress

Trim off the stalk ends, discard any discoloured leaves, thoroughly wash and serve.

Chicory (also known as Belgian endive)

Trim off the root end. Cut into 1 cm ($\frac{1}{2}$ in.) lengths, wash well, drain and serve.

Lettuce (round or cabbage)

Trim off the root end and remove the outside leaves. Wash thoroughly and drain well. The outer leaves can be pulled off and the head cut into quarters.

Cos lettuce

Trim off the root end and remove the outside leaves. Wash thoroughly and drain well. Cut into quarters.

Potato salad

200 g	8 oz	cooked potatoes
		1 tbsp vinaigrette
10 g	$\frac{1}{2}$ oz	chopped onion or chive (optional)
60 ml	$\frac{1}{8}$ pint	mayonnaise
		salt, pepper
		chopped parsley

1. Cut the potatoes in $\frac{1}{2}$ – 1 cm ($\frac{1}{4}$ – $\frac{1}{2}$ in.) dice; sprinkle with vinaigrette.
2. Mix with the onion or chive, add the mayonnaise and correct the seasoning.
3. Sprinkle with chopped parsley and serve.

Tomato salad

200 g	8 oz (approx.)	4 tomatoes
		$\frac{1}{4}$ lettuce
		1 tbsp vinaigrette
10 g	$\frac{1}{2}$ oz	chopped onion or chive
		chopped parsley (optional)

1. Peel tomatoes if necessary.
2. Slice thinly.
3. Arrange neatly on lettuce leaves.
4. Sprinkle with vinaigrette, onion and parsley and serve.

Mixed salad

Neatly arrange in a salad bowl. A typical mixed salad would consist of lettuce, tomato, cucumber, watercress, radishes, etc. Almost any kind of salad vegetable can be used.

Offer a vinaigrette separately.

Green salad

Any of the green salads, lettuce, cos lettuce, curled chicory, or any combination of green salads may be used. Neatly arrange in a salad bowl and serve with vinaigrette separately.

French salad

The usual ingredients are lettuce, tomato and cucumber, but these may be varied with other salad vegetables, in some cases with quarters of egg. A vinaigrette made with French mustard (French dressing) should be offered.

Sandwiches

An almost endless variety of sandwiches can be produced. They can be made from every type of bread, either fresh or toasted, cut into different shapes and with various fillings.

Types of sandwiches

1. 2 buttered slices of bread with a filling.
2. Double decker – 3 thin buttered slices of bread with 2 fillings.
3. Treble decker – 4 thin slices of buttered bread with 3 fillings.

Types of bread

White, brown, granary, rye, wholemeal, caraway seed, rolls, French sticks.

Toasted sandwiches can be made in 2 ways, as follows:

a) by inserting a variety of hot fillings, e.g. egg, bacon, ham, between two slices of hot, freshly buttered toast.
b) by placing the required filling, e.g. ham, cheese, between two slices buttered bread into a sandwich toaster.

Open sandwiches or Scandinavian smorgasbord are prepared from slices of any buttered bread, generously covered with any type of meat, fish, eggs, vegetables, salads, etc. For example:

1. Lettuce, prawns (peeled), mayonnaise, curl of lemon.
2. Scrambled eggs, mushrooms, capers.
3. Roast beef, sliced tomato, gherkin.
4. Pickled herring, chopped gherkin, hard-boiled egg.

Pinwheel sandwiches are prepared from slices of bread cut lengthwise from a sandwich loaf. The slices are buttered and the crusts removed. The slices are then covered with a soft filling, tightly rolled, wrapped in greaseproof paper and placed in a refrigerator to set, after which they can be cut into slices with a sharp knife.

Sandwich fillings

Fillings	Combinations of fillings	Added seasonings	Garnishes
ham	cheese and tomato	mayonnaise	mustard and cress
tongue	cucumber and egg	mustard	cress
beef	ham and coleslaw	vinaigrette	tomato
chicken	cottage cheese and pineapple	chutney	cucumber
turkey	prawn and mushroom	horseradish	lettuce
smoked fish			spring onions
tinned fish			radish
fish or meat pastes			gherkins
pâté			potato crisps
tomato			
cucumber			
egg			
crab			
prawn			

16

Savouries and snacks

Mushrooms on toast

150 g	6 oz	grilling mushrooms
10 g	$\frac{1}{2}$ oz	butter or margarine
		2 slices toast

1. Peel and wash the mushrooms.
2. Place on a baking tray.
3. Season with salt; brush with melted fat.
4. Gently grill on both sides for a few minutes.
5. Cut and trim the buttered toast into rectangles.
6. Neatly arrange the mushrooms on the toast.
7. Sprinkle with cayenne and serve.

Soft roes on toast

		6 soft roes
10 g	$\frac{1}{2}$ oz	butter or margarine
		2 slices toast
		cayenne

1. Pass roes through seasoned flour.
2. Shake off surplus flour.
3. Shallow fry on both sides or grill.
4. Dress on rectangles of buttered toast.

Scotch woodcock

		2 – 3 eggs
		salt, pepper
35 g	$1\frac{1}{2}$ oz	butter or margarine
		2 slices toast
5 g	$\frac{1}{4}$ oz	anchovy fillets
5 g	$\frac{1}{4}$ oz	capers

1. Break the eggs into a basin.
2. Season with salt and pepper.
3. Thoroughly mix with a fork or whisk.
4. Place 25 g (1 oz) of butter in a small, thick-bottomed pan.
5. Allow to melt over a low heat.
6. Add the eggs and cook slowly, stirring continuously until lightly scrambled.
7. Spread on 4 rectangles or round-cut pieces of buttered toast.
8. Decorate with 2 thin fillets of anchovy and 4 capers on each, and serve.

Sardines on toast

		8 sardines
10 g	$\frac{1}{2}$ oz	butter or margarine
		2 slices toast
		cayenne

1. If the sardines are large enough and firm enough, they can be skinned and boned.
2. Arrange on rectangles of buttered toast.
3. Reheat carefully under the salamander.
4. Sprinkle with cayenne and serve.

Welsh rarebit

25 g	1 oz	butter or margarine
10 g	$\frac{1}{2}$ oz	flour
125 ml	$\frac{1}{4}$ pt	milk
100 g	4 oz	Cheddar cheese
		1 egg yolk
		4 tbsp beer
		salt, cayenne
		Worcester sauce
		English mustard
10 g	$\frac{1}{2}$ oz	butter
		2 slices toast

1. Melt the butter or margarine in a thick-bottomed pan.
2. Add the flour and mix in with a wooden spoon.
3. Cook on a gentle heat for a few minutes without colouring.
4. Gradually add the cold milk and mix to a smooth sauce.

5. Allow to simmer for a few minutes.
6. Add the grated or finely sliced cheese.
7. Allow to melt slowly over a gentle heat until a smooth mixture is obtained.
8. Add the yolk to the hot mixture, stir in and immediately remove from the heat.
9. Meanwhile in a separate pan boil the beer and allow it to reduce to $\frac{1}{2}$ tbsp.
10. Add to the mixture with the other seasonings.
11. Allow the mixture to cool.
12. Spread on the 4 rectangles of buttered toast.
13. Place on a baking sheet and brown gently under the salamander and serve.
14. Cheese contains a large amount of protein, which will become tough and stringy if heated for too long or at too high a temperature.

Questions – Cold dishes, savouries and snacks

1. Name 3 single hors-d'oeuvre.

2. What should always be offered when serving a salad?

3. Which is the odd one out and why?
   green salad mixed salad
   French salad potato salad

4. With a double decker sandwich, how many slices of bread are used?

5. What have white, brown, granary, rye and wholemeal in common?

6. What fish is associated with Scotch woodcock?

7. What English sauce is used in Welsh rarebit?

Answers can be found on page 156.

17
Practices of cookery

General objectives To have a knowledge and understanding of kitchen practice.
Specific objectives To be able to explain the reasons for and to carry out the correct procedures with regard (a) to personal hygiene, food hygiene, kitchen hygiene; (b) to the prevention of accidents, fire and first aid; (c) to economic practice and methodical

A modern hygienic kitchen

procedures and practices; (d) to the legal obligations and complying with the law; (e) to developing a positive attitude to the employer, consumer and fellow employees.

Introduction

A skilled professional cook is one who works (a) hygienically (b) safely, (c) quickly (d) methodically (e) economically (f) artistically.

To become a competent and employable cook skills must be learned and learned correctly at the beginning, so that good habits and good standards are developed at the first stage of learning. Simple things such as wiping a cutting board after use, using the correct knife, and putting a little flour on a hot pan handle as a warning are examples of good practice.

When learning a skill, speed is not the most important thing to learn; it is essential that accuracy, attention to detail, the correct procedure and striving to improve performance come first. Increased speed will result from frequent repetition but during the process of practising a skill care must be taken so that bad habits do not creep in, as they are very difficult to get rid of. For example, one must not form the habit of putting the first finger on top of the back of a large knife when cutting instead of having the thumb and finger on the sides of the blade (thus giving better control of the knife).

It should be understood that in practice these aspects of work are not isolated or separate but interrelated and applied at the same time. For example, when filleting plaice the fish should be cut in such a way that the knife does not cut the person filleting or others nearby; that the board, knife and the person are clean; that no flesh is left on the bone, as this would be wasteful and uneconomic; that the bones are kept separate from the flesh, and white skin and black skin fillets are kept separate; that the fillets are whole, neat and perfect.

Acquiring good working skills and practices gives

a) job satisfaction and advancement in the job for the cook,
b) consumer or customer satisfaction from having eaten food cooked so that it is enjoyable to eat and promotes health,
c) satisfaction to the employer because of contented customers and employees, and increased business.

Work practice

It is important to know how to cook and to know the principles of cookery. It is essential to acquire the technical skills in order to use the tools and equipment of the trade. It is also essential that this knowledge, and this skill, are applied in such a manner that in every way cooking is successful and that the cook

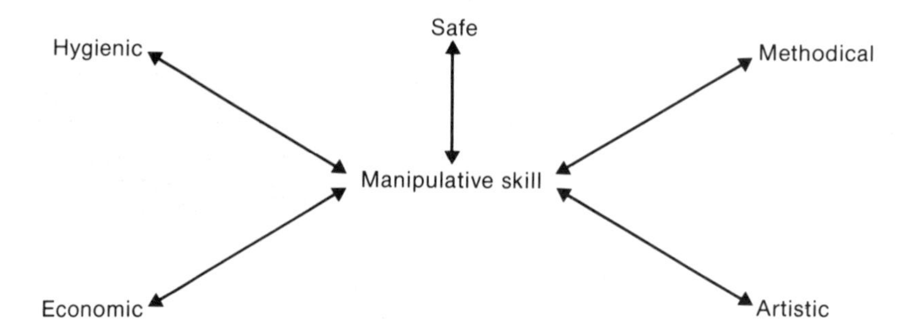

obtains job satisfaction. To achieve this aim the principles of

Hygiene
Safety = Good work practice
Economy

must be applied in the kitchen.

There are certain legal requirements which must be complied with. Because health and safety at work are so important, Parliament passed a law in 1974 known as the Health and Safety at Work Act. Under this law both the employer and the employees have a duty to take reasonable care of the health and safety of himself or herself, and of other persons who may be affected by his or her acts at work. In addition to the legal responsibility, good cooks have a moral responsibility for the health and happiness for those consuming the product of their work, whether they are patients in hospital, children at school, or people eating in an industrial canteen, restaurant, aircraft or wherever.

Kitchen clothing

The function of clothes which are worn in the kitchen, known as whites, is twofold:

a) they protect the food from the wearer, and
b) they protect the wearer from heat and spillage.

Cooks' clothing should be chosen so that all the following points are considered. They should be:

a) hygienic – easily washable; show when they need washing,
b) protective – of a material which protects the body from heat and absorbs liquid if spilled on to the wearer,
c) comfortable – not too tight or too heavy,
d) hard-wearing – able to withstand frequent washing,
e) smart in appearance – so that they can be worn with pride.

1. White clothes reflect heat and therefore help to reduce discomfort, particularly when working in hot conditions.

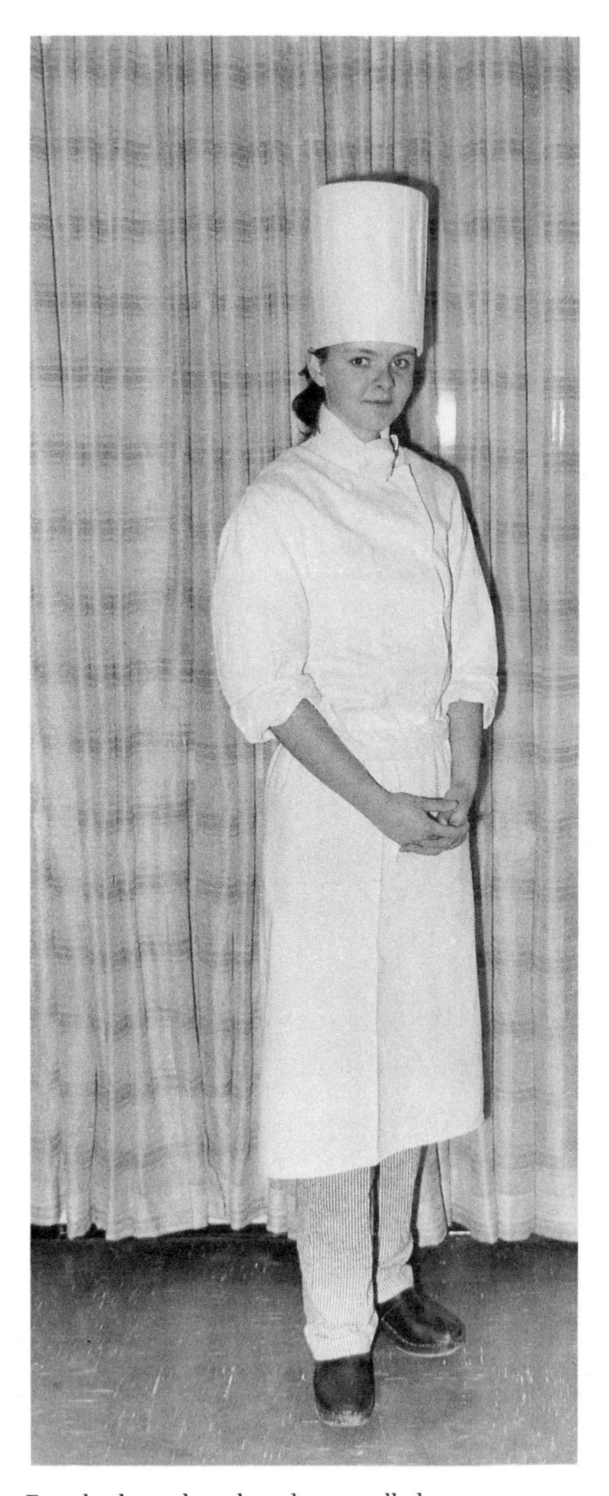

Female shown here has sleeves rolled up . .

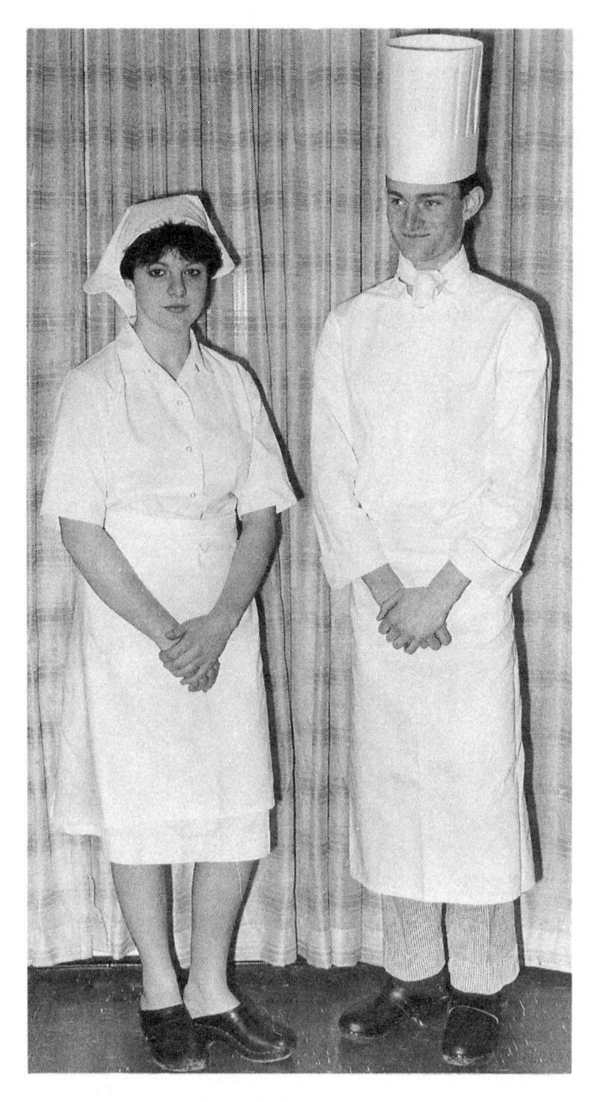

Examples of kitchen clothing

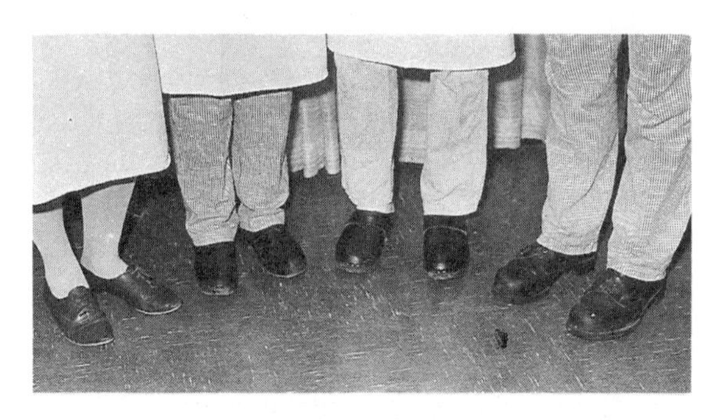

Footwear

2. White shows dirt and stains more clearly than any other colour so that the need to change into clean whites is made obvious.
3. Kitchen clothing requires frequent professional laundering in order to remove the various food stains.
4. In hot kitchens cooks perspire and perspiration stains clothes and leaves an unpleasant smell.
5. Cooks should therefore have an ample supply of kitchen clothing.

Kitchen clothing is available in

a) pre-shrunk cotton drill, which requires starching and laundering,
b) a mixture of man-made/natural fibres such as polyester/cotton or terylene/cotton, which are easily washed, do not require laundering and may be drip dry, with a minimum of ironing.

Hats are available in disposable materials, they are very light on the head, adjustable to head size and have a cloth headband to absorb perspiration.

Footwear

Since cooks are on their feet, often for long periods of time, footwear must be: comfortable; non-absorbent; durable (long-lasting); non-slip; sound – kept in good repair not too heavy. Boots, shoes or clogs will be suitable but training shoes, plimsolls or sandals are not suitable (see below left).

Use and care of knives

Knives must be handled with respect, used correctly and taken care of, so that a professional performance can be achieved. Blunt knives are likely to be the cause of accidents, since more pressure has to be applied than if a sharp knife is used. Sharp knives enable the work to be completed more quickly with less expenditure of energy and with better finish, thus giving greater job satisfaction.

Safety rules

Always observe the rules of safety for the benefit of yourself and others.

1. If carried, the knife point must be held downwards.
2. Knives on the table must be placed flat, so that the blade is not exposed upwards.
3. Do not allow knives to project over the edge of the table.
4. When using knives keep your mind and eye on the job in hand.
5. Use the correct knife for the correct purpose.
6. Always keep knives sharp.
7. After use always wipe the knife with the cutting edge away from the hand.
8. Keep the handle of the knife clean when in use.
9. Never leave knives lying in the sink.
10. Never misuse knives; a good knife is a good friend but it can be a dangerous weapon.

Selecting the correct knife for the purpose

Specific tools have been designed for certain functions to be performed in the kitchen so that work can be done successfully. A basic set of tools could comprise (see diagram below):

1.	A vegetable peeler	for peeling vegetables and fruit.
2.	A vegetable knife, 4 in. blade	for general use on vegetables and fruit.
3.	A filleting knife, 6 in. blade (flexible)	for filleting fish.
4.	A medium large knife 10 in. blade	for shredding, slicing, chopping foods.
5.	A carving knife (in addition)	for carving.
6.	A boning knife (when and if needed)	for butchery.
7.	A palette knife	for spreading and turning items over.
8.	A trussing needle	for trussing poultry and game.
9.	A fork	for lifting and holding joints of meat.
10.	A steel	for sharpening knives.

When you have chosen the correct tool there are occasions when extra care needs to be taken.

1. When using a knife to cut sideways there is less control than when cutting downwards, e.g. cross cuts when chopping onion or slicing long sandwich loaves lengthwise.
2. When shredding or chopping it is necessary to keep the fingertips and nails clear of the blade, since they are not visible all the time. When chopping, keep the fingers of the hand not holding the handle on top of the blade.
3. Never bone out or fillet frozen meat or fish in the frozen state; however, when thawed the centre may still be very cold and cause the fingertips to be numbed. Cuts are then more likely to occur.
4. When using a large knife use the thumb and first finger on the sides of the blade near the handle in order to control the sideways as well as the downward movement of the knife.
5. When using a trussing needle take extra care when drawing the needle and string upwards towards the face.
6. When scoring pork rind take care lest the surface being scored offers varying degrees of resistance, which could cause the knife to move out of control.

Sharpening

Two tools are available for sharpening knives – a steel, which should be well grooved, and a carborundum stone, which should not be too coarse as a saw edge may result. Knives need to be ground regularly; this is usually done by a knife grinder.

When using a stone *always* draw the blade of the knife away from the hand holding the stone because few stones are provided with a guard. When using a steel, for preference use one with a guard. Should you however have a steel with no guard *always* draw the knife being sharpened away from you. When using a stone or a steel, angle the blade of the knife to 45° and sharpen alternate sides of the knife using considerable pressure and drawing almost the whole length of the blade edge along the stone or steel. Having used the stone always follow up by using the steel and then wipe the knife on a cloth before use. The reason for drawing the knife across at an angle is to produce an edge to the blade, and to obtain a sharp edge it is necessary to apply both sides of the blade to the steel or stone. As the stone produces a rough edge it is necessary to follow with a steel to provide a smooth, sharp edge. The knife must be wiped after using the stone, since small particles of the stone will adhere to the blade.

The steel may be used in 3 ways, as follows. Whichever way is chosen care must be taken to sharpen the knife safely.

1. Holding the steel in one hand and the knife in the other (right-handed people will hold the knife in the right hand), draw the blade down the steel at an angle of 45° some 6 or 7 times on each side of the steel (thus, both sides of the blade), exerting pressure. Before doing so, *check* that the steel has a guard. See below.

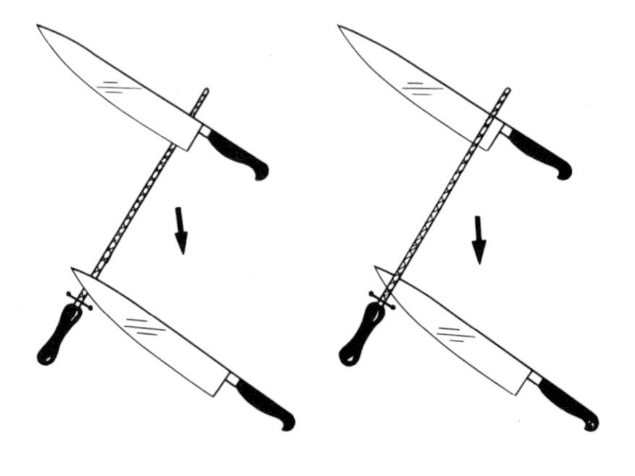

2. Holding the steel and knife as point 1, draw the knife away from you towards the end of the steel at an angle of 45° some 6 or 7 times on each side of the steel (thus, both sides of the blade), exerting pressure. See above opposite.

3. Placing the pointed end of the steel on a wooden block or heavy board, draw the knife downwards towards the block at an angle of 45°, exerting pressure and making certain the steel does not slip. As with the two previous methods, both sides of the blade are drawn down the steel some 6 or 7 times for each side. See below.

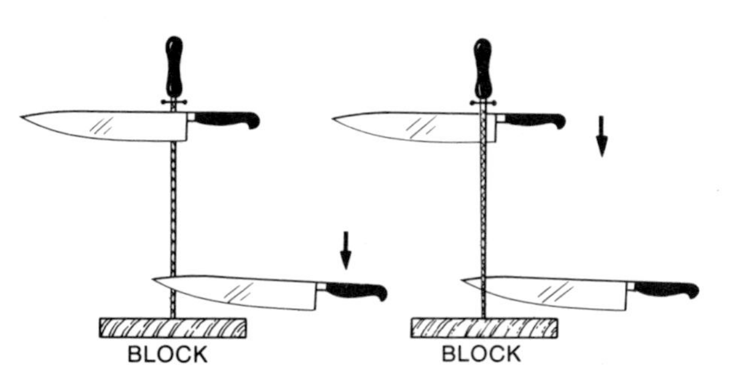

To test for sharpness, the skin of a tomato is a good indicator. To retain sharpness always use a wooden surface or suitable cutting surface of a cutting board. Never cut on stainless steel. Clean knives during and after use and particularly after using on acid items such as lemon. Stains on the blade can be cleaned with a fine cleaning powder or abrasive pad.

Some stainless steel knives for professional cooks are available which need less sharpening, as they retain their sharpness and of course do not stain.

It should be remembered that a good craftsperson never blames the tools, since, being a good craftsperson, he or she always takes care of them.

Accident prevention

Principle

To prevent accidents happening it is necessary to know why and how they occur. With this knowledge a positive attitude to preventing accidents must be taken. A positive attitude means that the cook thinks and takes action because he or she *cares* and does not want accidents to happen in the kitchen.

Practices

In the working situation, at all times

a) concentrate on the work in hand,
b) do not be distracted,
c) do not use excessive haste.

Prevention of cuts

1. Use the correct knife for the job.
2. Keep knives clean and sharp.
3. Keep knife handles free from grease.
4. Carry knives with the point held downwards.
5. Knives when not in use should be flat on the table or board, so that the blade is not exposed upwards.
6. Knives should be wiped clean with the edge away from the hand.
7. Do not put knives in a washing up sink.
8. When chopping do not have other knives on the board or chopping block.
9. Ensure that guards are in place on machines with cutting blades.
10. Take extra care when cleaning machines with blades, remove the electric plug so that the machine cannot be accidentally switched on.
11. Allow frozen meat to thaw before boning out.
12. Take extra care when handling items which have sharp or jagged bones.

Prevention of burns and scalds

Burns are caused by dry heat and scalds by wet heat. Both can be very painful and have serious effects.

1. Kitchen whites should be worn with the sleeves rolled down and the apron at a sensible length, so that it gives protection.
2. A sound, thick cloth should be used for handling hot utensils. It should not be used wet and is best folded to give greater protection.
3. When carrying trays containing liquid, one hand should be on the side and the other on the end to balance the tray.
4. A hot pan brought out of the oven should have a little flour placed on the handle and lid as a warning that it is hot.
5. Handles of pans should not protrude over the edge of the stove, as the pan may be knocked off.
6. Extra care is needed when moving pans containing liquid.
7. When hot, certain foods require particular care when being handled because of their high temperature, e.g. sugar, fats and oils.
8. When frying add food away from you when placing in the fat.
9. Drain foods well; do not put wet food into hot fat.
10. When opening a steamer door, turn off the steam and wait about 30 seconds before opening the door.

Prevention of explosions

When using gas certain precautions need to be taken to prevent accidents.

1. Always check that gas is properly lit.
2. With ranges with pilot lights it is important to see that the main jet has ignited from the pilot.
3. With solid top ranges the centre ring should not be replaced until a few minutes after the stove is lit, as the gas may go out.

Prevention of falls, etc.

1. Any liquid spilt on the floor should be cleaned up immediately.
2. No article should be left in a position on the floor which could cause a person to fall over it.
3. When lifting heavy articles from the floor do not bend the back, bend at the knees.
4. Do not put containers with liquid above eye level, as they may be pulled down by someone else.

Prevention of accidents with machinery

1. The machine should be in correct working order before use.
2. The controls of the machine should only be operated by the person using the machine.
3. Assemble machine correctly and use only the correct tools.
4. Ensure that hands do not come into contact with revolving blades, whisks or hooks.
5. When cleaning machines remove plugs to prevent machine being accidentally switched on.

First aid

Principle

Accidents do happen and the correct immediate action must be taken. First aid is *first* aid, and the first rule to observe is that if the injury resulting from the accident seems to be serious qualified assistance must be sought. If there is a qualified person on the staff, he or she should deal with the accident as soon as possible.

Practices

Cuts

Slight cuts. Wash around the cut, dry well with a clean cloth, apply an antiseptic and cover with a waterproof plaster.
Serious cuts. Bandage a dressing firmly in place on the cut and immediately obtain the assistance of a nurse, doctor or hospital.

Burns and scalds

Place the injured part under slowly running water or immerse in cool water for 10 minutes until the pain eases. If serious, the burn or scald should be covered lightly with a clean cloth to exclude the air, and the person sent to hospital.

Waste disposal unit

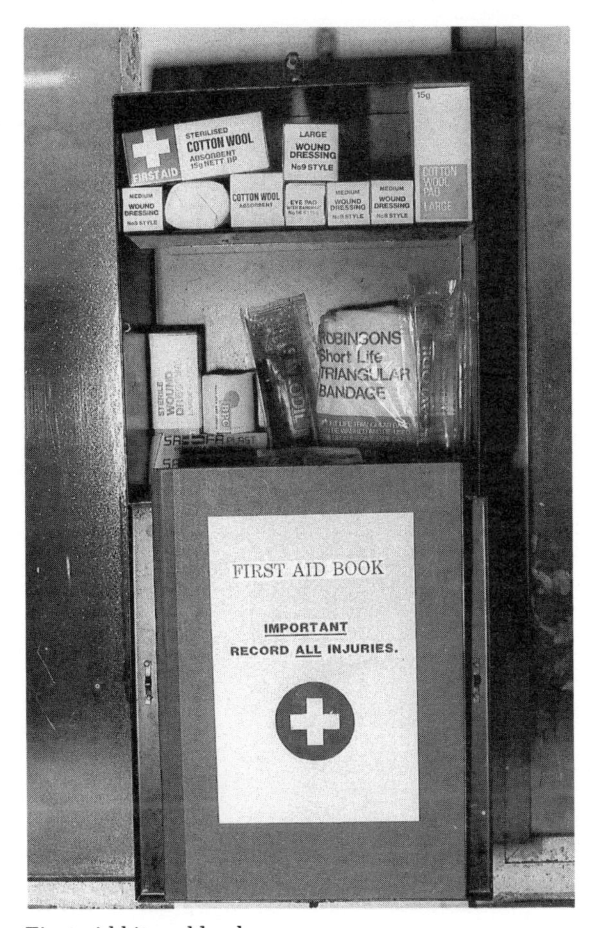

First-aid kit and book

Fire prevention

Fires often start in kitchens and frequently result in injury to the employee and other people on the premises. It is essential that every catering worker should be aware of the dangers and always be on guard to minimise the risk of starting a fire.

Principles

The first principle is that 3 things are needed for a fire to start and that if 1 of them is removed the fire is extinguished. The 3 are:

fuel – something which burns
air – which keeps the fire going
heat – gas, electricity, etc.

The second principle is that fires started by electricity are only to be extinguished by using black (CO_2) or green (halon) extinguishers. Water or foam would conduct electricity. Water should not be used on oil or fat fires as it may cause ignited fat to spread.

Practices

Should a fire start, the following procedure should be followed:

1. Do not panic.
2. Warn other people of the fire.
3. Do not put yourself or others at risk.
4. Follow the fire instructions of the establishment.
5. Close all doors and windows.
6. Turn off gas, electricity and fans.
7. Do not wait for the fire to get out of control before calling the fire brigade.
8. If it is a small fire use the appropriate extinguisher.

In the event of the clothes of a person working in the kitchen catching alight:

Action to be taken Quickly wrap a fire blanket round the person and roll them on the floor. The blanket cuts off the air and the flames will be smothered and put out.

In the event of a fire breaking out in the kitchen:

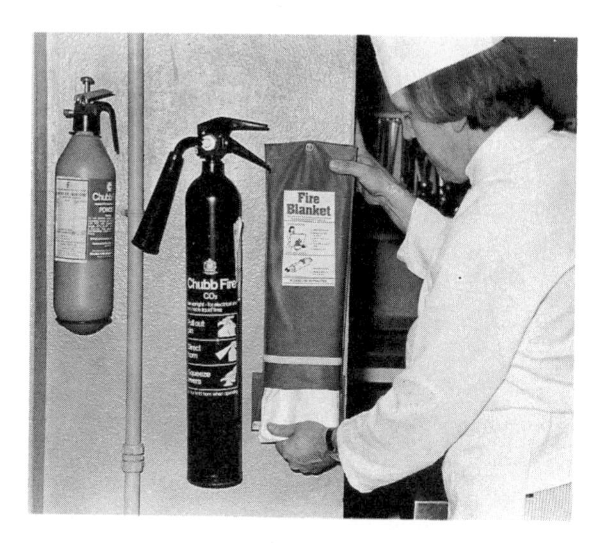

Fire extinguishers and fire blanket

Action to be taken Warn other people and close doors and windows to restrict entry of air. Turn off gas and electricity to remove the fuel. Use the appropriate extinguisher to remove the heat.

In the event of fat or oil igniting and bursting into flames:

Action to be taken Immediately cover the pan with a lid, cloth or fire blanket to exclude air, and quickly turn off the heat.

Working methods

Principles

To obtain efficiency in the kitchen it is necessary (a) to cut waste to a minimum and (b) for cooks to use their time and energy in the most effective manner. To achieve this people working in the kitchen need to know how to work efficiently.

Practices

Cooks need to be able to organise:

a) themselves,
b) the materials and equipment used,
c) the place in which they work.

Self-management

The acquiring of good working habits is most important, as follows:

a) standing well balanced, to distribute the body weight evenly in order to reduce tiredness;
b) working at tables which are the right height;
c) developing a positive mental attitude to do the job to the best of one's ability;
d) to improve performance by taking less time but doing the work better;
e) thinking out the best sequence to adopt when several things have to be done;
f) considering if a more effective method can be employed;
g) developing the habit of cleaning and clearing 'as you go';
h) wearing comfortable clothes and footwear.

Materials and equipment

To improve performance in the kitchen thought should be given to how best to use energy to produce the best results. These examples may be helpful:

a) arrange items to be prepared so that the sequence of work requires the least movement;
b) work methodically, for example, if preparing sprouts, etc., do not drop the trimmings on to the unprepared sprouts, have a separate container for the trimmings;
c) when preparing large quantities of food organise the food so that lifting and moving items is reduced to the minimum;
d) have equipment readily to hand;
e) use mechanical equipment when suitable to save energy and time. Sometimes for small amounts it may not be a saving if the equipment takes a long time to clean after use;
f) fuel should not be wasted – when not required, as appropriate, gas or electricity should be turned down or off.

Organised food preparation

Disorganised food preparation

A well planned kitchen

The kitchen

A well planned kitchen is a great help when trying to saving time and energy. However, in any kitchen the cook can probably work more efficiently by considering these points:

a) ventilation – fans and windows should be used to cool the kitchen without cooling the foods which are to be served hot;
b) noise – excess noise affects working efficiency, therefore noise should be kept to a minimum;
c) movement – siting of tables, sinks, salamanders, services, hot plates, etc., will be fixed but some thought as to the way they are reached may cut down walking.

Hygiene

One of the most important things about cookery is cleanliness – the need for cooks to be clean, for commodities to be used hygienically and for the kitchen to be kept clean. Harmful germs (pathogens) are present, which cannot be seen but may cause illness. Therefore, people, food, equipment and premises must not only look clean, they must *be* clean.

Principles

A knowledge, understanding and application of the law related to cleanliness is essential.

All cooks should have a desire to produce food which is not only enjoyable to eat but *safe* to eat.

Cooks must take pride in their personal hygiene and in the kitchen's hygiene.

Food hygiene regulations

These are legal obligations which can be enforced by an Environmental Health Officer.

Equipment
This must be clean and in good condition at all times.

Personal requirements
1. Clothing must be kept as clean as possible.
2. Cuts, etc., must be covered with a waterproof dressing.
3. All parts of the person liable to come into contact with food must be kept as clean as possible.
4. Spitting is forbidden.
5. Smoking and the use of snuff is forbidden in any room where food is stored or prepared.
6. As soon as a person is aware of suffering from or is a carrier of infection such as typhoid, paratyphoid, dysentery, salmonella or staphylococcal infection the employer must be notified. The employer must notify the Medical Officer of Health.

Premises
1. Toilets must be clean, well lit and ventilated.
2. No food room shall contain or directly communicate with a toilet.
3. A notice requesting people to wash their hands after using the toilet must be prominently displayed.
4. The ventilation of soil drainage must not be in a food room.
5. The water supply to food rooms and toilets is only permitted through an efficient flushing system.

Washing facilities
1. Hand basins with an adequate supply of hot water must be provided.
2. Soap, nail brush, clean towels or warm air machines must be available by hand basins.

Other points
1. First aid bandages, waterproof dressing and antiseptics must be easily accessible.
2. Lockers must be provided for outdoor clothes.
3. Lighting and ventilation must be suitable.
4. Sleeping in food rooms and sleeping rooms adjacent to food rooms are not permitted.
5. Refuse must not be allowed to accumulate in a food room.
6. Buildings must be in good repair to enable them to be cleaned and to keep out rats, mice, etc.

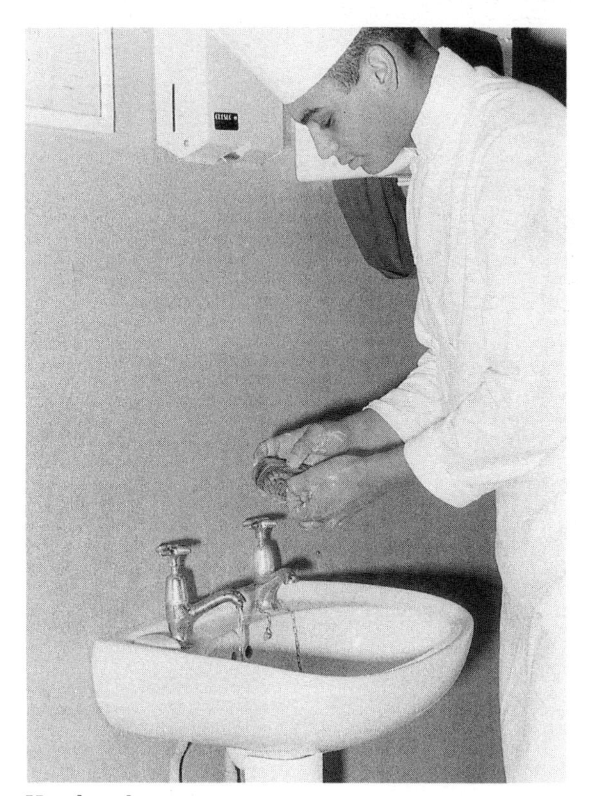

Handwash point

Hygienic disposal

Unhygienic disposal

7. The temperature of meat, fish, gravy, milk, cream and egg products must be kept at temperatures below 10°C.
8. Stored foods must not be placed in a yard, etc., lower than 0.5 metres (18 in.) unless properly protected from possible contamination.

Practices

Personal hygiene

Self-respect and respect for others is important for all people working in kitchens; a high standard of personal hygiene and physical fitness is essential. To help achieve a high standard these points should be practised to prevent germs contaminating food.

1. Bathing – peferably a daily shower or bath.
2. Hands – thoroughly washed frequently, particularly after using the toilet.
3. Jewellery, rings and watches – should not be worn in the kitchen. Rings may harbour food particles, jewellery may fall into food and food may not be properly washed by someone wearing a watch.
4. Hair – should be washed regularly and kept covered when food is handled.
5. Nose, mouth, ears – these should not be

handled as germs from these areas can be transferred on to food.
6. Cuts, burns, etc., should be covered with a waterproof dressing.
7. Smoking must never take place where food is handled – germs can be transferred to the fingers from the mouth or on to work surfaces when the cigarette is put down.
8. Spitting should never occur.
9. Clean clothing – both protective whites and underclothes should be clean and outdoor clothing kept in a locker away from the kitchen.
10. Adequate sleep, relaxation, exercise and fresh air as well as wholesome food and pure water are necessary to maintain good health.

Kitchen hygiene
Kitchens should be well ventilated and well lit and should have ample supplies of hot and cold water. The walls, floors and equipment should be designed with materials which are easy to keep clean.

These guide rules apply to cleaning large and small equipment.

1. Wash in hot water containing detergent.
2. Rinse in hot water.
3. Dry thoroughly.
4. Pay particular care to items difficult to clean, e.g. conical strainers and sieves. Hold under running tap water to force particles out of the holes.
5. Cloths, muslin and piping bags should be boiled, rinsed and dried. Plastic or nylon piping bags should be washed in very hot water and then dried.
6. Remove plugs before cleaning electrical equipment.
7. For cleaning fixed mechanical equipment wash with hot detergent water, rinse and dry both removable and fixed parts.

Food hygiene
It is of the utmost importance that everyone handling food should know how food poisoning is caused and how it must be prevented.

Food poisoning is an illness which develops between 1 and 36 hours after eating affected food, causing stomach pains and diarrhoea, and sometimes vomiting. It may be caused by chemicals accidentally entering food during production, e.g. at the farm or from the container the food is cooked in. Most cases of food poisoning are caused by harmful germs (bacteria) and since these germs can only be seen under a microscope, knowing how their growth can be prevented is essential.

Certain conditions are necessary for bacteria to multiply:

food is of the right kind;
temperature is suitable;
moisture is adequate;
time has elapsed.

Factors in bacterial growth

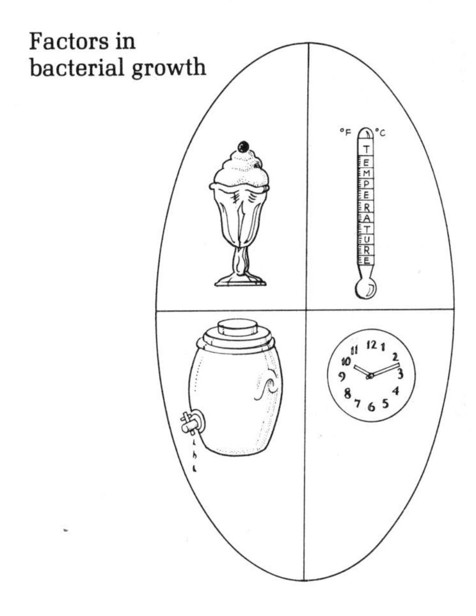

Foods most easily contaminated include the following:
1. Stock, sauces, gravies, soups.
2. Meat and meat products (sausages, pies, cold meats).
3. Milk and milk products.
4. Eggs and egg products.
5. All foods which are handled.
6. All foods which are reheated.

Temperature

1. Bacteria multiply at temperatures between 10°C and 63°C.

2. Foods should therefore not be stored or kept between these temperatures – they should be below 10°C or above 63°C.
3. Washing up water should be at a temperature above 63°C.
4. Boiling kills bacteria.
5. To destroy the poison that bacteria produce requires 30 minutes boiling.
6. Certain bacteria that are more heat-resistant require 4 – 5 hours boiling.
7. Bacteria are not killed by cold, they only stop multiplying.

Moisture
Bacteria require moisture for growth, they cannot multiply on dry foods. Ideal for their growth are jellies, creams, sauces, etc.

Time
Under ideal conditions 1 germ divides into 2 every 20 minutes. Therefore, foods for example stored overnight in a warm place could be contaminated with millions of bacteria by the morning.

Prevention of food poisoning
Two major sources of bacteria are (a) salmonella – from the intestines of animals and humans and (b) staphylococci – from human hands, nose, throat and other parts of the skin.

Salmonella (animal source)
1. Insects and vermin (rats, mice) droppings.
2. Food itself infected, e.g. as with some duck eggs.
3. Cross-contamination, e.g. germs conveyed from cleaning a chicken on a board then cutting cold meat on the uncleaned board.
4. Conveyed by a human being who has the disease or who is a carrier (one who doesn't suffer from food poisoning but passes on the germs to others).

Staphylococci (human source)
Bacteria are present on hands, in the nose and throat, and on sores, spots and boils, etc. Other bacteria which cause food poisoning are found in the soil.

To prevent food poisoning:

1. Stop bacteria multiplying.
2. Prevent bacteria being moved from place to place (cross-contamination).

This is done by:

a) eliminating conditions favourable to growth by controlling the temperature at which food is kept;
b) preventing entry into premises, e.g. excluding vermin, flies, etc.,
c) leaving no food about uncovered;
d) keeping dustbins and swill bins clean and covered with lids;
e) maintaining a high standard of cleanliness of kitchens and equipment;
f) ensuring that washing up is effective and carried out at the correct temperature;
g) storing foods at the correct temperature;
h) paying particular attention to those foods most likely to be contaminated;
i) reheating thoroughly food which has to be reheated.
j) develop clean personal habits in the kitchen, i.e. refraining from smoking, coughing, sneezing, etc., where there is food.

Questions – Practices of cookery

1. The Health and Safety at Work Act states that certain people have responsibilities. Who are they?

2. Why should those working in the kitchen try to do well? In order to obtain j—— s—————————————— .

3. Hygienic, protective, comfortable, hard-wearing and smart, describes what?

4. What is a *carrier* and what must be done when someone is discovered to be a carrier?

5. With what should a small cut on the finger be covered?
6. What must be available by hand basins?
7. Explain why smoking is forbidden in kitchens.
8. State the four conditions necessary for bacteria to multiply.
9. Food should not be stored between which temperatures?
10. What is the source of salmonella and the source of staphylococci bacteria?
11. What is cross-contamination?
12. Why may accidents occur?
13. Why are knives never put in the washing up sink?
14. How does one warn that a handle or lid of a pan removed from the oven is hot?
15. Why should anything spilt on the floor be cleaned up immediately?
16. Before cleaning electrically operated machinery what should be done first?
17. What treatment should be applied to scalds or burns?
18. Three things are required to keep a fire going. What are they?
19. How is a fire put out?
20. In the event of a fire, what is the first thing to be done and what must you not do?
21. Cooks need to organise 3 things. What are they?

Answers can be found on page 156.

18

Principles and practices of presentation

General objectives To understand the principles of presenting food and the need to appreciate the artistic side of cookery.
Specific objectives To develop the skills of use of colour, decoration and garnishing; to acquire the skills of flavouring, seasoning and consistency.

The aim of a cook is to present food so that it is as near perfect as possible. Using both small and large equipment effectively and applying the principles of cooking correctly are two aspects of the cook's work. A third aspect is acquiring and applying artistic skills. These skills are learned through training and experience, and by developing the senses of what smells right, what looks right, what feels right and what tastes right.

Decorated sweets

1. Consistency
2. Texture
3. Flavour
4. Seasoning
5. Colour
6. Decoration
7. Garnishes
8. Accompaniments

These are areas of cooking often concerned with personal opinion and preference, and because of this they require considerable skill on the part of the cook. Personal opinion needs to be guided, and while the creativeness of cooks should be encouraged, it should be developed from a sound foundation of knowledge. Professional cooks have to satisfy the consumer, therefore acceptable standards have to be learned. The principle is that the customer must always think he or she is right. The needs and wants of the consumers must be considered – for example children and the elderly may find what is pleasing to them to be quite different. For example, the texture and taste of marmalade on bacon could appeal to some children, and very green-coloured sweet cakes may not appeal to many people.

To learn artistic skills it is necessary to compare and contrast. If, for example, ten people have made tomato soup, a small amount of each soup could be tasted to assess taste (seasoning and flavour), texture, colour and consistency.

When adjusting seasoning, colour, etc., do so with care. Gradually alter to obtain the required result – a little at a time is the best way. As a general guide, therefore, do not over season, over colour, over decorate or over fill the serving dish. Slightly less rather than slightly more should be the rule.

Foods which should be served at a hot temperature should be hot; cold food should be served cold but not frozen. The consistency of, for example, soups, sauces, stews should be checked when hot. The texture of, for example, ice cream, should be checked so that it is not frozen solid when about to be eaten.

Consistency

The thickness or thinness, that is the consistency, of a soup or sauce depends on a variety of factors:

a) the size of pan – large surface area allows more evaporation, e.g. tomato soup;
b) the faster the cooking the greater the evaporation e.g. white sauce;
c) the quality of the commodities used, e.g. oils in mayonnaise, cornflour;
d) the amount of cooking-out of flour when making a roux or making choux paste.

The skilful cook will correct the consistency during the cooking process and particularly before presentation. It is easier to thin soups or sauces than to thicken them. To thin, add appropriate liquid to obtain the required thickness. To thicken, further cooking may produce evaporation and increase thickness. Sauces such as mayonnaise can be thinned with the addition of vinegar or water, according to taste.

The degree of thickness or thinness will vary according to the use required, e.g. masking or pouring for serving. The proportion of flour to fat in a roux, and the ratio of cornflour to liquid can be varied to affect the thickness of the finished result.

There is a tendency for the sauce in stews and for purée and cream soups to be served too thick. To test for thickness a ladle can be used; soups and sauces should just coat the back of the ladle.

A portion of stew can be plated to check thickness, and to check masking consistency a spoonful of sauce can be spooned over a portion of food on a plate.

Texture

One of the functions of the cook is to give pleasure through the senses of the persons eating the food and this includes the satisfaction from feel. For example, celery or lettuce should feel crisp, steaks should be tender not tough, custard should be smooth not lumpy.

A competent cook knows what the texture should be like when eaten and how to produce the right texture. This means that tasting to test is essential in most instances. To cook spaghetti so that the centre is a little firm (*al dente*), or French beans so that they are just cooked, requires the cook to sample and test with his or her own teeth. Likewise, the smoothness of soup, for example, is best tested with a tasting spoon.

To obtain crisp lettuce it may be necessary to allow it to be in cold water for a time, then drain well and refrigerate. To tenderise meat to alter the texture it may be marinated (steeped or soaked in liquid containing wine or vinegar). Meat carved across the grain produces a much more edible texture than if the cuts are made with the grain, e.g. silverside of beef. If the texture of a soup or sauce is not smooth enough it may be improved by passing through a finer meshed sieve or strainer, or by using a blender or liquidiser for longer time, and then straining.

Cooking alters the texture of foods and the skilled cook will have learned when the right amount of heat has been applied so that the texture is at its best when eaten, e.g. grilled steaks.

Contrasting textures are important for bringing variety and interest to meals, e.g. *croûtons* with purée soup, wafers with ice cream, and crisp biscuits with soft cheeses have contrasting textures.

Flavour and seasoning

Taste is of the utmost importance in cookery. The cook will need to know (a) how to retain the flavour of food and (b) how to alter the flavour of food:

i) so that the flavour is brought out, and
ii) by a combination of ingredients to produce different tastes.

Cooks need to cultivate the ability to discriminate and identify flavour – this will be the result of training and knowledge.

To retain flavour it is necessary to:

a) use foods which are as fresh as possible, e.g. green vegetables, fruit, fish, eggs;
b) use the least amount of cooking liquid, e.g. root vegetables, stews;
c) use the cooking liquid, e.g. fish sauces;
d) use cookery methods best suited to the type of food (refer to section on cookery principles);
e) prepare, cook and serve in as short a time as possible, e.g. fish, eggs and vegetables;
f) take care not to use excess seasoning, as this may prevent the consumer tasting the natural flavour, e.g. too much pepper, salt; too much sugar will not allow the natural flavour to be predominant, e.g. raspberries, strawberries;
h) use herbs and strongly flavoured foods such as onions with care, e.g. half a bayleaf may be better than a whole one as it is strong, and cauliflower soup should taste of cauliflower, not onions;
i) season – the addition of salt and pepper may be before, during, and at the end of cooking; tasting during cooking and adjusting the seasoning at the finish is essential; care should be taken to adjust little by little to prevent over seasoning; a clean spoon should be used, which should be thoroughly washed between each taste.

Herbs and spices are used to bring variety of tastes as well as to stimulate the appetite. They can be used singly, or several can be used together to produce different flavours, e.g. curry powder, mixed spice, faggot of herbs.

Essences

Concentrated flavours can be used in natural or chemical form to increase flavour. For example, fish stock or meat stock can be reduced by boiling until a thick essence of natural flavour is produced. Marmite, which is a vegetable extract, Bovril, which is a meat extract, and stock cubes can be used to give flavour.

Natural and synthetic essences, e.g. almond, vanilla, lemon and raspberry, are available and convenient to use. However, the use of vanilla pods, real lemon juice, fresh raspberries, etc., will give the true flavour.

Flavouring and seasoning is very much a matter of taste but, like all other culinary skills, the ability to taste has to be learned.

Colour

Colour in cookery takes two forms:

a) natural – e.g. red in raw tomatoes, green in cooked cabbage, brown in roasting chicken, baking cakes;
b) artificial – chemical colourings, e.g. red, green, yellow, etc.

Natural colour

Some foods are naturally colourful, others acquire colour during the cooking process and some change colour when cooked.

Competent cooks take care to retain colour of green vegetables such as sprouts, cabbage, spinach. This is achieved by quickly bringing the vegetables to the boil, not covering them with a lid when on the boil and cooking for the minimum time necessary.

Discoloration needs to be prevented, e.g. potatoes must be put into water as soon as they are peeled, lemon juice prevents peeled apples and bananas from going brown.

Browning occurs in the cooking processes of grilling, roasting, frying and baking, and the satisfaction obtained from achieving an appetising brown colour is most rewarding. This skill is learned from experience – from knowledge of the commodities and equipment used, and from developing an aesthetic sense, that is, the developing of an 'eye' to how much colour, or how little, gives the best result.

Commodities such as tomato purée, stock cubes, gravy browning, and strawberry or raspberry purée are examples of items used to give colour. Truffle, which is very expensive and is a form of fungi, is black in colour and used for decorating and flavour.

Ingredients such as parsley, picked or chopped and used sparingly, brighten up the dish. Tomatoes give colour, peas mixed with carrots, and mixed vegetables give plate appeal. Glacé cherries, angelica or crystallised violets can be used to give a colourful effect to pastry dishes.

Decorating and arranging

How foods are arranged on the serving dishes or plate and how they are decorated so that they have eye appeal is a most important aspect of cookery. How to arrange foods so that they look attractive is a skill which is learned, and while individual creativity should be encouraged, certain guidelines should be considered.

Attractive presentation of food

1. Over decorating spoils the effect.
2. Contrasting colours are effective.
3. Dishes or plates should not be overloaded.
4. Variety of ingredients used for decoration makes meals/dishes more attractive.
5. For hygienic reasons foods used for decorating should be handled as little as possible.
6. Foods should be neatly arranged on the dish or plate.
7. Garnishes as a rule are to enhance appearance and taste of the main part of the dish.
8. Some forms of decorating, e.g. cold buffet work, wedding cakes, are of prime importance and can be time-consuming. However, a knowledge of simple, attractive, quickly prepared decoration is important.

Items used for decorating

In the kitchen	Example of use
chopped parsley	sauté potatoes
picked parsley	grilled fish
watercress	roast chicken
lemon	fried fish
In larder work	
cooked vegetables	cold meat dishes and salads
raw vegetables	salads
tomatoes	cold fish dishes and salads
truffle	cold poultry dishes
In pastry work	
glacé cherries	pear condé
whipped cream	meringues, gâteaux
toasted nuts	ice cream, sweets
angelica	trifle

Garnishes

Garnishes are part of the dish and are used to supplement the main ingredient in order to:

a) add contrasting or interesting flavour or appearance,
b) extend, for economic reasons, the bulk of the dish.

Garnishes are served on the dish as a rule because they are part of it, e.g. lamb stew and vegetables, roast beef and Yorkshire pudding, pancakes and lemon, boiled beef and dumplings.

Certain kitchen items are descriptive of traditionally recognised and accepted meaning. When these terms are used on the menu, then the dish would be an accurate representation of the term. For example the use of Doria indicates cucumber.

Examples of garnishes

Main dish	Garnish
Pea soup	peas
Clear soup celestine	pancake strips
Poached eggs florentine	spinach
Tomato omelette	tomato concassé
Fried fish	lemon
Poached fish bonne femme	sliced mushrooms
Boiled salt beef	carrots and dumplings

The term *garnish* is not applied to sweet dishes.

Accompaniments

Many dishes have another item or items served separately, which are known as accompaniments. These items served from the kitchen are part of the dish and are usually separate because:

a) they are best kept away from the main part of the dish until the last moment, e.g. sauce could make the main ingredient soggy;
b) not every person wants the accompaniment, or some may require a little, others a lot, e.g. horseradish sauce;
c) the accompaniment can best be served in this way, e.g. gravy.

Examples of accompaniments

Main dish	Accompaniment
purée, soup	croûtons
fried cod	tartar sauce
roast lamb	mint sauce
curried chicken	rice, poppadums, Bombay duck
ice cream	wafer
smoked salmon	brown bread & butter

19

Menu planning, principles and practices

General objective To understand and apply the knowledge required for the compilation of menus.
Specific objectives To compile menus, considering: portion/cost control, together with nutritional requirements; balance; texture, flavour and colour for various types of people under differing circumstances.

When planning a menu, that is when deciding which dishes are to go together to make up a meal, certain information is required:

a) *who* is to eat the meal?
b) *when* is the meal to be eaten?
c) *where* is the meal to be eaten?

When this is known consideration can be given to producing a *balanced* menu, taking into account:

1. Nutritional needs
2. Variety of ingredients
3. Variety of colour
4. Variety of texture
5. Variety of flavour
6. Facilities available
7. Cooking method
8. Ability of the cook
9. Cost, and portion size

Having considered and decided on these issues, the person producing the menu uses organising skills so that it is correctly cooked, well presented and on time.

Who is to eat the meal?

Meals are planned for people with different requirements, for example men doing heavy manual work will need a different meal to women who sit typing. Children, adolescents, expectant mothers, senior citizens and those with illnesses requiring special diets will all have different needs. Meals for special social occasions, e.g. weddings, parties, discos, etc., will be planned to meet the needs of the occasion.

As a guide, when planning menus the daily requirements to produce a nutritionally satisfactory diet would be:

milk	$\frac{1}{2}$ litre (1 pt), more for children
meat, fish or poultry	once a day
egg, cheese or pulses	daily
fruit	once a day, preferably citrus fruit
vegetables	daily, in addition to potatoes
fats (butter, margarine)	daily
cereals (wholemeal bread or oatmeal)	daily
sugar	daily
water	$1\frac{1}{2}$ litres liquid daily

Food provides energy for the body and the energy value of food is measured in calories or kilojoules. Foods with a high fat content will have a high energy value, those with a lot of water a low energy value. Fats, cheese, bacon and sugar have a high energy value. Men require more calories than women, big men and women more than small men and women. People engaged in energetic work require more calories than those doing less energetic work.

Menus offered in most hotels and restaurants and many schools and hospitals offer a choice of dishes. The responsibility of deciding on a well balanced meal then rests with the person making the selection.

When is the meal to be eaten?

The time of day influences the type of meal to be eaten, so do people's working hours such as shift work, school hours and hospital routines. Social background and geographical area may also dictate when a meal will be eaten. Examples of meal patterns may be:

A	B	C
Breakfast	Breakfast	Breakfast
Dinner	Lunch	Lunch/Dinner/
High tea	Afternoon tea	Snack
Snack	Dinner	Evening meal

Pattern A may be followed in families with children. High tea may be taken by people in the north of England and in Scotland.

Pattern B will be found in hotels. Confusion may occur with the use of the words 'dinner' and 'lunch'. Dinner in hotels is always an evening meal, whereas school dinners are at midday. Influences of tourism and people from other countries living in Britain have broadened eating habits. Both the time of day that meals are served and the kind of dishes served have been affected by such things as TV and advertising.

Light meals and snacks which can be eaten at any time are very popular, as shown by the increase in fast food and self-service operations.

Where is the meal to be eaten?

Originally food was eaten in the home or at the place of work, such as in the fields for those working on the land. Today food is prepared and eaten in a variety of establishments, and this has an effect on the menu.

Hotels	Hospitals	Aeroplanes
Take-aways	Hostels	Licensed premises
Ships	Motels	School
Restaurants	Trains	

Limitation of space on trains and aeroplanes, and the fact that in hospitals and on aeroplanes the food is taken to the person rather than the person going to where the food is, are examples where special consideration needs to be given to how the food is to be prepared and served.

What is to be eaten?

A balanced meal is one in which the nutritional needs are met and variety of ingredients, colour, texture, flavourings and seasoning is taken into account. When compiling a meal or menu, cooking facilities, serving equipment and the capability of the cooks must also be considered.

Colour can be introduced by using vegetables such as carrots, peas or tomatoes, and by using contrasting colouring in a soup or sweet. Different cooking methods are necessary – to serve fish and chips followed by apple fritters would be unwise, as both colour and texture are similar. Repetition of flavour should be avoided, e.g. cauliflower soup followed by a main course served with cauliflower.

Tomato soup	*Egg mayonnaise*
–	–
Roast beef *Yorkshire pudding* *buttered cabbage* *roast potatoes*	*Fried fillet of plaice* *tartar sauce* *fried potatoes* *broccoli*
–	–
Fruit trifle	*Strawberry flan*

These are examples of menus planned according to these principles. In addition, it is usual in some forms of catering to serve more filling types of dish at midday rather than in the evening, e.g. steak and kidney pudding. The number of courses served will depend on the establishment and on the occasion but because a large number of courses may be offered it does not necessarily mean that the meal is a heavy one – it obviously depends on the style of menu and the quantity of food at each course.

Cost

When planning menus the following issues relating to cost should be taken into account:

1. Foods in season will be at their best and cheapest.
2. Foods which are in the store should be utilised, e.g. leftovers should be correctly prepared hygienically, and not wasted.
3. The cheapest food may not necessarily be the best buy.
4. On delivery, check that the quality and quantity meet your requirements.
5. Do not over or under order; reference to recipes will give a guide to amounts to order.

Portion control and costing

Portion control means controlling the size or quantity of food to be served to each customer. The amount of food allowed depends upon the following:

1. The type of customer or establishment.
2. The quality of the food.
3. The price paid for the food.

Portion control should be closely linked with the buying of food and the golden rule should be 'a fair portion for a fair price'.

Portion control equipment can assist in regulating the size of portions, e.g. measured ladles, fruit juice glasses, milk dispensers, tea-measuring machines, individual pie dishes, pudding basins and moulds.

Costing – a catering business like any other business must make sufficient profit in order to survive. It is important, therefore, to know the exact cost of each process and every item produced. Cost control is an important function of management. Every catering worker should be cost conscious and it is useful for cooks and chefs to be able to cost the dishes they prepare. For example, bread and butter pudding (4 portions) could be costed as follows:

Portion control equipment

Portion control equipment

			pence
$\frac{1}{2}$ litre milk	@ 42p per litre	=	21
3 eggs	@ 8p each	=	24
60 g sugar	@ 50p per kilo	=	25
30 g sultanas	@ 100p per kilo	=	4
2 slices buttered bread			8
vanilla essence			2
			84p

The cost of ingredients for 4 portions = 84p, i.e. 21p for 1 portion.

Food cost	To find the selling price multiply the cost price of the food by	If the cost price of food is £1 the selling price is	If cost price is 20p the selling price is	Gross profit
60%	$1\frac{2}{3}$	£1.66	32p	40%
55%	$1\frac{3}{4}$	£1.75	35p	45%
50%	2	£2	40p	50%
45%	$2\frac{2}{9}$	£2.22	44p	55%
40%	$2\frac{1}{2}$	£2.50	50p	60%
$33\frac{1}{3}$%	3	£3	60p	$66\frac{2}{3}$%

Management decides the selling price, which has to take into account cost of labour, rent, rates, heating, lighting, equipment, repairs, maintenance and a fair profit. A typical example would be for the cost of the ingredients to equal 40% of the selling price, with 60% added for all the other expenses. For example, the cost of 1 portion = 21p or 40% (this figure is known as the food cost). To calculate the selling price:

$$\frac{21\text{p} \times 100}{40} = 52.5\text{p}$$

Nutrition

Nutrition is the study of foods and why foods are so important to the body. Without food the body would die. Some foods are better for the body than others, and this needs to be considered if we are to be healthy and free from disease.

1. Energy giving foods

Some foods give the body energy to do all the jobs they have to do and to provide warmth. These foods are known as energy givers and consist of sugars, starches and fats.

fats

sugars

starch

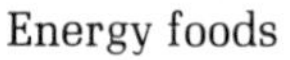

Energy foods

For example:

Sugars
Cakes, pastries, jams, honey, sugar, syrup, fresh and dried fruits

Starches
Potatoes, cereals, bread, flour, pastries

Sugars and starches are called carbohydrates. They supply the body with most of its energy.

Fats
Lard, margarine, butter, dripping, vegetable fats, cooking oils

Fatty foods – meat, bacon, sausages, fried foods, dairy produce, nuts, fatty fish, e.g. herring, salmon

Fats and fatty foods are concentrated sources of energy.

2. Body building foods

This group of foods helps us to grow, and foods within this group all contain a substance called *protein*. There are two types of protein:

Animal protein
Meat, fish, eggs, milk, cheese – excellent body building foods.

Vegetable protein
Peas, beans, lentils, nuts, cereals – good body building foods.

3. Body protecting foods

This group of foods looks after the health of our bodies. These foods contain substances called mineral elements and vitamins, which are found in small quantities in most foods.

Mineral elements
These are required by the body in very small quantities. Calcium, iron, and iodine are the most important of the 19 mineral elements.

Vitamins
These are substances vital to life. They are found in fresh fruits, vegetables, milk, cheese, butter and eggs. Vitamins are named after the letters of the alphabet and the most important ones are A, B, C and D.

Water
This is present in nearly all foods, it is responsible for cleansing the body and helps to keep the body healthy.

Proteins, fats, carbohydrates, vitamins, minerals and water are all known as *nutrients*.

Questions – Menu planning, portion control, costing, nutrition

1. When making a menu there are 9 important considerations. What are they?

   COST — TEXTURE
   COLOUR — STAFF
   BALANCE — WORDING
   SUPPLY — SEASON
   REPETITION

2. Some terms used on menus always refer to an ingredient. What are the ingredients for the following terms?

   a) Lyonnaise (Onion) d) Washington – Sweetcorn
   b) Dubarry (Cauli) e) Condé – Rice
   c) Parmentier (Potatoe)

3. What's where? Complete these places with a suitable word to make an item which is eaten. For example,

   Yorkshire – – – – – – –, the missing word is *pudding*.

   Cornish PASTY
   Chelsea BUN

Devonshire CREAM
Lancashire HOTPOT
Swiss ROLL
Bakewell TART
Eccles CAKE
Brussels SPROUTS
Danish PASTRIES

4. Briefly explain portion control.

5. Name six items of portion control equipment.

6. Who gains when a policy of 'a fair portion for a fair price' is practised?

7. How do honey, and bread and butter, for example, benefit the body? ENERGY PROVIDING

8. Give examples of two body building foods.

MEAT FISH EGGS
cheese milk

They assist in maintaining health of the body

9. What is the function of vitamins?

10.

E V E N P E A S	Every letter helps to
M I N E R A L S	make a word or
U T M U O T Y T	words, 13 of them to
F A T H T W G A	do with nutrition. How
G M S O E A R R	many can you find?
M I L K I T E C	Having found the
F N B O N E N H	words, check that you
I S U G A R E O	know their nutritional
	purpose or function.

11. When will foods be cheapest and at their best?

Answers can be found on page 157.

20

Purchasing

General objectives To be aware of and understand the need for knowledge in buying food and to know the principles of purchasing related to menu planning.
Specific objectives To be able to recognise, select, buy and correctly store foods according to their quality and value for money; to be aware of current market prices of all foodstuffs.

Introduction to purchasing

Purchasing principles

Before a dish of food or a complete meal can be produced, the following six factors must be considered, regarding the purchase of the required ingredients.

1. Recognition
2. Quality
3. Selection
4. Quantity
5. Cost
6. Buying
7. If stored – how stored

Selection of the most suitable ingredients will depend upon the situation in which the dish or meal will be served. As a guide, the following points should be noted:

a) cheapest may not be best;
b) foods will cost less in season and be at their best;
c) fresh foods should be as fresh as possible and used as soon as possible after purchase.

Irrespective of the kind of establishment – hospital, hotel, restaurant, school, or whether in an aeroplane, train or wherever, cooks need to learn to recognise quality and to distinguish the various foods used in cookery, and to discriminate so that the best use is made of what is available. Competency in purchasing is acquired by experience based on knowledge of the ingredients and commodities used in the kitchen.

Meat

A knowledge of meat is necessary before buying, preparing, cooking and serving – the various types, joints and cuts of meat; how to recognise quality; joints that are tender, and those that are tough; the cost and the food value should be understood.

Storage of meat

1. Fresh meat must be hung to allow it to become tender.
2. The approximate time for hanging is up to 14 days at 1°C.
3. Meat carcasses should be hung on meat hooks.
4. Joints of meat should not remain in the blood issuing from them.
5. Meat should be kept refrigerated at all times.

Nutritive value
Meat contains protein, fat, water, iron and vitamins. It is therefore an important body building food and a source of energy.

Beef

How to recognise quality in beef

1. Lean meat should be bright red with small flecks of white fat in the meat (known as marbling).
2. Fat should be firm, creamy white in colour and odourless.

Offal is the name given to the edible parts taken from the inside of the animal. Most beef offal is known as ox, e.g. ox heart, ox tongue, etc.

Beef offal

Name	Use	Cost per lb
Tripe	boiling, braising	
Heart	boiling, braising	
Ox liver	braising, frying	
Ox kidney	braising, stewing, soup	
Ox tongue	salting then boiling, braising	
Ox tail	braising, soup	

Use	Joint	Cost per lb
Roasting	sirloin ribs topside wing fore ribs	
Frying	fillet sirloin rump	
Stewing	shin thick flank chuck	
Boiling	silverside brisket thin flank	
Braising	topside middle rib fore rib	
Grilling	rump sirloin in steaks – fillet	

Sticking piece, leg of mutton cut and shank are used for various purposes, e.g. stewing, mincing etc.

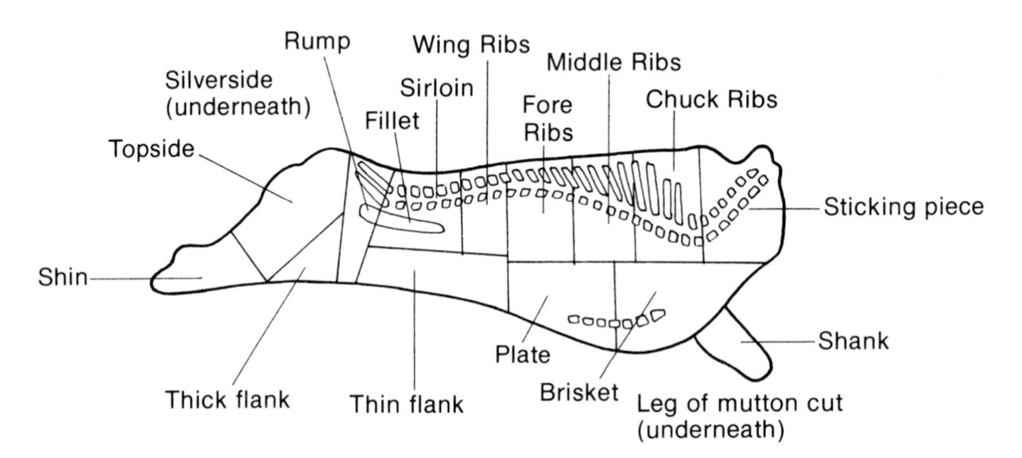

Side of beef

Veal

Veal is the meat from the young cow (calf).

Quality and purchasing points

1. The flesh of veal should be pale pink, and firm, not soft and flabby.
2. Cut surfaces must not be dry, but moist.
3. Bones in young animals should be pinkish white, porous and with a small amount of blood in their structure.
4. The fat should be firm and pinkish white.
5. The kidney ought to be firm and well covered with fat.

Uses	Joints	Cost per lb
Roasting	loin best end leg	
Frying and grilling	loin (chops) best end (cutlets) leg (escalopes)	
Braising	shoulder knuckle and leg	
Stewing	shoulder breast knuckle	
Sauté	shoulder leg	

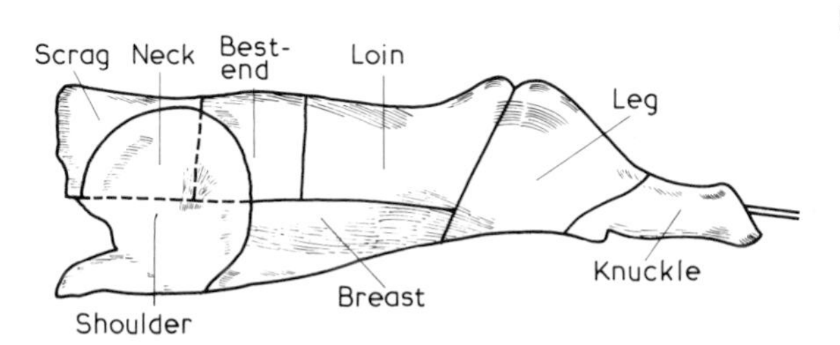

Side of veal

Lamb and mutton

Quality and purchasing points

1. Lamb is under 1 year old – after 1 year it is termed mutton.
2. The carcass should be compact and evenly fleshed.
3. The lean flesh of lamb and mutton ought to be firm, a pleasing, dull red colour and have a fine texture or grain.
4. The fat should be evenly distributed, hard, brittle, flaky and clear white in colour.
5. The bones should be porous in young animals.

Use	Joint	Cost per lb
Roasting	leg shoulder best end loin saddle breast	
Grilling and frying	cutlets (from the best end) loin chops double chops (from the saddle) fillet	
Stewing	shoulder breast middle neck	
Boiling	leg (mutton)	

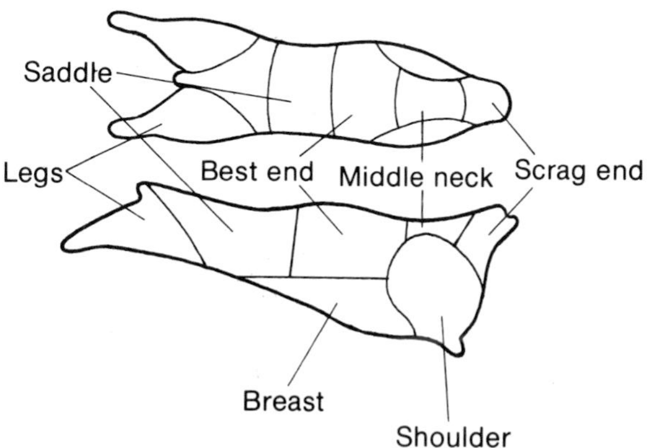

Carcass

Pork

The keeping quality of pork is less than that of any other meat, therefore the greatest care is needed in its handling, preparation and cooking. Pork must always be well cooked and never left underdone.

Quality and purchasing points
1. Lean flesh of pork should be pale pink.
2. The fat should be white, firm, smooth and not excessive.
3. Bones must be small, fine and pinkish.
4. The skin, or rind, ought to be smooth and without hair.

Use	Joint	Cost per lb
Roasting	leg loin spare rib shoulder	
Boiling	leg belly	
Frying and grilling	loin (chops)	
Pies and sausage	shoulder spare rib	

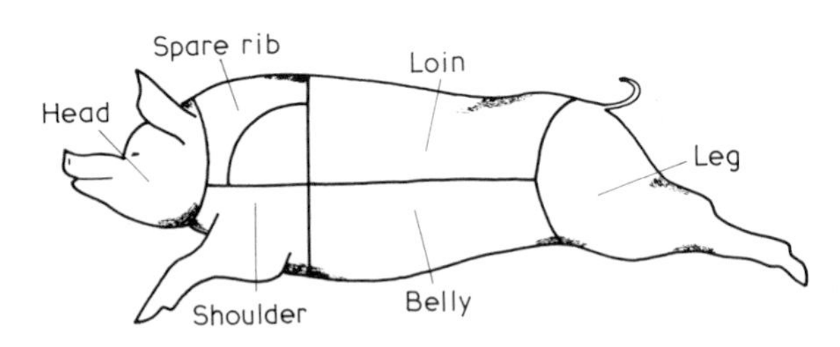

Side of pork

Bacon

Bacon is the cured flesh of the pig. *Green bacon* is cured in brine but not smoked. *Smoked bacon* is cured and smoked – the keeping quality of smoked bacon is longer than that of green bacon.

Quality and purchasing points
1. There should be no sign of stickiness.
2. There must be no unpleasant smell.
3. The rind should be thin, smooth and free from wrinkles.
4. The fat ought to be white, smooth and not excessive in proportion to the lean.
5. The lean meat of bacon should be deep pink in colour and firm.

Use	Joint		Cost
Boiling	gammon hock collar		
Grilling and frying	collar back streaky gammon	in rashers	

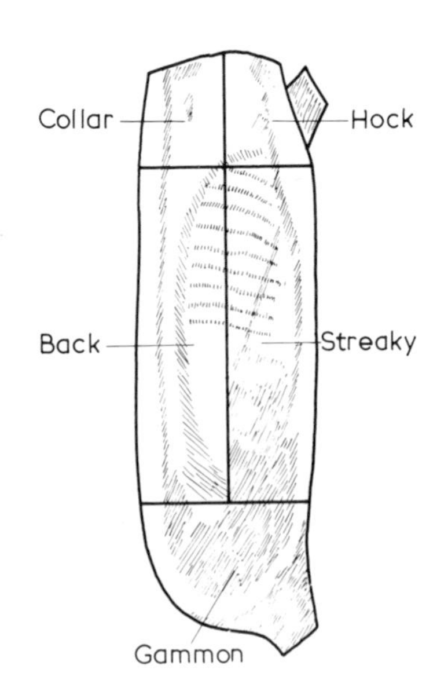

Side of bacon

Ham

A ham is the hind leg of a pig, which is preserved by curing, drying and smoking.

English hams are cooked by boiling or steaming and are eaten either hot or cold in a variety of ways. Some imported hams, e.g. Parma (Italy), Bayonne (France), are cured, dried and smoked, then cut into paper-thin slices and eaten raw as an hors d'oeuvre or in salads and sandwiches.

Poultry

Poultry is the name given to domestic birds which are bred for food.

Structure and food value
Poultry flesh has a similar composition to meat; it contains protein and is therefore useful for building and repairing body tissues and providing heat and energy. But because the fibres are shorter and the flesh is not interlaced with fat it is more easily digested than meat. The flesh of the legs is coarser and darker because of greater muscular activity and is less digestible than the breast and wing. Poultry legs divide into two pieces, the drumstick and thigh. These are known as dark meat. The breast and wing are referred to as white meat.

Storage
Once poultry has been *drawn* (the innards removed) it should be put in a refrigerator.

Frozen birds must be stored in a deep freeze cabinet and should always be removed in sufficient time for them *to thaw out completely* before being used. This is important because of the dangers of contamination by salmonella bacteria, which cause food poisoning (see page 120).

Quality and purchasing points
1. Birds must be free from any unpleasant smell.
2. The flesh must be firm and show no trace of blue or greenish tinge.
3. The breast should be plump.
4. The vent end of the breast bone should be pliable when squeezed between the fingers.
5. The skin should be unbroken.

Fish

Fish can be divided into three groups, as follows:

Oily fish
This group includes herring, mackerel, salmon. All oily fish are round in shape and, when filleted, give two fillets.

White fish
These are:
a) round in shape, e.g. cod, whiting, haddock;
b) flat in shape, e.g. plaice, sole, turbot.

All flat fish, when filleted, give four fillets, two large and two small.

Shellfish
This group includes crabs, prawns, lobster.

Food value
Fish are valuable not only because they contain protein and are a good body building food but also because they are suitable for lots of menus and can be cooked and presented in a wide variety of ways.

Quality
The points of quality to look for when buying fresh fish are as follows:

1. Eyes – bright, full and not sunken.
2. Gills – bright and fresh looking.
3. Flesh – firm to the touch.
4. Scales – should be moist and plentiful.
5. Skin – should be covered with a fresh sea slime or be smooth and moist.
6. Smell – a pleasant, fishy smell.

Purchasing points for fresh fish
1. It is essential to buy absolutely fresh as it deteriorates very quickly, especially oily fish and shellfish, therefore buy daily.

2. Where possible buy direct from the market or supplier.
3. Fish should be transported refrigerated and covered with crushed ice, so that it arrives in good condition.
4. The flesh of the fish must not be broken or damaged.
5. Fish may be bought on the bone or off the bone (filleted).
6. Fish of moderate size are superior in flavour and have finer flesh than large fish.

When filleting the approximate loss from boning and waste is 50 – 60%.

Storage
1. Fresh fish are stored either in a fish box containing ice, in a separate refrigerator, or in a part of a refrigerator used only for fish.
2. The temperature must be kept just above freezing point.
3. Frozen fish must be stored in a deep freeze cabinet.
4. Smoked fish should be kept in a refrigerator.

Preservation
Fish are preserved in four ways:
1. Freezing – many varieties of fish, either on the bone or filleted, are deep frozen.
2. Tinning – oily fish, e.g. sardines and salmon, are tinned (a) in their own juice (b) in oil or (c) in tomato sauce.
3. Salting and smoking – e.g. haddock, salmon, mackerel, trout, eel, sprats, cod's roe and herring (which are then known as kippers).
4. Pickling – herring are filleted, rolled and pickled in vinegar (then known as rollmops).

Cooking fish
Fish may be cooked by steaming, poaching, boiling, grilling, baking, shallow and deep frying. Certain fish are not cooked, apart from the smoking or curing process, e.g. salmon, smoked trout, smoked mackerel, smoked eel.

Vegetables

Vegetables are important foods. They may be used in many ways, both cooked and raw:
a) as accompaniments to meals;
b) as separate courses within a menu;
c) for soups;
d) for flavouring stocks and sauces, and fish, meat, poultry and game dishes;
e) in hors-d'oeuvre and salads;
f) as a substitute for meat in vegetarian cookery.

Food value
If vegetables are fresh, correctly handled and correctly cooked they contribute vegetable protein, carbohydrates and vitamins to the body.

All vegetables are parts of plants.

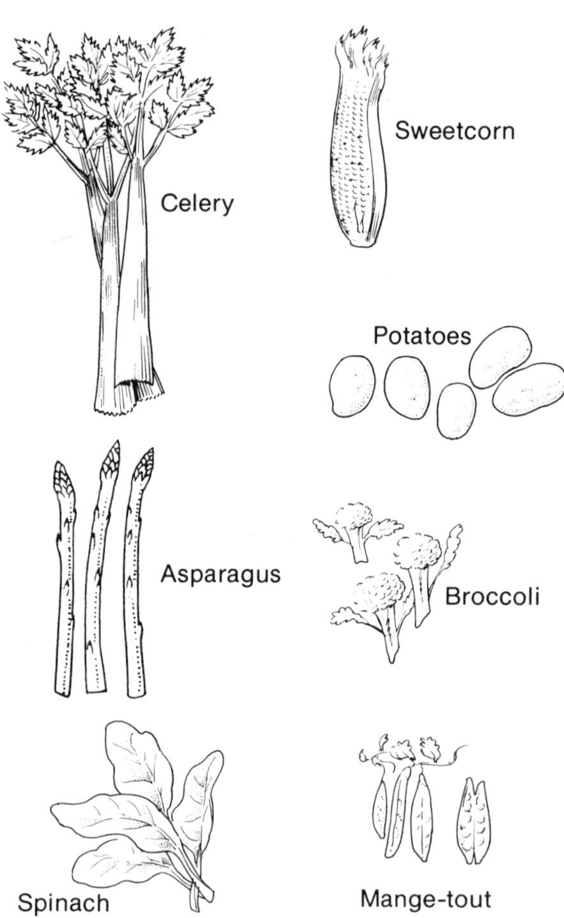

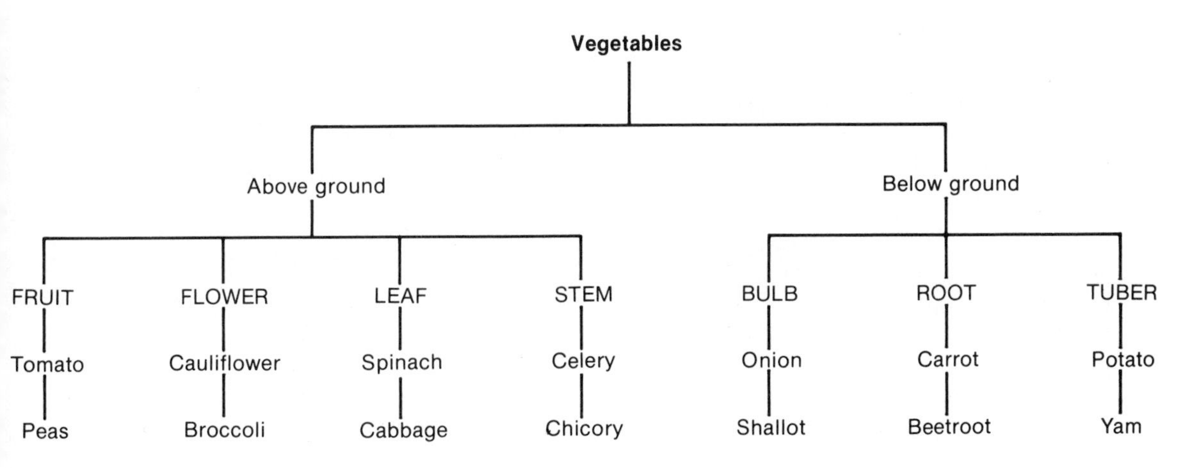

Root vegetables

These are of different types, e.g.
Roots – carrots, turnips, beetroot;
Bulbous roots – onions, shallots, leeks;
Tubers – potatoes, Jerusalem artichokes yams, sweet potatoes.

1. All root vegetables should be clean and free from soil – earth increases weight and consequently the price.
2. They should be sound, firm and undamaged.
3. There should be no sign of sprouting.

Green vegetables

These are of different types, e.g.
Flowers or head – cauliflower, broccoli;
Leaves – cabbage, lettuce, spinach, sprouts;
Fruit – cucumber, tomato, beans, peas;
Blanched stems – celery, chicory, sea-kale.

1. The leaves should be a fresh green colour, crisp and not wilted.
2. Cabbage and sprouts should be compact, with tightly growing leaves.
3. Cauliflower should have closely grown flower which is firm and white, with no excess of stalk or outside leaves.
4. Peas and beans should be crisp and of medium size. Pea pods should be full and beans not stringy.
5. Blanched stems must be firm, white, crisp and free from soil.

Fungi

Mushrooms, cèpes, morels.

Fruit seeds

When dried, these are known as pulses, e.g. peas, beans.

Quality and purchasing points
Freshness in all vegetables is very important, therefore they should be bought daily. The best flavour and food value is found in freshly picked vegetables.

Storage
1. Storage destroys some of the vitamin C in vegetables, therefore do not store unnecessarily.
2. Green vegetables and salad vegetables should be stored on well ventilated racks in a cool temperature.
3. Root vegetables should be emptied from containers and stored on well ventilated racks in a cool, dry place.
4. Potatoes should be stored in a cool, dark, dry place because warmth will cause them to sprout, light turns them green and damp causes rot.

Preservation of vegetables
Vegetables are preserved in the following ways:

1. Tinning – e.g. carrots, celery, peas, tomatoes.
2. Dehydration – e.g. onions, carrots, cabbage, potatoes are shredded and quickly dried to remove most of their water content.
3. Drying – e.g. peas, beans are removed from the pods and dried, reducing their moisture content to 10%. These are known as pulses.
4. Pickling – e.g. onions, red cabbage are pickled in spiced vinegar.
5. Accelerated freeze drying – e.g. peas, beans, sprouts, spinach, cauliflower.

Fruit

Fruit is an important source of food because:

a) there is such a wide variety,
b) they are so popular,
c) they can be eaten raw,
d) they can be cooked in a variety of ways.

Food value
Fruit contains vitamins and is helpful to the body as a protective food.

When fresh vegetables are in season

Spring		
asparagus	greens	broccoli – white and purple
artichokes, Jerusalem	cauliflower	new potatoes
new carrots	new turnips	
Summer		
artichokes, globe	turnips	asparagus
cauliflower	aubergine	cos lettuce
beans, broad	peas	radishes
beans, French	carrots	sea-kale
sweetcorn		
Autumn		
artichokes, globe	parsnips	field mushrooms
artichokes, Jerusalem	aubergine	peppers
beans, runner	cauliflower	red cabbage
salsify	celery	shallots
celeriac	swedes	marrow
turnips		
Winter		
Brussels sprouts	chicory	cabbage
kale	celery	parsnips
cauliflower	broccoli	red cabbage
Savoy cabbage	celeriac	swedes
turnips		
All the year round		
Although the following vegetables are available all the year round, nevertheless at certain times, owing to bad weather, a heavy demand or other circumstances, supplies may be temporarily curtailed.		
beetroot	leeks	cabbage
mushrooms	carrots	onions
cucumber	spinach	lettuce
tomatoes	watercress	potatoes

Types of fruit

Soft fruits	Stone fruits	Citrus fruits	Hard fruits	Other fruits	
Raspberries	Cherries	Oranges	Apples	Bananas	Kiwi
Strawberries	Damsons	Lemons	Pears	Pineapples	Passion fruit
Loganberries	Plums	Limes		Dates	Mango
Gooseberries	Apricots	Grapefruits		Figs	Lychee
Blackberries	Greengages	Tangerines		Grapes	Papaya
Redcurrants	Peaches	Kumquat		Melon	
Blackcurrants				Rhubarb	

For kitchen purposes fruit can be classified as above:

Quality and purchasing points
1. Because soft fruits deteriorate quickly they must be undamaged and not over-ripe when bought.
2. Soft fruit should look fresh – there should be no sign of wilting, shrinking or mould.
3. The colour of soft fruits is a good indication of their quality and ripeness, but this needs to be learnt by experience.
4. Hard fruits such as apples and pears should not be bruised.
5. Hard fruits should be purchased just before peak ripeness is reached. This can be tested in pears by gentle pressure with the thumb at the base of the fruit.

Storage

Hard fruits, e.g. apples, are left in boxes in a cool store.

Soft fruits, e.g. raspberries are left in punnets or boxes in a cold room.

Stone fruits, e.g. plums, are placed on trays. Peaches are left in their delivery trays.

Bananas should not be stored in too cold a place, otherwise the skins go black.

Preservation of fruit

Fruits are preserved in many ways:

1. Drying – apples, pears, apricots, figs. Plums when dried are called prunes, and currants, sultanas and raisins are produced by drying grapes.
2. Canning – almost all fruits may be canned.
3. Candied – orange and lemon peel.
4. Glacé – cherries.
5. Jam – most fruits can be made into jam.
6. Freezing – strawberries, raspberries, loganberries, apples and plums.
7. Cold storage – apples can be stored at a temperature 1 – 4°C.
8. Gas storage – fruit can be stored in an atmosphere in which the oxygen content is decreased and carbon dioxide increased.

Uses

With the exception of certain fruits, e.g. lemon, rhubarb, cranberries, fruit can be eaten cooked or raw. If fruit is to be eaten at its best when raw, then extra care is needed with its selection. To obtain maximum flavour and sweetness from any fruit it must be eaten at peak ripeness.. Some fruits, e.g. apples, pears, cherries, gooseberries, have both dessert and cooking varieties.

Nuts

Nuts are the kernel (seed) of the tree or plant from which they come; they are perishable and may easily become rancid or infested with insects.

Uses

Nuts are used extensively in pastrywork, confectionery, vegetarian cooking, the making of some liqueurs and as snacks, e.g. almonds, Brazils, hazelnuts, walnuts, peanuts.

Food value
Nuts are highly nutritious because they contain protein, fat and mineral salts, and therefore are a food that helps with the building and repair of the body, and provision of energy to the body. Nuts are difficult to digest.

Quality and purchasing points
1. Nuts should be of good size.
2. They should be heavy for their size: this indicates that they are well filled.
3. There must be no sign or smell of mildew.

Storage
1. Dessert nuts – those with the shell on keep in a dry ventilated store.
2. Shelled nuts, whether whole, ground, nibbed or flakes, keep in airtight containers.

Milk

Milk is the liquid produced by all female mammals for feeding their young, as it is an ideal food for the very young of each particular species. Cow's milk is used almost exclusively in catering. Milk contains fat (known as butterfat); skimmed and semi-skimmed milk have lower fat content.

Food value
Because of the high nutritive value of milk it is the most complete single food known. Milk contains all the nutrients for growth, repair, energy, protection, and regulation of the body.

Storage
Milk is an excellent food for human beings. It is, unfortunately, also an excellent food for bacteria, therefore it must be stored carefully.

1. Milk should be kept in the container in which it is delivered.
2. Milk must be stored in the refrigerator.
3. It should be kept covered, as it absorbs smells such as fish.
4. Milk and cream should be purchased daily.
5. Tinned milk should be stored in a dry, ventilated room.
6. Dried milk is kept in airtight tins in a dry store.
7. Imitation cream is kept in the refrigerator.

Preservation of milk
Powdered milk – once reconstituted treat it as carefully as fresh.
Evaporated milk – is concentrated homogenised milk without sugar. Unopened it keeps almost indefinitely.
Condensed milk – is condensed to twice the concentration of fresh milk, with sugar added. Unopened it keeps indefinitely.

Uses of milk
1. Soups and sauces.
2. Cooking of vegetables, fish and gnocchi.
3. Puddings, cakes, sweet dishes.
4. Hot and cold drinks.

Cream

This is the concentrated milk fat which is skimmed off the top of the milk, and it should contain 18% butterfat. Cream for whipping must contain more than 30% butterfat.

Cream	Fat content	Cost	Uses
Single	18%		Pouring cream for sweet dishes, finishing stews, sauces and soups.
Whipping	35%		Decorating sweet dishes, cakes.
Double	48%		Decorating sweet dishes, cakes.
Clotted	55%		Served with cream teas and fresh fruit.

Use of cream
1. Cream must be cold when required for whipping.
2. Whip in a china or stainless steel bowl.
3. Over-whipping turns cream into butter. This is more likely to happen in hot weather. To prevent this happening, put the bowl of cream in a bowl of ice while whisking.
4. When adding cream to hot liquids dilute

the cream with some of the liquid before adding to the main bulk to prevent the cream separating.

Yoghurt

Yoghurt is a curd-like food prepared from milk fermented by the action of bacteria.

Types of yoghurt

1. Fat free – less than 5% milk fat.
2. Low fat – contains maximum 1.5% milk fat.
3. Whole milk – contains fat as in whole milk.
4. Real fruit – contains whole fruit.
5. Fruit flavoured – contains fruit juice.

Cheese

Cheese is made from the milk of cows, goats or ewes. There are many hundred varieties of cheese, most countries manufacturing their own special cheeses.

Food value

Cheese is a highly concentrated form of food, with a very high nutritive value. It is therefore an excellent body building, energy giving, protective food. Cheese is difficult to digest because it contains a high percentage of fat.

Quality and purchasing points

1. The skin or rind of cheese should not show spots of mildew – this is a sign of damp storage.
2. Cheese, when cut, should not give off an over-strong smell – this is an indication of ammonia.
3. Hard, semi-hard and blue vein cheese when cut should not be dry.
4. Soft cheese when cut should not appear runny but should have a delicate, creamy consistency.
5. Freshly cut cheese should look fresh, with no dry areas or beads of fat on the surface.
6. Cut, pre-wrapped cheese should show no evidence of mould, moisture, or greasiness inside the packing.
7. Vacuum-packed cheese will keep longer than loosely wrapped cheese.

Storage

1. Cheese should be kept in a cool, dry, well ventilated place.
2. Whole cheeses should be turned occasionally.
3. Cheese should be kept away from other food which may be spoilt by the smell, e.g. eggs.

Preservation of cheese

Certain cheeses may be preserved by processing. A hard cheese can be ground to a fine powder, melted with milk, poured into moulds and wrapped in foil, e.g. Kraft, Primula.

Types

There are four main types of cheese, with numerous varieties of each – hard, semi-hard, soft or cream, and blue vein. Each type of cheese is usually named after its place of origin, e.g. Stilton. Hard cheeses, e.g. Cheddar, Cheshire, Leicester and Parmesan have better keeping qualities than soft cheeses because they contain less water.

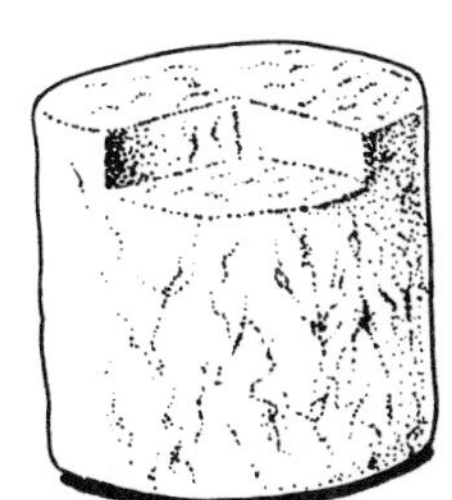

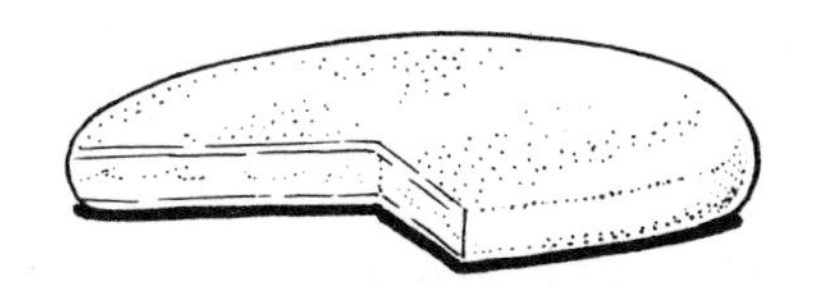
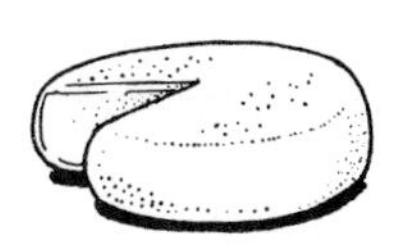

Stilton, Edam, Brie and Camembert

Uses

Cheese has many uses in cookery:

1. Soups – grated on top of the soup and browned or offered separately, e.g. onion soup.
2. Pasta – grated hard cheese (traditionally Parmesan) is mixed in or served with almost all pasta dishes, e.g. macaroni cheese.
3. Eggs – grated cheese mixed in or as a topping for a wide variety of egg dishes, e.g. omelets, poached eggs, soft and hard boiled eggs.
4. Vegetables – grated cheese mixed in with a number of potato dishes and used as a topping for many potato and vegetable dishes, e.g. cauliflower.
5. Fish – grated cheese as a topping for some fish dishes.
6. Pancakes – stuffed savoury pancakes often include cheese among the fillings, and may be topped with a cheese sauce.
7. Quiche or savoury flans – these are prepared with a wide variety of fillings, many of which include cheese.
8. Savouries and soufflés, e.g. Welsh rarebit, cheese soufflé.

Fats and oils

A wide choice of fats and oils is available but they should be carefully selected for specific cooking needs if the best possible results are to be obtained.

Animal fats

These must all be kept in a cold store, preferably under refrigeration. Butter is produced from the cream of milk – 1 litre (2 pints) of cream produces approximately $\frac{1}{2}$ kg (1 lb) butter.

Food value

Because butter is a high fat food it gives energy to the body.

Quality

1. A good butter is sweet and nutty, not over salty and free from oiliness, acidity and excessive moisture.
2. Butter should smell fresh and taste creamy and pleasant.
3. The texture should be soft and smooth and the colour almost white or pale yellow.
4. Fresh butter should be used fairly quickly, otherwise it goes rancid, which means that it acquires an unpleasant taste and smell.

Uses of butter

Good butter adds a pleasant flavour to all foods and has the following uses in cookery:

1. Soups, sauces, pot roasting, finishing vegetables.
2. Cakes, biscuits, pastry.
3. Shallow frying certain foods.
4. Eggs – omelets, scrambled and fried eggs.

Lard is the rendered fat from the pig. Good quality lard is a pure white fat. Mixed with butter or margarine, it can be used for certain cakes and pastry. It can also be used for shallow and deep frying.

Suet is prepared beef fat, the best of which is obtained from around the kidneys of the animal. Beef suet is used for suet pastry, stuffing and mince meat (sweet).

Dripping is obtained from clarified animal fats and can be used for shallow or deep frying.

Vegetable fats

Margarine is manufactured from milk and an oil produced from a vegetable, e.g. palm, ground-nut, coconut, cotton-seed, sunflower, sesame, soya or tea-seed.

Food value

Margarine is an energy giving and protective food. Vitamins A and D are added during its production.

Quality

There are several grades of margarine and some are blended with butter. Taste is the best guide to quality.

Uses of margarine in cookery

Margarine can be used in place of butter but neither the smell nor the flavour are so pleasant. It is not as suitable as butter for finishing sauces. Margarine is equally nutritious and may be cheaper than butter.

Compound fats are produced from refined, extracted vegetable oils, to give fats which may be used for cooking purposes, e.g. frying, cakes and pastry.

Vegetable oils

Vegetable oils are often preferred to animal fats for deep frying because higher temperatures can be reached without smoking. Varieties of oil include olive, corn, ground-nut, sunflower-seed, walnut, grape seed, sesame seed, almond and wheatgerm.

Storage

1. Oil should be kept in a cool place.
2. If refrigerated, some oils congeal; they return to a fluid state in a warm temperature.
3. Oils keep for a fairly long time, but they will go rancid if not kept cool.

Uses of oil in cookery

1. High quality oils are used in making vinaigrettes, mayonnaise, hors-d'oeuvre and salads.
2. Oils are used in making some pasta.
3. For shallow frying (and certain oils for deep frying).
4. For lubricating trays, moulds, utensils and marble slabs to prevent sticking.

Eggs

The term 'eggs' applies not only to hens' eggs, which are one of the most valuable ingredients in cooking because of their many uses, but also to the eggs of other birds such as turkeys, geese, ducks, guinea-fowl, quail and gulls, which are also used but in a much more limited way.

Food value

As eggs contain most nutrients, they are a protective food and provide energy and material for growth and repair of the body.

Quality and buying points

1. Eggshells should be clean, well shaped, strong and slightly rough.
2. When broken there should be a higher proportion of thick white to thin white.
3. Yolks should be firm, round and of a good even colour.

Stale eggs

As eggs become stale, the thick white gradually changes into thin white, the yolk loses shape and begins to flatten, water evaporates from the eggs and is replaced by air, so as air is lighter than water, fresh eggs are heavier than stale ones.

Egg sizes – hens eggs are graded in 7 sizes according to weight:

Size 1 – 70 g 4 – 55 g 6 – 45 g
2 – 65 g 5 – 50 g 7 – under 45 g
3 – 60 g

Storage

1. Eggs must be stored in their packing trays, blunt end upwards, in a cool but not too dry place. A normal refrigerator temperature is ideal.
2. Because eggshells are porous eggs can absorb strong odours, so keep them away from strong smelling foods such as cheese, onions and fish.

Uses of eggs in cooking

1. Hors-d'oeuvre – hard-boiled for egg mayonnaise and salads.
2. Soups – clarifying clear soups, enriching soups.
3. Egg dishes – scrambled, poached, boiled, omelet, etc.
4. Farinaceous – making pastes for noodles, ravioli, etc.
5. Fish – in frying batters, for egg and crumbing.
6. Sauces – mayonnaise, hollandaise, sabayon.
7. Meat and poultry – for binding mixtures, e.g. Vienna steaks, chicken cutlets and for coating for crumbing.
8. Salads – usually hard-boiled and included in many composed salads.
9. Sweets and pastries – used extensively in many ways.
10. Savouries – e.g. Scotch woodcock, savoury flans.

Cereals

Cereals are the seeds or grains of cultivated grasses, and are important for they are the staple foods in the diets of most human beings. They are easily grown, easy to transport, relatively cheap, can be stored for long periods and are easily prepared and cooked.

Food value

Cereals are one of the best of the energy giving foods because they contain large percentages of starch. Wholegrain cereals provide vitamin B and are therefore a protective food.

Storage of cereals

1. Store in a cool, dry, well ventilated place.
2. Damp air must never be allowed near cereals, for they will absorb moisture and go mouldy.
3. The store must not be warm otherwise mould may develop on the cereals.
4. Keep cereals in pest-free containers and examine them periodically for insects.

Types of cereal

Wheat

This is milled in various ways to produce the following products:

Rice

This is available in several types, as follows:

1. Long grain white or brown Patna or Basmati types, which have a slender pointed grain, a firm structure which when cooked remains fluffy and dry, and are suitable for savoury dishes.
2. Medium grain – absorbs more liquid than long grain; suitable for sweet and savoury dishes. Carolina type.
3. Short grain – the cheapest rice. Small, chalky coloured round or oval grains which absorb a great deal of liquid. Used for puddings and sweet dishes.
4. Wild rice – the seed of an aquatic plant related to the rice family. It has a distinctive nutty flavour suitable for savouries and is expensive.
5. Ground rice – used for milk puddings.
6. Rice flour – used for thickening soups and stews.
7. Rice paper – thin, edible paper used for macaroons and nougat.

Tapioca is prepared from the tuber of the cassava plant. There are four types: seed pearl, medium pearl, pearl, and flake. Tapioca is used for milk puddings and for thickening soups, stews.

Cereal	Type	Uses
Flour	Strong	bread, buns puff pastry
Flour	Medium or general purpose	cakes, scones, pastry
Flour	Soft	sponges, biscuits
Flour	Wholemeal	bread, pastry
Semolina		milk pudding, gnocchi, pasta
Oats	coarse medium fine	porridge, muesli, oatcakes
Barley	pearl fine flour roasted	soups, stews barley water, thickening soups malt – for making vinegar
Maize (corn)		breakfast cereals, cornflour, corn oil
	cornflour	thickening soups, sauces, custard powder, cakes
Rye		black (rye) bread, rye biscuits

Sago is prepared from the pith of the sago palm, shaped into small round pellets, and used for milk puddings and soups.

Arrowroot is prepared from the underground stems of the maranta plant. It is easily digested, has a delicate flavour and is used for milk puddings, cakes, biscuits and thickening sauces and glazes.

Potato flour is a preparation from potatoes suitable for thickening soups, sauces, and stews.

Raising agents

A raising agent is added to some frying batters, cake and bread mixtures to give lightness to the mixture. This lightness is based upon the principle that gases expand when heated. The gases used are air, carbon dioxide or steam (water vapour).

Types of raising agent

1. *Baking powder* is made from 1 part sodium bicarbonate to 2 parts cream of tartar. When used under the right conditions baking powder produces carbon dioxide gas. *Uses*: sponge puddings, cakes, scones, suet puddings, dumplings.
2. *Yeast* is a living organism and a plant of the fungi group, of which there are several types. When yeast in a mixture is fed with sugar and moisture (water or milk) and given warmth it ferments and produces carbon dioxide.

Food value
Yeast is rich in vitamin B and protein. It therefore helps to build and repair the body and gives it protection.

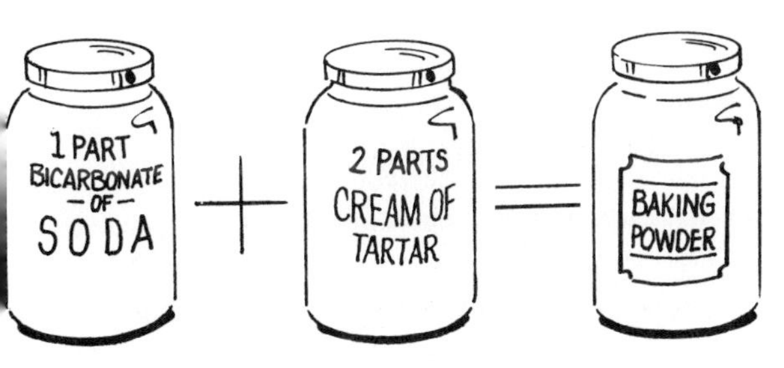

Chemical raising agent

Quality and buying points
Fresh yeast should:

a) be pale grey in colour, and look fresh and moist,
b) have a pleasant smell,
c) crumble easily,
d) cream readily when mixed with sugar,
e) be ordered only as required.

Storage
Yeast should be wrapped and stored in a cold place.

Types of yeast
1. Compressed yeast – sometimes known as German yeast or barm. This is the most widely used; it is very pure, and is packed and sold in packets. It will only keep 2 – 3 days in a cold place.
2. Brewer's yeast – taken from the top of the vats during the brewing of beer. It has a strong taste and does not keep well.
3. Dried yeast – usually dried brewer's yeast. Dried and sealed it keeps indefinitely.

Uses of yeast

1. Bread and rolls.	4. Croissants, brioches.
2. Bun doughs.	5. Danish pastry.
3. Baba, savarin.	6. Frying batters.

Air expands very quickly when heated. Air can be introduced into mixtures by:
a) sifting the flour – all mixtures,
b) rubbing fat into flour – short pastry,
c) creaming of fat and sugar – cake mixtures,
d) beating mixtures – batters,
e) whisking – egg whites,
f) folding and rolling – flaky and puff pastry.

Sugar

Sugar is produced from sugar cane and sugar beet and is available

a) unrefined, e.g. demerara or brown;
b) refined, e.g. castor, granulated, cube and icing.

By-products include golden syrup and treacle.

Food value
Sugar is invaluable for producing energy.

Storage
Always store sugar in a cool, dry place.

Uses
Sugar is chiefly used for pastry and bakery goods.

Substitutes
Artificial sweeteners are also available.

Herbs

The leaves of herbs contain an oil, which gives the characteristic smell and flavour. Wherever possible herbs are best used fresh, but the majority are dried to ensure a continuous supply throughout the year.

Food value
Herbs have no food value but they are important because they help to stimulate the appetite by heightening flavours and are an aid to digestion because they stimulate the flow of gastric juices.

A list of the more popular herbs appears in the table below.

Spices

This is a general term covering a wide variety of aromatic seasonings which are used to flavour savoury and sweet dishes. Spices are natural products obtained from fruits, seeds, roots or the bark of the numerous trees and shrubs.

A list of the more popular spices appears in the table opposite.

Condiments

Salt

This is used in almost every form of cooking and preserving foods. When used in sensible proportion salt helps bring out flavour in cooked food. Low sodium salt is also available.

Food value
Salt is required in all body fluids and also prevents muscular cramp. (This is why you frequently see sportsmen taking salt tablets after vigorous exercise.)

Basil	Small leaf, pungent flavour, sweet aroma. Uses – tomato dishes, sauces, salads, lamb dishes.
Bay leaves	Leaf of the bay laurel or sweet bay tree or shrub. Uses – soups, sauces, stews, fish, vegetable dishes.
Chervil	Small, neat-shaped leaves with delicate flavour. Uses – decorating cold dishes, in the mixture '*fines herbes*'.
Chive	Bright green member of onion family, resembles coarse grass, delicate onion flavour. Uses – soups, salads, hors-d'oeuvre, fish, poultry, meat dishes.
Mint	Many varieties. Uses – peas, new potatoes, mint sauce and jelly.
Parsley	Uses – garnish, flavour and decorate a wide variety of dishes.
Sage	Strong, pungent flavour. Uses – stuffings for pork, duck and goose.
Tarragon	Bright green attractive leaf, pleasant flavour. Uses – salads, hors-d'oeuvre, fish and meat dishes, sauces.
Thyme	Small neat leaves, strong flavour. Uses – soups, sauces, stews, stuffings, vegetables.
Fines herbes	Mixture of chervil, tarragon, parsley. Used in many recipes.

Allspice	The unripe fruit of the pimento tree. It has a flavour like a blend of cloves, cinnamon and nutmeg. Reddish-brown colour. Uses – sauces, sausages, cakes, milk puddings.
Cloves	Dark-brown, dried unopened flower buds of a tree. Uses – flavouring stocks, sauces, apples, and studding roast ham.
Cinnamon	The bark of small branches of the cinnamon shrub. Pale brown colour, available in stick or powdered form. Uses – chiefly in pastry and bakery work.
Nutmeg	The kernel of the fruit of the nutmeg tree. Available whole or ground. Uses – soups, sauces, vegetable and cheese dishes, sweet dishes.
Mace	The outer bright red covering of the nutmeg, delicate flavour. Uses – flavouring sauces and certain fish and meat dishes.
Coriander	Pleasant, yellowish-brown spice obtained from the seed of a plant. Tastes like a mixture of sage and lemon peel. Uses – sauces, mixed spice, curry powder.
Ginger	The root of a reed-like plant. Available whole and ground. Uses – sauces, pickles, curries, pastry and bakery work.
Saffron	Dried stigmas of crocus, bright yellow colour and distinctive flavour. Uses – soups, sauces, rice dishes.
Mixed spice	A mixture of allspice, coriander, cloves, nutmeg, cinnamon, ginger. Uses – chiefly in pastry work.
Curry powder	Many Asian cooks make up their own curry powder. A typical recipe could include: bay leaves, ginger, chillies, nutmeg, saffron, garlic, caraway, coriander, clove, allspice, cinnamon, mace, pepper, turmeric.

Storage
Salt must be stored in a cool, dry store, as it readily absorbs moisture. Salt should be kept in airtight containers.

Uses
Salt is used for the following purposes:

1. Curing fish and meat, e.g. herring, haddock, ham, bacon.
2. In making cheese and butter.
3. Pickling many foods, e.g. beef, tongue.
4. In the cooking of almost all foods.
5. As a condiment on the table.

Pepper

This is obtained from the berry of a tropical shrub – these berries are black peppercorns. When the outer skin is removed from black peppercorns white peppercorns remain. Both black and white pepper are available in ground form. Black pepper is more pungent than white.

Use
Peppercorns are used whole in stocks, sauces and dishes where the liquid is strained. They are freshly ground in a pepper mill when used for general seasoning, both in food preparation and cooking and at the table as a condiment.

Green peppercorns are fresh, unripe pepper berries, milder than dried peppercorns, and available in tins or frozen.

Ground pepper is used as a whole seasoning and as a condiment at the table.

Cayenne or red pepper is the hottest of the peppers, it is obtained from grinding chillies and capsicums.

Paprika is a bright red milk pepper used chiefly in a Hungarian style stew called goulash. It is produced from capsicums.

Mustard is obtained from the seed of the mustard plant, sold in powder form and diluted with water, milk or vinegar for table use. Mustard is also used as a seasoning in the kitchen for special dishes of a hot, spicy nature. Continental type mustards are mixed with herbs and wine vinegar.

Vinegar – malt vinegar is made from malt, which is produced from barley. Yeast is added, which converts it to alcohol. Bacteria are then added to convert the alcohol into acetic acid.

Artificial vinegars are chemically made. They are cheaper and inferior, and have a pungent odour and a sharp flavour.

Wine vinegars (red or white) are made from grapes and are more expensive but have a more delicate flavour. Cider vinegar is also available.

Colour – the colour of vinegar is no indication to its strength, as burnt sugar is added to give colour.

Uses of vinegar

1. As a preservative.
2. For tenderising meats, poultry and game before cooking.
3. For flavouring sauces.
4. As a table condiment.

Questions – Purchasing: meat and poultry

1. Meat is a body building food and a source of energy and contains
   pROTIEN, fAT, wATER, iRON, vITAMINS.

2. Match the following:

Roasting	Thick flank	STEWING
Frying	Silverside	Boiling
Stewing	Fillet	GRILL
Boiling	Rib ROAST	
Braising	Sirloin steak	FRY
Grilling	Topside	BRAISE

3. Name 4 types of offal. Kidney liver tripe heart

4. What is veal? meat from calf

5. From where are these cuts of lamb obtained?

   (a) cutlet (b) chop (c) chump chop

   Best end Saddle loin Saddle

6. Pork should be lean and pale pink, with smooth, firm but not excessive fat. True or false?

7. Explain why frozen chickens must be thawed completely before use.

Answers can be found on page 157.

Questions – Purchasing: fish and vegetables

1. Name

   a) 3 oily fish
   b) 3 white fish

   and explain what effect this difference has in choosing a method of cookery.

2. Are fish and meat of equal nutritional value?

3. How do you know if fish is fresh?

4. State 3 ways of preserving fish.

5. Name 3 shellfish.

6. Give an example of each of the following types of vegetable:

   a) root e) leaf
   b) bulb f) fruit
   c) tuber g) stem.
   d) flower

7. When dried the seeds of peas and beans are known as . . . .

8. Give an example of vegetables cooked by the following methods of cookery (a different vegetable for each).

Roasting	Deep frying
Braising	Shallow frying
Boiling	Grilling
Baking	Steaming

Answers can be found on page 157.

Questions – Purchasing: fruit and dairy produce

1. What is the food value of fruit?
2. Give two examples of each of the following types of fruit:
   a) soft d) hard
   b) stone e) other.
   c) citrus
3. State a fruit or fruit dish cooked by the following methods:
   a) steaming c) baking
   b) poaching d) deep fried.
4. What food is the most complete single food?
5. What is contained in cream that enables it to be whipped?
6. How many grades of eggs are there?
7. Eggs have a variety of uses in cookery: state 3 of them.
8. What is cheese?
9. Give an example of cheese used with:
   a) a pasta dish c) a snack.
   b) a vegetable dish
10. From which countries do these cheeses come?
    a) Roquefort d) Edam
    b) Parmesan e) Gruyère
    c) Stilton f) Wensleydale

Answers can be found on page 158.

Questions on general commodities

1. Match the following:
   Butter Beef
   Lard Cow's milk
   Margarine Pork
   Suet Vegetable oil
2. Why are oils often preferred to animal fats for deep frying?
3. What are cereals?
4. Strong flour is used for bread, soft flour for sponges – true or false?
5. Which types of rice would be suitable for
   a) sweet dishes
   b) savoury dishes?
6. What have cornflour, potato flour and arrowroot in common?
7. What is yeast?
8. What conditions are essential when using yeast in cooking?
9. Explain what a spice is and what it does.
10. What are condiments?

Answers can be found on page 158.

Answers

Answers Recipes *Questions page 3*

1. The proportion of one ingredient to another, e.g. equal ratios are 4 oz flour, 4 eggs, 4 oz sugar.
2. THE RECIPE
3. Recipes for pastrywork.
4. It could be any or all of these. That is why it is necessary to correct the consistency.
5. Heat.

Answers Boiling *Questions page 29*

1. c) fully covered with liquid.
2. To remove excess salt, so that they are not too salty to eat.
3. False.
4. Hot liquid.
5. Boiling.
6. Green vegetables – boiling liquid.
   Fresh beef – cold liquid.
7. c) bring to boil with lid on, remove lid and cook quickly.
8. Fish, meat, vegetables, eggs, pasta.
9. All of them.
10. c) slightly firm.

Answers Poaching *Questions page 34*

1. Slow cooking in the minimum amount of liquid.
2. Eggs.
3. Sauce.
4. Compôte.
5. 8 cm, 3 in.
6. Minimum amount just to cover, and gentle movement of the liquid.
7. To retain the steam and heat, thus enabling the fish to cook quicker and also to prevent the surface drying out.

Answers Steaming *Questions page 39*

1. Cooking by moist heat.
2. Either

   a) on a plate over a saucepan,

b) in a steamer,
c) in a pressure cooker,
d) in a perforated container steamer.

3. They are light and digestible.

4. Less heat is required, as foods cook quickly.

5. To prevent penetration of moisture.

6. Quickly.

7. a) VEGETABLES
b) CHEAPER
c) ECONOMICAL

Answers Stewing *Questions page 43*

1. Tougher, cheaper cuts.

2. True.

3. Gently.

4. Slow.

5. Yes.

6. 1 – shoulder
3 – breast
4 – middle neck
5 – scrag end.

Answers Braising *Questions page 48*

1. Stewing.

2. Carrots, onions, bouquet garni, seasoning.

3. To seal the pores so as to retain some of the juices and flavour in the meat and give colour.

4. Celery, cabbage, chicken, rice.

5. Slices of carrot and onion cut thickly.

6. Tougher cuts of meat.

7.

Grill	Poach
Braise	Bat
Simmer	Meats
Fry	Eats

8. Because the goodness is retained in the cooking liquor.

9. Against the grain – it is more difficult to eat if carved with the grain.

Answers Roasting *Questions page 56*

1. Fat.

2. Potatoes, parsnips.

3. Pouring some of the fat, in which the meat is cooking, over the joint to keep it moist and help it to cook and colour evenly.

4. Tender meat.

5. To seal the pores of the meat to retain juices and flavour.

6. Best end of lamb, sirloin of beef and leg of pork.

7. If there is the sound of spluttering of the fat, and if it is colouring too quickly.

8. Beef – horseradish
Lamb – mint
Pork – apple
Chicken – bread
Turkey – cranberry

9. a) by weight – by approx amount of time per pound,
b) by use of meat thermometer,
c) by pressure of finger to test resistance,
d) by colour of juices.

10. Cooking on a bed of roots in a covered pan with the aid of butter, using good quality meat or poultry.

11.

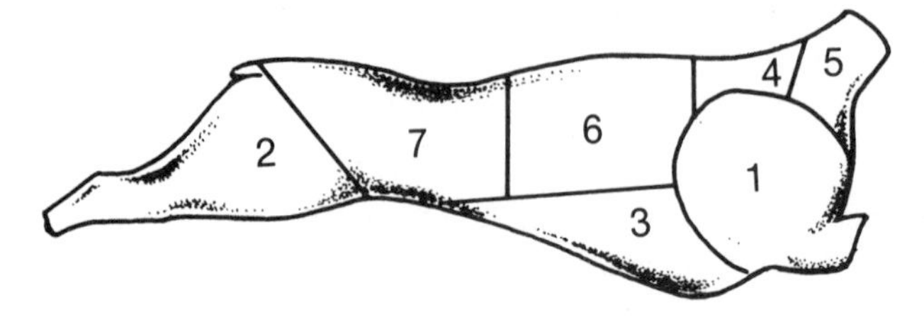

Lamb used for roasting

1. shoulder
2. legs
3. breast
6. best end
7. saddle

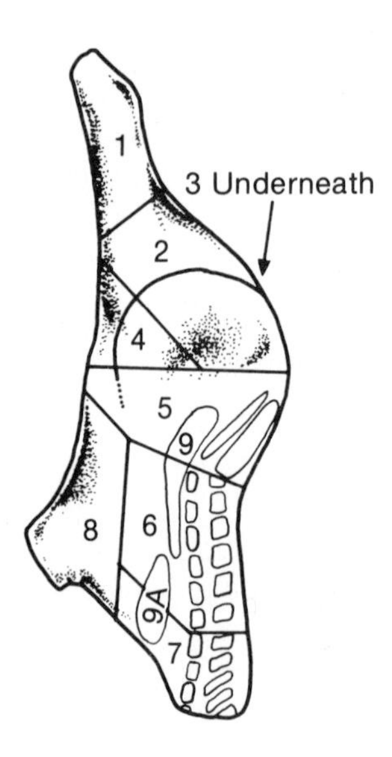

Beef hindquarter

2. topside
6. sirloin
7. wing ribs
9. fillet

Answers **Grilling** *Questions page 64*

1. Grilling is very quick cooking of tender foods using a grill or salamander.

2. Meat – steaks, chops, etc. Fish – whole plaice, cod steaks, etc. Vegetables – mushrooms, tomatoes.

3. A grill with the heat above the item to be grilled.

4. To enable even cooking and colouring on both sides.

5. Cutlet, kidney, sausage, bacon, tomato, mushroom.

6. Ox kidney – it is too tough to grill.

7. | | |
   |---|---|
   | CUTLET | CLOCK |
   | COD | DOVE |
   | STEAK | LEG |
   | PORK | PET |
   | | EEL |
   | | POT |

8. Current prices should be obtained, if possible both retail and wholesale. Ideally the restaurant price should be obtained from different types of establishment.

9. Gas, electricity, charcoal.

Answers **Frying** *Questions page 76*

1. Because of the danger of fat catching fire; because the high temperature of fat can cause severe burns; because of the quantity of fat; because, if ignited, the deep fat could cause considerable damage.

2. It could catch fire – ignite.

3. Presentation side – that is, the side uppermost on the dish, because being fried first it will have the best appearance. This side of the fillet will have been next to the bone.

4. Batter; flour, egg and crumbs; flour and milk. Oil and crumbs would slide off, the other 3 would stick or adhere to the surface of the item to be fried.

5. Word 1 down: SPIDER

				S	A	F	E	T	Y
			A	P	P	L	E		
		F	R	I	T	U	R	E	
				D	E	E	P		
B	A	S	K	E	T				
			B	R	O	W	N		

6. Pancakes – they are shallow fried and not coated.

7. a) Frying pan b) Sauté pan c) Spider d) Basket

8. The amount of fat and the type of equipment used.

9. Check the points given on safety in the list on page 68.

10. Sauté is shallow frying, as with potatoes in a frying pan or when using chicken or meat, when the sauté pan is swilled out so that no flavour is lost.

    Sauté potatoes, sauté chicken, tender cuts of meat.

Answers **Baking** *Questions page 92*

1. *Dry* heat.

2. Choux paste – chocolate eclairs
   Short paste – meat pies
   Puff paste – jam puffs
   Sweet paste – apple flans

3. a) 225 – 300°F or 110 – 150°C
   b) hot
   c) Regulo 4 – 6

4. b) Currant buns

5. b) and c)

6. Puff pastry – steam
   Bread rolls – yeast
   Small cakes – baking powder

7. 1. Paste
   2. Air
   3. Scone
   4. Time
   5. Rolls
   6. Yeast

8. Puff pastry goods – steam. Bread rolls – yeast. Small cakes – eggs and baking powder.

9. a) cream slice, jam puffs, b) flans, tartlets c) cream buns, éclairs.

10. a), b) and d). Yeast is not used in scones and baked potatoes require no fat – roast potatoes do.

Answers **Microwave cookery** *Questions page 95*

1. Because less time is taken, therefore less electricity is required.

2. Glass, ceramic, paper, plastic. *Never* metal.

3. Seal.

4. i) defrosting food,
   ii) small amounts of food can be very quickly cooked, and
   iii) frozen meals can be reheated as required, thus reducing waste.

5. i) for large quantities of food,
   ii) for thick or large items of food, and
   iii) for eggs cooked in their shell.

Answers Cold dishes, savouries and snacks *Questions page 104*

1. a) grapefruit
   b) egg mayonnaise
   c) avocado pear
   d) smoked salmon
   e) melon
   f) pâté

2. A salad dressing.

3. Potato salad – it has only one main ingredient.

4. Three.

5. All are types of bread which can be used for sandwiches.

6. Anchovy.

7. Worcester sauce.

Answers Practices of cookery *Questions page 120*

1. Employers and employees.

2. Job satisfaction.

3. Cooks' clothing.

4. A person conveying infection such as typhoid, dysentery, etc. They must inform their employer.

5. A waterproof dressing.

6. Soap, nail-brush and clean towel or warm air hand dryer.

7. Because of the possibility of conveying germs from the mouth to foods or work surface via the fingers. Cigarette ends which have been in the mouth may be put down on work surfaces. Ash may fall into food.

8. Food, temperature, moisture, time.

9. 10°C and 63°C.

10. Salmonella – intestine of animals and humans.
    Staphylococci – humans hands, nose, throat, etc.

11. Bacteria being moved from place to place, contaminating clean foods, surfaces, etc.

12. Usually through lack of care and concentration, being distracted or excessive haste.

13. Someone may plunge their hand into the water and cut themselves.

14. Sprinkle with something white, e.g. flour.

15. Someone may slip on it.

16. Remove the plug.

17. Apply cool running water until pain eases.

18. Fuel, air and heat.

19. By removing the source of heat (gas, electricity), excluding air or removing the items which could burn.

20. Warn others of the fire and do not panic.

21. i) themselves,
    ii) their materials, equipment and utensils,
    iii) the kitchen.

Answers Menu planning, portion control, costing, nutrition *Questions page 131*

1. COST, TEXTURE, COLOUR, STAFF, BALANCE, WORDING, SUPPLY, SEASON, REPETITION

COST	TEXTURE
COLOUR	STAFF
BALANCE	WORDING
SUPPLY	SEASON
REPETITION	

2. a) Onions d) Sweetcorn
   b) Cauliflower e) Rice
   c) Potatoes

3. Cornish pasty, Chelsea bun, Devonshire split, Lancashire hotpot, Swiss roll or buns, Bakewell tart, Eccles cake, Brussels sprouts, Danish pastries

4. Deciding the size and quantity of food to be served to each person and ensuring that this is done.

5. Scoops, measuring ladles, individual serving dishes, pre-packed individual items, e.g. tea bags, butter, jam.

6. Everybody – the customer, the employer, and the staff because they are all satisfied.

7. They are energy providing foods.

8. Meat, fish, eggs, milk, cheese, etc.

9. They assist in maintaining the health of the body.

10.

Even	Vitamins	*Also*
Peas	Water	Fume
Minerals	Energy	Lot
Fat	Protein	No
Milk	Game	In
Bone	Eat	Starch
Sugar	Nut	

11. When in season.

Answers Purchasing – meat and poultry *Questions page 150*

1. protein, fat, water, iron, vitamins.

2. Roasting – rib
   Frying – sirloin steak
   Stewing – thickflank
   Boiling – silverside
   Braising – topside
   Grilling – fillet

3. Kidney, liver, tripe, heart.

4. The meat from the calf.

5. a) best end b) saddle or loin c) saddle or loin.

6. True.

7. To enable the chicken to be thoroughly cooked through so as to prevent possible food poisoning.

Answers Purchasing – fish and vegetables *Questions page 150*

1. a) mackerel, herring, salmon
   b) cod, haddock, plaice

   The oily fish are not deep fried; because of their oily nature they are often grilled. Salmon is less oily and is also poached. Mackerel and herring are soused. White fish are cooked by deep frying and by other methods of cookery.

2. Yes

3. Eyes – bright
   Gills – red

Flesh – firm
Skin – covered with fresh sea slime
Smell – pleasant

4. Freezing, smoking, tinning, pickling.

5. Lobster, crab, prawns, shrimps, mussels.

6. a) root – carrot, turnip, parsnip
   b) bulb – onion, shallot, leek
   c) tuber – potato, Jerusalem artichoke
   d) flower – cauliflower, broccoli.
   e) leaf – cabbage, spinach, sprouts.
   f) fruit – cucumber, tomato, peas, beans
   g) stem – celery, sea kale

7. Pulses.

8. Roasting – parsnips
   Braising – cabbage
   Boiling – sprouts
   Baking – potatoes
   Deep frying – onions
   Shallow frying – mushrooms
   Grilling – tomatoes
   Steaming – beetroot

You may have chosen other suitable examples.

Answers Purchasing – fruit and dairy produce *Questions page 151*

1. It is a protective food.

2. a) raspberries, strawberries, gooseberries, etc.
   b) cherries, damsons, plums, etc.
   c) oranges, lemons, grapefruit, etc.
   d) apples, pears.
   e) pineapple, bananas, melons.

3. a) steamed puddings – apples, sultanas, etc.
   b) poached – plums, pears.
   c) baked – fruit pies, tartlets.
   d) fried fritters – pineapple, bananas.

4. Milk.

5. Fat.

6. 7.

7. Thickening, colouring, binding, clarifying, providing nutritive value.

8. Concentrated milk from cows, goats or ewes.

9. a) macaroni cheese c) Welsh rarebit.
   b) cauliflower

10. a) France d) Holland
    b) Italy e) Switzerland
    c) England f) England

Answers General commodities *Questions page 151*

1. Butter – Cow's milk
   Lard – Pork
   Margarine – Vegetable oils
   Suet – Beef

2. Because higher temperatures can be reached without smoking.

3. Seeds or grains of cultivated grasses.

4. True.

5. a) short grain
   b) long grain

6. All are used for thickening.

7. A living organism – a plant of the fungi group.

8. Warmth, liquid, time and suitable food.

9. Spice – natural fruit seeds, roots or bark, used for flavouring and seasoning.

10. Salt and pepper, mustard, vinegar.

General questions

These posers are intended to stimulate your curiosity, so that you will seek the answers and enjoy broadening your knowledge of cookery.

1. Whose zoo? What are these?
   a) Bombay duck
   b) Welsh rarebit
   c) cat's tongue
   d) extra duck
   e) salamander
   f) spider
   g) buck rarebit
   h) toad in the hole
   i) bat

2. Who's who? These names have culinary associations. What are they?
   a) Rosemary
   b) Olive
   c) Charlotte
   d) Victoria
   e) Hélène

3. Musical equipment? What cookery items are these?
   a) cornets
   b) triangles
   c) drumsticks
   d) horns

4. What do you make of these?
   e.g., a) to grumble – grouse
   b) not worth bothering with
   c) drunken fish
   d) stupid cut of meat
   e) rubbish
   f) almost sounds dreadful
   g) was in a race
   h) game in prison

5. What foods do you associate with the following?
   a) Kate and Sydney
   b) bangers and mash
   c) purée of nip and nip
   d) bubble and squeak

Answers can be found on page 163.

Questions Fruit and vegetable alphabet

E.g.,	Eve fell for it	Apple
	Used in Russian soup	Beetroot
	Good for the eyes	CARROT
	Every day has one	DATE
	No yolks or whites on this one	EGGPLANT
	Well known for its leaf	FIG
	Popular starter on menu	GRAPEFRUIT
	Type of bean	HARICOT
	Palestine tuber	Jerusalem/ARTICHOK
	Curly	KALE
	Rabbit food!	Lettuce
	Honeydew, for example	Melon
	Early common vegetable	New Pot
	Makes the eyes water	Onion
	Dried vegetables	Pulse
	Base of Melba sauce	Raspberry
	Popeye food	Spinache
	Used a lot in purée	Tomatoe
	Grows in wet beds	WATERCRESS
	Sweet potato	YAM

Answers can be found on page 163.

Alphabet quiz

How quickly can you complete this?

E.g.,	Sauce served with pork	Apple
	Pouring fat over meat when roasting	B
	Served with boiled mutton	C
	A stone fruit	D
	Goes into cups	E
	Boneless	F
	Cheese is this when served separately	G
	Type of bean	H
	Part of every recipe	I
	Kind of artichoke	J
	Smoked herring	K
	Citrus fruits	L
	Essential in the diet	M
	Almonds are	N
	Colourful fruit	O
	Saturated in vinegar	P
	Every cook should strive for this	Q
	Food kept in this	R
	Essential in every kitchen	S
	An aspect of menu planning	T
	Degree of grilling	U
	Cover cuts with this	W
	Part of an egg	Y
	Live meat here	Z

Answers can be found on pages 163 – 64.

Sauces crossword

Questions

1. Served with roast chicken
2. Served with roast lamb
3. A coloured sauce
4. A sauce of another colour
5. Served with roast beef
6. Cold sauce
7. With ice cream
8. Goes with fish
9. Served with grilled herrings
10. Hard boiled and diced
11. Served with many English sweets
12. Goes with roast mutton

Solution can be found on page 164.

Cookbusters

These quizzes can be played in various ways. A quiz master may pose the question in response to a contestant selecting a letter. The opportunity to answer the question may be given to the first one calling out 'cook' or by having two different bells or items to sound. If one contestant marks the correct answers in blue, the other in red, then the first to complete top to bottom in red or side to side in blue wins (you must first agree who is to be blue and who red). The next letter is selected by the contestant who gives the correct answer. If incorrectly answered by one contestant, his or her opponent has a chance to answer. Instead of just two contestants, the game can be played with pairs or teams of contestants.

Another way to play is for two people to compete, and the first one to complete all or the most letters in an agreed time wins. A third way is for two students to compete to score the most correct answers using all the letters.

The nutrition cookbuster is an example of other topics on which students could construct a quiz. Other subject areas include hygiene, safety, etc.

Single-letter cookbuster

Questions

E laid down by chickens
S not allowed in kitchens
C best end are cut into these
P dried vegetables
B to make or keep white
M list of dishes
D stone fruit
W essential for life
R principle of cooking
F protein food
U small equipment
J preserved fruit
O all good cooks are
H common fish
G tomatoes and mushrooms are cooked this way
K mixed grills include these
X multiplication sign
Q the answer is the reply to this
I on top of the cake
L citrus fruit
N not gross
T in the hole
V a common soup
Y some split peas are this
A vinegar is this

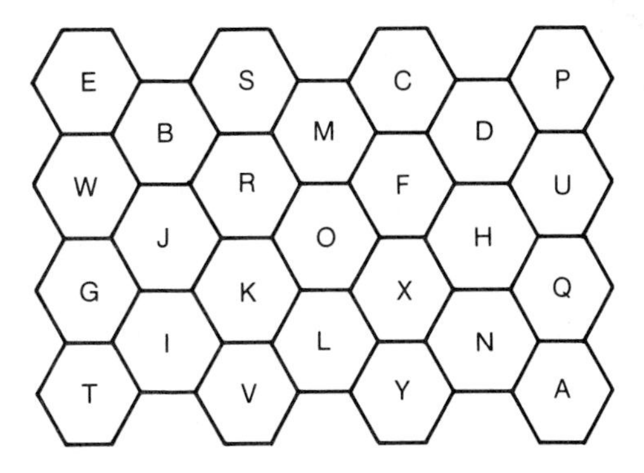

Answers can be found on page 164.

Nutrition cookbuster

Questions

C	coarse structure vegetables and cereals
I	a mineral element
G	protein helps this
V	essential chemical substances
M	almost perfect food
P	both vegetable and animal
O	contains vitamin C
B	diets should be this
S	a main group of carbohydrate
F	source of protective food
L	white fish store oil here
D	the breaking down of food

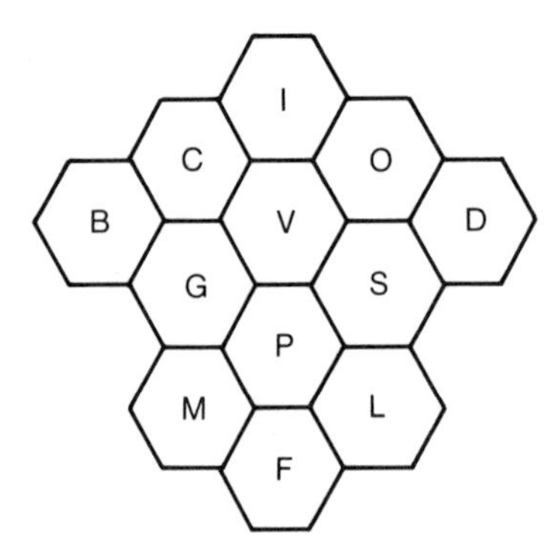

Answers can be found on page 164.

Multi-letter cookbuster

Questions

ALC	type of menu
MS	served with roast lamb
CB	first meal of day in France
SKP	popular meat dish
FA	cuts and burns need this
SP	what it's sold for
MO	modern piece of equipment
VP	economical tool
RP	used by pastry cooks
BW	puts air into egg whites
FHR	important law
T	three-sided pot rest
R	used to thicken sauces
S	also means to jump
CC	cause of much food poisoning
WYH	after visiting the toilet
UD	beef is usually roasted thus
BBP	sweet cooked in a bain-marie
ATD	essential to get best results
CSC	before serving thick soup do this
JS	work well done gives this
FB	used to smother flames
CF	saves time, space and work
CP	sprinkled on many dishes
FE	puts out flames

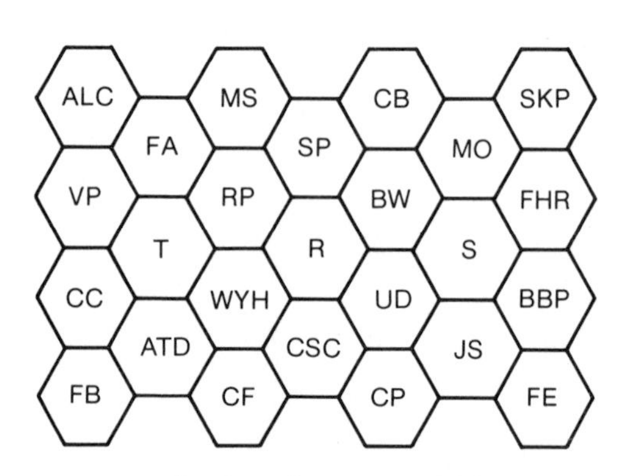

Answers can be found on page 164.

General answers

Questions on pages 159–162.

1. Whose zoo?

   a) dried fish served with curry
   b) cheese mixture on toast
   c) a type of biscuit used as a *petit four*
   d) a part-time waiter
   e) type of grill heated from above
   f) a utensil used in deep frying (like a spider's web)
   g) Welsh rarebit with a poached egg
   h) sausage or chop cooked in Yorkshire pudding
   i) bat – cutlet bat – used to flatten meat

2. Who's who?

   a) Rosemary – a herb often used with lamb
   b) Olive – fruit of olive tree used as garnish, hors d'oeuvre, etc.
   c) Charlotte – a mould or a sweet
   d) Victoria – a type of plum
   e) Hélène – pear hélène – ice cream, pear and chocolate sauce

3. Musical equipment:

   a) cornets – wafer biscuits for ice cream; also foods, e.g. ham, smoked salmon, shaped like a cone
   b) triangle – a wooden or iron triangle-shaped item for hot pans to rest on
   c) drumsticks – the lower part of the leg of chicken
   d) horns – cream horns – puff paste shapes on a cream horn mould

4. a) grouse
   b) trifle
   c) soused herrings
   d) chump chop
   e) tripe
   f) offal
   g) runner bean
   h) jugged hare

5. a) slang for steak and kidney
   b) sausages and mash
   c) purée of turnips and parsnips
   d) fried potatoes and cabbage

Answers Fruit and vegetable alphabet

Apple
Beetroot
Carrot
Date
Eggplant (aubergine)
Fig
Grapefruit
Haricot
Jerusalem artichoke
Kale
Lettuce
Melon
New potato
Onion
Pulse
Raspberry
Spinach
Tomatoes
Watercress
Yam

Answers Alphabet quiz

Apple
Basting
Caper sauce
Damson
Eggs
Filleted
Grated
Haricot
Ingredients
Jerusalem
Kipper
Limes and lemons
Mineral salts
Nuts

Orange (or olive)
Pickled
Quality
Refrigeration
Safety
Texture
Underdone
Waterproof dressing
Yolk
Zoo

Sauces crossword

Solution

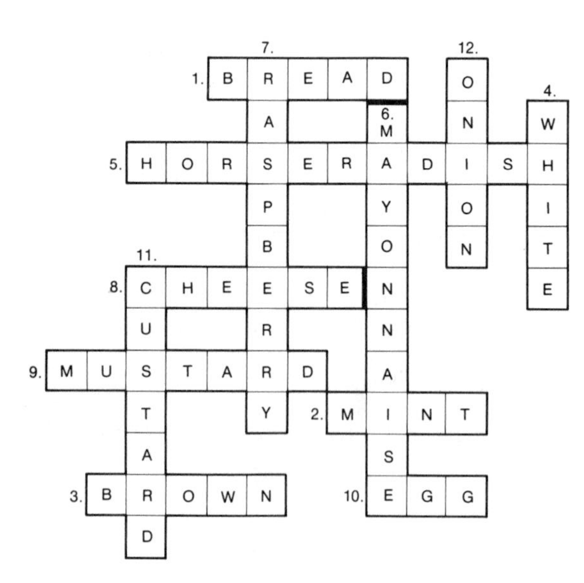

Single-letter cookbuster

Answers

Eggs
Smoking
Cutlets
Pulse
Blanch
Menu
Damson
Water
Roasting
Fish
Utensil
Jam
Organised
Haddock
Grilled
Kidney
X
Question
Icing
Lemon
Net
Toad
Vegetable
Yellow
Acid

Nutrition cookbuster

Answers

Cellulose
Iron
Growth
Vitamins
Milk
Protein
Orange
Balanced
Sugar/starch
Fat
Liver
Digestion

Multi-letter cookbuster

Answers

à la carte
Mint sauce
Continental breakfast
Steak and kidney pie/pudding
First aid
Selling price
Microwave oven
Vegetable peeler
Rolling pin
Balloon whisk
Food Hygiene Regulation
Triangle
Roux
Sauté
Cross-contamination
Wash your hands
Underdone
Bread and butter pudding
Attention to detail
Correct seasoning, consistency
Job satisfaction
Fire blanket
Convenience food
Chopped parsley
Fire extinguisher

Recipe index

General index